The Atom
Bomb

Other Books in the Turning Points Series:

Turning Points
IN WORLD HISTORY

The Atom Bomb

Tamara L. Roleff, *Book Editor*

David L. Bender, *Publisher*
Bruno Leone, *Executive Editor*
Bonnie Szumski, *Editorial Director*

Greenhaven Press, Inc., San Diego, California

Library of Congress Cataloging-in-Publication Data

The Atom Bomb / Tamara L. Roleff, book editor.
        p.   cm. — (Turning points in world history)
    Includes bibliographical references and index.
    ISBN 0-7377-0214-1 (pbk. : alk. paper). —
ISBN 0-7377-0215-X (lib. : alk. paper)
    1. Atomic Bomb—United States. 2. Hiroshima-shi (Japan)—
History—Bombardment, 1945. 3. Nagasaki-shi (Japan)—History—
Bombardment, 1945. 4. Atomic bomb—Moral and ethical aspects.
I. Roleff, Tamara L., 1959–   . II. Series: Turning points in world
history (Greenhaven Press)
UG1282.A872 2000
355.8'25119—dc21   99-34739
                                                                              CIP

Cover photo: © Smithsonian Institution

©2000 by Greenhaven Press, Inc.
P.O. Box 289009, San Diego, CA 92198-9009

Printed in the U.S.A.

Contents

Foreword

Certain past events stand out as pivotal, as having effects and outcomes that change the course of history. These events are often referred to as turning points. Historian Louis L. Snyder provides this useful definition:

> A turning point in history is an event, happening, or stage which thrusts the course of historical development into a different direction. By definition a turning point is a great event, but it is even more—a great event with the explosive impact of altering the trend of man's life on the planet.

History's turning points have taken many forms. Some were single, brief, and shattering events with immediate and obvious impact. The invasion of Britain by William the Conqueror in 1066, for example, swiftly transformed that land's political and social institutions and paved the way for the rise of the modern English nation. By contrast, other single events were deemed of minor significance when they occurred, only later recognized as turning points. The assassination of a little-known European nobleman, Archduke Franz Ferdinand, on June 28, 1914, in the Bosnian town of Sarajevo was such an event; only after it touched off a chain reaction of political-military crises that escalated into the global conflict known as World War I did the murder's true significance become evident.

Other crucial turning points occurred not in terms of a few hours, days, months, or even years, but instead as evolutionary developments spanning decades or even centuries. One of the most pivotal turning points in human history, for instance—the development of agriculture, which replaced nomadic hunter-gatherer societies with more permanent settlements—occurred over the course of many generations. Still other great turning points were neither events nor developments, but rather revolutionary new inventions and innovations that significantly altered social customs and ideas, military tactics, home life, the spread of knowledge, and the human condition in general. The developments of writing, gunpowder, the printing press, antibiotics, the electric light, atomic energy, television, and the computer, the last two of which have recently ushered in the world-altering information age, represent only some of these innovative turning points.

Each anthology in the Greenhaven Turning Points in World History series presents a group of essays chosen for their accessibility. The anthology's structure also enhances this accessibility. First, an introductory essay provides a general overview of the principal events and figures involved, placing the topic in its historical context. The essays that follow explore various aspects in more detail, some targeting political trends and consequences, others social, literary, cultural, and/or technological ramifications, and still others pivotal leaders and other influential figures. To aid the reader in choosing the material of immediate interest or need, each essay is introduced by a concise summary of the contributing writer's main themes and insights.

In addition, each volume contains extensive research tools, including a collection of excerpts from primary source documents pertaining to the historical events and figures under discussion. In the anthology on the French Revolution, for example, readers can examine the works of Rousseau, Voltaire, and other writers and thinkers whose championing of human rights helped fuel the French people's growing desire for liberty; the French *Declaration of the Rights of Man and Citizen*, presented to King Louis XVI by the French National Assembly on October 2, 1789; and eyewitness accounts of the attack on the royal palace and the horrors of the Reign of Terror. To guide students interested in pursuing further research on the subject, each volume features an extensive bibliography, which for easy access has been divided into separate sections by topic. Finally, a comprehensive index allows readers to scan and locate content efficiently. Each of the anthologies in the Greenhaven Turning Points in World History series provides students with a complete, detailed, and enlightening examination of a crucial historical watershed.

A Brief History of the Atom Bomb

"We were lying there, very tense, in the early dawn, and there were just a few streaks of gold in the east; you could see your neighbor very dimly," writes I.I. Rabi, a physicist with the Manhattan Project who witnessed the first atom bomb test in the New Mexico desert on July 16, 1945. He continues:

> Suddenly there was an enormous flash of light, the brightest light I have ever seen or that I think anyone has ever seen. It blasted; it pounced; it bored its way right through you. It was a vision which was seen with more than the eye. It was seen to last forever. You would wish it would stop; altogether it lasted about two seconds. Finally it was over, diminishing, and we looked toward the place where the bomb had been; there was an enormous ball of fire which grew and grew and it rolled as it grew; it went up into the air, in yellow flashes and into scarlet and green. It looked menacing. It seemed to come toward one.
>
> A new thing had just been born; a new control; a new understanding of man, which man had acquired over nature.[1]

The detonation of the world's first atom bomb at the Trinity test site near Alamogordo, New Mexico, proved the theory that the atom had a tremendous energy that could be used to fuel the world's most dangerous weapon. The atom's power was fully demonstrated when an atomic bomb was dropped on the Japanese city of Hiroshima (population 350,000) on August 6, 1945, and another one three days later on Nagasaki (population 270,000). The two bombs killed approximately 150,000 people outright and injured another 125,000. Within five months, another 60,000 people had died from their injuries or from radiation sickness; within five years, about 275,000 people had died from the atom bombs. In addition, 90 percent of Hiroshima was destroyed by the bomb that was dropped on the city. Nagasaki's damage was less severe due to its differing geography.

This total destruction wreaked havoc on society in the two cities. Fires burned for days in the cities because the firemen were killed and their equipment destroyed. Hospitals and clinics were just empty shells, destroyed by the bombs' blasts. The few surviving doctors and nurses were overwhelmed with injured victims and medical supplies were quickly exhausted. The streets were impassable due to the fires and the rubble from the destroyed buildings. Communication with the outside world was nonexistent, as the telephone and telegraph lines were destroyed, as were the railways. The police, army, and Japanese government were unprepared for such a calamity and were able to provide little, if any, assistance to the survivors. Naomi Shohno, who became a nuclear physicist after searching for her family in the rubble of Hiroshima, describes how the survivors attempted to cope:

> All buildings such as shrines, factories, and barracks, not to mention the schools that had already been designated as refuges and the hospitals that remained unburned, were used as temporary relief camps. Most buildings in the city, even if their superstructures remained intact, were half-destroyed, with their windowpanes and walls blown out and a heap of debris laying scattered on the floor. Medical treatment was most difficult, because many doctors and nurses were injured—in Hiroshima, for example, 90 percent of its doctors (270) and 93 percent of its nurses (1,650) suffered death or injury in the bombing—and medical supplies and equipment had been destroyed.[2]

The deaths, injuries, and destruction were so devastating and overwhelming that the survivors were the victims of sensory overload, unable to cope with anything other than their own needs. The cries of many injured people, which would have brought help in different circumstances, were ignored as people rushed by to escape the fires, to seek help for their own injuries, or to reach their homes to search for family members. A few people did stop and help, but there were so many in need that it was impossible to help them all. Shohno explains why years later, some atomic bomb survivors feel a deep sense of shame and guilt:

> The memories of the shocking sights and terror at the time of the bombing is another source of agony for the atomic bomb victims. Some feel guilt because, in the desperate situation confronting them at the time, they could not save others dear to them. Overwhelmed by the disaster and deprived of a sense of direction, many of them deserted their family members, friends, and neighbors who were buried under crushed buildings; it was all they could do to run to their own safety.[3]

A New Type of Energy

Japanese and American news reports of the dropping of the atom bombs on Japan, only reported that "a new type of bomb"[4] had been used. Most people had no concept of what an atom bomb was or why it was so powerful. The theory that made the atom bomb possible was discovered in 1938 when two German physicists, Otto Hahn and Fritz Strassman, were experimenting with uranium. With the help of Otto Frisch and Lise Meitner, they discovered that bombarding uranium atoms with neutrons did not create a new element as they had expected. Instead, the uranium atoms split into two other elements, in this case, barium and krypton.

By following Albert Einstein's theory of relativity about mass and energy ($E = mc^2$), Meitner and Frisch knew that a tremendous amount of energy would be released during fission, as Frisch called the splitting process. (Einstein's theory means that the energy in matter is exactly equal to the matter's mass multiplied by the speed of light squared.) The two new atoms (barium and krypton) weighed less together than the single uranium atom; therefore, according to Einstein, the difference in mass must be energy. Frisch and Meitner calculated the energy to be 200 million electron volts, which is an immense amount of energy from just one atom. Extrapolating the figures reveals that a pound of matter converted to pure energy would produce more than half the amount of electricity generated in the United States in a week. Scientists later realized that pound for pound, fission could produce more than 20 million times the energy of TNT.

The Worry About the Germans

At the time of Hahn and Strassman's discovery, very few physicists were still working in Germany. During the 1920s and 1930s, Germany was the center of the scientific world, and physicists from all over the world flocked to Göttingen University to work and study with such notable physicists as Max Born and Werner Heisenberg, among others. Heisenberg was one of the leading atomic researchers in the late 1920s and early 1930s. He authored the Uncertainty Principle which states that it is impossible to determine an electron's position and momentum with certainty, because measuring one will influence the other. In the years after Hitler came to power, though, many scientists in fascist-controlled nations fled to Scandinavia, England, and the United States to avoid religious persecution. Among the émigrés were Frisch and Meitner of Austria; Enrico Fermi of Italy; Leo Szilard, Edward Teller, and Eugene Wigner of Hungary; and James Franck, Albert Einstein, and Max Born of Germany. Despite pleas from many of his friends and coworkers, Heisenberg, who was 100 percent German, refused to leave his homeland. During World War II, Heisenberg was appointed the director of Germany's atomic bomb research project by Hitler.

Fermi and Szilard, who were now in the United States, immediately realized the possibilities of fission. Fission could create a chain reaction if one uranium atom emits two neutrons during fission, and those two neutrons cause two other uranium atoms to fission, which then release a total of four more neutrons, which cause four more uranium atoms to fission, releasing eight neutrons, and so on. Since each fission process creates 200 million electron volts, a nuclear chain reaction could produce a very powerful explosion and hence a very destructive weapon. Szilard feared that the Germans were already working on developing an atom bomb. He wanted all experiments about uranium fission and chain reactions to be kept secret and unpublished to slow down the Germans' research as much as possible. Szilard writes in his memoirs:

> At that time it was already clear, not only to me but to many other people—certainly it was clear to Wigner—that we were at the threshold of another world war. And so it seemed to us urgent to set up experiments which would show whether in fact neutrons are emitted in the fission process of uranium. I thought that if neutrons are in fact emitted in fission, this fact should be kept secret from the Germans.[5]

Szilard knew that if Germany developed an atom bomb it would use it against its enemies in the coming war. Not everyone agreed with Szilard's desire for secrecy, however, and some papers exploring uranium fission were published in the early 1940s.

The United States Commits to the Atom Bomb Project

Atomic research was also ongoing in Great Britain. Frisch, now in exile in Birmingham, England, and another German physicist, Rudolf Peierls, wrote a paper for the British government in the spring of 1940 in which they concluded that an atomic bomb would need only a little bit over two pounds of uranium in order to explode with more force than had ever been seen before. They theorized that if two one-pound masses of uranium are kept apart, the bomb will remain stable. If the two one-pound masses are brought together, however, the mass becomes critical and will explode. A year later a British committee studied the Frisch-Peierls memorandum and another study and concluded it was "quite probable that the atom bomb may be manufactured before the end of the war."[6] The British belief in the prospects of an atom bomb seemed to pique Washington's interest in developing the bomb. One day before the Japanese attacked Pearl Harbor, Roosevelt committed the United States to building an atomic bomb.

With the support of the U.S. government, research and

development of the atom bomb proceeded rapidly. Physicist Emilio Segré and chemist Glenn T. Seaborg discovered that a product of uranium-235 decay was plutonium, which showed greater promise than uranium as a fissile material for nuclear chain reactions. General Leslie R. Groves and J. Robert Oppenheimer, who were selected in the fall of 1942 to head the secret atom bomb project known as the Manhattan Project, selected the site for a secret laboratory. Construction began almost immediately to prepare the laboratory, situated on a secluded mesa called Los Alamos thirty-five miles north of Santa Fe, New Mexico, for the influx of scientists who would soon be arriving. Factories and towns were also built in Oak Ridge, Tennessee, and Hanford, Washington, to produce the uranium and plutonium and to house the workers needed for the bomb project. When Fermi proved in early December 1942 that a nuclear chain reaction could be controlled, the development of the atom bomb moved from theory to fact.

The German Bomb

Spurring on the American effort to make the atom bomb was the fear that the Germans, who were very much involved in the beginnings of atomic research, were at least a year ahead of the Americans. "We were told day in and day out that it was our duty to catch up with the Germans,"[7] recalls Leona Woods Marshall, one of the few women physicists working on the Manhattan Project. Oppenheimer predicted that the Americans would have a bomb ready to use by early 1945; therefore, the Germans, who began their research in 1939, should have a bomb by the end of 1943. Hans Bethe and Edward Teller, two physicists working on the Manhattan Project, wrote Oppenheimer a memo in August 1943 expressing their fears about the German effort:

> It is possible that the Germans will have, by the end of this year, enough material accumulated to make a large number of gadgets [atomic bombs] which they will release at the same time on England, Russia, and this country. In this case there would be little hope for any counter-action. However,

it is also possible that they will have a production, let us say, of two gadgets a month. This would place particularly Britain in an extremely serious position but there would be hope for counter-action from our side before the war is lost, provided our own tubealloy program [the British code name for the atom bomb project] is drastically accelerated in the next few weeks.[8]

Reports that the Germans were using heavy water to act as a coolant in their reactors led the British to sabotage the heavy water installation at Vemork in southern Norway. A raid by fourteen British commandos in October 1942 was unsuccessful; the gliders transporting the soldiers crashed into a mountain and the survivors were executed by the Germans. A second raid in February 1943 by Norwegian special forces was more successful; the stored heavy water was spilled down a drain and the destruction caused by the raid would take weeks to repair. However, by April, the Germans had restarted production at the heavy water plant. When Neils Bohr, an eminent Danish physicist escaped the Nazis and fled to Scotland in October, he showed British authorities a drawing of an experimental heavy-water nuclear reactor that had been given to him by Werner Heisenberg in Copenhagen two years earlier. The British realized they would have to stop production at the Norwegian plant once and for all. American B-17s bombed the Norsk Hydro Plant in November, effectively shutting it down. The Nazis decided to rebuild in Germany, and in February 1944 shipped the heavy water from Norway to Germany. However, during the transport, Norwegian resistance fighters blew up the ferry on which the water was being carried, and the train cars with the barrels of heavy water quickly sank to the bottom of a lake.

The *Alsos* Mission

Groves was anxious to learn something more concrete about the Germans' progress with the atom bomb. He had sent some scientists and army intelligence officers to Italy in December 1943 to discover what they could about the German project, but they had learned little. The unit, code-named *Alsos*, which is Greek for "grove," was led by Lieutenant Colonel Boris T. Pash and physicist Samuel A. Goudsmit. Goudsmit was probably chosen because he had never worked on the Manhattan Project, and therefore could not give away secrets if he was captured.

When the Allied forces invaded Normandy in June 1944, the eyes and ears of the Manhattan Project were right behind them. In France, Goudsmit learned that Frédéric Joliot, who had remained in Paris when the Germans invaded, knew very little of the German attempt to build an atom bomb, despite the fact that Germans had taken over his laboratory. However, reports reached the *Alsos* team that Strasbourg looked promising as a site for the German project. The unit hurried to Strasbourg, arriving just after Allied troops captured the town on November 15, 1944. Goudsmit and Pash found a physics laboratory in the Strasbourg hospital, along with four physicists and many papers and documents. Among the documents Goudsmit found a whole stack of papers dealing with the German atom bomb project. The *Alsos* team was relieved by the contents of the documents; the Germans were far behind the Americans in the atomic bomb research, and had not yet been able to sustain a nuclear chain reaction. Goudsmit writes:

> It is true that no precise information was given in these documents, but there was far more than enough to get a view of the whole German uranium project. We studied the papers by candlelight for two days and nights until our eyes began to hurt. . . . The conclusions were unmistakable. The evidence at hand proved definitely that Germany had no atom bomb and was not likely to have one in any reasonable form.[9]

Although Germany did not have an atom bomb, Groves wanted to make sure that no German physicist was carrying on atomic experiments, or that any German physicists were captured by the Russians. The *Alsos* mission was to round up all the physicists remaining in Germany and remove them to England. Along the way, the unit discovered in early April 1945 twelve hundred tons of uranium ore hidden by the

Germans. The ore was packed up for shipment to the United States where it would be processed at the Oak Ridge plant for the Little Boy bomb. Documents placed the German scientists at a small town in the Black Forest region. The *Alsos* mission went there and found the mother lode; in a cave in the side of an eighty-foot cliff was the German atomic pile. The Germans were still using heavy water as a moderator for their pile, a material Fermi and Szilard had rejected years earlier because the water absorbed too many neutrons to permit a chain reaction to occur. Within a few days of the pile's discovery, Germany's top physicists— Werner Heisenberg, the leader of the atom bomb project, Otto Hahn, who had discovered fission, and others—were all captured. Pash writes:

> The fact that the German atom bomb was not an immediate threat was probably the most significant single piece of military intelligence developed throughout the war. Alone, that information was enough to justify *Alsos*.[10]

The German scientists spent the rest of the war in confinement in England.

The Work at Los Alamos

Meanwhile, in August 1943 the United States and Great Britain had secretly agreed at a conference in Quebec that the two countries would collaborate on the atom bomb project. Britain sent several distinguished refugee physicists in December, including Bohr, Frisch, Hans Bethe, Rudolf Peierls, and Klaus Fuchs, among others, to work at Los Alamos; after the war, the United States would share its atomic bomb secrets with England. In return, the United States would receive all the patents and any commercial or industrial benefits from atomic energy research.

The scientists at Los Alamos began their research on an atom bomb by trying to devise a gun-type bomb. A "bullet" of uranium or plutonium would be fired into a target of the same element; the combined weights of the bullet and the target would form a critical mass and start the chain reaction, thus setting off the atomic explosion. A second technique developed for the atom bomb was implosion, the opposite of explosion. A ball of uranium or plutonium would be surrounded by an explosive; the force of the explosion would be directed inward toward the plutonium ball. The explosion's shock waves would compress the fissionable ball until it reached criticality, thus setting off the atom bomb.

A major drawback to the development of the bomb, however, was the lack of fissionable U-235 and plutonium. Up until early 1945, the total amount of uranium and plutonium available in the United States was about the size of a grain of salt. However, the lack of uranium did not stop the gun-type bomb design. A prototype had already been made and test bombs, using TNT, were exploded in the desert. Then it was discovered the plutonium would not work in a gun-type bomb; the plutonium bullet would vaporize before it reached its target. With that discovery, more energy was poured into developing the implosion-type bomb.

In early 1945, the first U-235 was shipped from the processing plant in Tennessee to Los Alamos. However, Groves was informed that there would only be enough uranium produced by July 1945 to build one bomb. By necessity, the uranium would be used in the gun-type bomb, which was nicknamed Little Boy. Plutonium would be used in the implosion bombs, and the engineers at Hanford predicted they would have enough plutonium by the middle of August 1945 for three bombs. Since the implosion-type bomb had never been used before Groves and Oppenheimer decided they would test it in the desert first before dropping it on Japan. The plutonium bomb was rounder than Little Boy; consequently, it was nicknamed Fat Man.

Truman Becomes President

Before any of the bombs became reality, Roosevelt died at his retreat in Warm Springs, Georgia, on April 12, 1945. His vice president, Harry S. Truman, was sworn in as president that afternoon. Truman, who as a senator was in charge of the Special Committee for Investigating the National Defense Program, had twice asked Henry L. Stimson, Roosevelt's secretary of war, for information about a military project in Hanford, Washington. The committee had received reports, he wrote in a letter to Stimson, that "the undertaking . . . is being carried out in a wasteful manner."[11] He requested that Stimson inform two army officers of the purpose of the project so that they could determine if the project's $2 million was being properly spent. Stimson replied:

> I am sorry that your committee is being pressed by members of the Congress with suggestions that the project is being carried out in a wasteful manner. I assure you that this question as to such waste cannot be justly or properly ascertained until the project has been carried out and its necessity and purpose understood.[12]

Now, a little over a year later, Truman was finally informed about the atom bomb. Groves and Stimson, who met secretly with Truman two weeks after he assumed office, told him they expected to have bombs ready to use in August or September.

Not long after Truman took office, the German scientists were captured and sent to England, Hitler committed suicide April 30 in Berlin, and Germany surrendered May 7, 1945. The war in Europe was officially over.

Trinity

Meanwhile, at Los Alamos, the scientists were beginning preparations to test a plutonium, implosion-type bomb. The test site, twenty-four miles by seventeen miles, was two hundred miles south of Los Alamos and was chosen for its isolation. At Trinity, Oppenheimer's name for the site and the test, a hundred-foot steel tower was built to hold the bomb. The tower would be ground zero. The scientists wanted the bomb off the ground to more closely simulate the actual conditions of the bomb drop and to reduce the amount of sand that would be sucked up by the blast and later rain down as radioactive dust. Observation posts were built ten thousand yards south, north, and west of ground zero to record the blast's effects. A base camp was also built ten miles south of the tower, and twenty miles north of ground zero was Campania Hill, where other observers gathered to watch the explosion.

The plutonium bomb was new and extremely complicated and many of the Los Alamos scientists were certain it would be a dud. Their attitude can best be expressed in a poem known as the *Los Alamos Blues*:

> From this crude lab that spawned the dud,
> Their necks to Truman's axe uncurled,
> Lo, the embattled savants stood
> And fired the flop heard round the world.[13]

Bets wagered by the scientists on the size of the bomb's blast were mostly pessimistic, ranging from zero, a complete dud, to the equivalent of 45,000 tons of TNT. Most believed that Oppenheimer's bet of 300 tons to be the most likely yield. Physicist Edward Teller was optimistic with his wager of 45,000 tons. When I.I. Rabi arrived at the laboratory a few days before the test, the only choice left for his $1 bet was 18,000 tons.

Groves and Oppenheimer selected July 15 or 16, 1945, as the date for the test. Truman would be in Potsdam, Germany, then meeting with Churchill and Joseph Stalin of the Soviet Union to discuss war reparations in Europe, Soviet involvement in the Pacific war, the future of Germany, and the Soviet Union's role in Europe. Truman believed a successful atom bomb test would be his "ace in the hole"[14] for his negotiations with Stalin.

During the night of July 15, a thunderstorm swept through the Trinity test site area, postponing the explosion until 5:30 a.m. on July 16. The waiting seemed interminable to those who had been working on the bomb for years. James B. Conant, president of Harvard University and a leader of the Manhattan Project, later told Groves he never imagined seconds could last so long.

The first impression the observers had was the brilliant flash of light, so intense that it blinded those who looked at it directly. According to a popular story, a blind girl named Georgia Green was traveling in a car with her brother-in-law fifty miles away from the Trinity site. When the bomb exploded, she clutched his arm and is said to have asked him what caused the flash of light. Within milliseconds of its detonation, the fireball had become so large that some feared it would never stop growing. Next came the shock wave. Fermi, instead of watching the explosion, was slowly dropping small pieces of paper. When the shock wave blew the pieces of paper across the desert floor, he paced off the distance. Quick estimations in his head placed the bomb's yield at approximately 20,000 tons. Measurements taken after the blast indicated the bomb's yield was 18,600 tons. Rabi won the betting pool pot of $102.

The thunder from the blast echoed across the desert. Oppenheimer's brother Frank was amazed at the noise from the blast.

> And the thunder from the blast. It bounced on the rocks, and then it went—I don't know where else it bounced. But it never seemed to stop. Not like an ordinary echo with thunder. It just kept echoing back and forth. . . . It was a very scary time when it went off.[15]

Fermi's wife, Laura, later said of her husband, "He was so profoundly and totally absorbed in his bits of paper that he was not aware of the tremendous noise"[16] from the bomb.

After the mushroom cloud dissipated, Rabi felt a chill come over the observers.

> [It] was not the morning cold; it was a chill that came to one when one thought, as for instance when I thought of my wooden house in Cambridge, and my laboratory in New York, and of the millions of people living around there, and this power of nature which we had first understood it to be— well, there it was.[17]

A survey of ground zero later found a crater four hundred yards in diameter. The steel tower was completely vaporized, with just a few twisted feet of metal sticking out of the cement footings. The sand in the crater had melted into glass the color of jade.

The Potsdam Conference

Groves and Oppenheimer had little time to appreciate their success. They had to write a memo to Stimson, who was in

Germany with Truman at the Potsdam Conference, and give him the results of the test. Truman received a preliminary report the same day, and the news elated him and gave him confidence with his meetings with Stalin. Truman felt that with the bomb, the United States would no longer need the Soviet Union's help with the war in the Pacific. Truman hinted obliquely at the bomb to Stalin, telling him that the United States had "a new weapon of unusual destructive force." Stalin seemed to show no particular interest in the news except to reply he was glad to hear it and hoped America would make "good use of it against the Japanese."[18] Some historians believe Stalin showed so little interest in Truman's news because he was already aware of the atom bomb through the German spy Klaus Fuchs, who had been screened and sent to work on the Manhattan Project by the British.

It was at the Potsdam Conference on July 26 that the United States, Great Britain, and China released the Potsdam Declaration, an ultimatum to Japan ordering it to surrender or else face "prompt and utter destruction."[19] The United States had already intercepted secret messages between Japan and the Soviet Union in which the Japanese asked the Soviets to mediate a peace agreement. However, the United States had not yet received any formal request for peace at the time of the Potsdam Declaration. The Soviets also secretly agreed to declare war on Japan in August. Now that the United States had the atom bomb, it was not as eager to have the Soviet Union join the war against Japan as it knew the Soviets would want concessions and territory in the Pacific for its participation, which the United States was not willing to give. Two days after the Potsdam Declaration, the Japanese gave their answer in a radio broadcast. The terms of surrender were "unworthy of consideration," "absurd," and "presumptuous."[20] Truman gave the order to proceed with the atomic bombing as scheduled.

Preparations to Drop the Bomb

Now that the bomb had been proven to work, the disassembled pieces of Little Boy and Fat Man could be shipped to a small island in the Pacific known as Tinian Island. From there, B-29 bombers would fly to Japan and drop the bombs on their targets. A meeting among military and scientific advisors selected five possible cities for possible targets for the atom bomb: Kyoto, Hiroshima, Yokohama, Niigata, and Kokura. Stimson, however, refused to allow Kyoto to be bombed. He argued that Kyoto, as the longtime cultural center and former capital of Japan, was too important to the Japanese to permit its destruction. Nagasaki was substituted instead. Further discussions established that the bomb's first target would be Hiroshima; Kokura would be the second city destroyed. Yokohama, Niigata, and Nagasaki were alternates in case of bad weather over the selected primary targets.

General Carl Spaatz, the commanding officer of the 509th Composite Group, a squadron of B-29 bombers that had been specially modified to carry and drop the atom bomb, received his official orders July 25 to bomb the first target city as soon as weather permitted anytime after August 3. His squadron was to continue to bomb the Japanese cities as soon as he had atomic bombs to drop on them.

Hiroshima

During the early morning hours of August 6, 1945, three B-29 Superfortresses from the 509th Composite Group took off from Tinian Island and started flying toward Japan. Piloting the lead plane, the *Enola Gay*, which carried the atom bomb, was Lieutenant Colonel Paul W. Tibbets. Accompanying him were two observation planes—the *Great Artiste* and the *Necessary Evil*—carrying personnel and equipment to photograph and record the first combat use of the atomic bomb.

At 8:15 A.M., a single B-29 bomber was seen flying over Hiroshima. Some Japanese reported seeing an object and then some parachutes dropping out of the planes; thinking that American pilots were bailing out of their shot-up airplanes, they cheered. The parachutes were carrying observation equipment, however, to record the effects from the bomb's blast. Forty-three seconds later, Little Boy exploded at 1,900 feet above ground level.

Survivors on the ground reported seeing a brilliant white flash followed by a searing wave of heat that burned exposed skin. Almost every building within a radius of one mile from ground zero was demolished by the bomb. Houses three miles away from the bomb's hypocenter were flattened. American reconnaissance planes flew over Hiroshima four hours later and could not see the city below due to the smoke from the fires that raged out of control throughout the city.

The Japanese had no idea about what had happened to Hiroshima. An official radio broadcast told the Japanese people, "Hiroshima suffered considerable damage as the result of an attack by a few B-29s. It is believed that a new type of bomb was used. The details are being investigated."[21] Military officials could hardly believe that an entire city was destroyed by a single bomb. A Japanese general sent to investigate reported:

> There was but one black dead tree, as if a crow was perched on it. There was nothing there but that tree. As we landed at the airport all the grass was red as if it had been toasted. . . . Everything had burned up simultaneously. Some schools with blow-off roofs and broken windows were left standing at some distance from the center of the city. But the city itself was completely wiped out. That must be the word, yes, completely wiped out.[22]

Despite the devastation suffered by Hiroshima, and even after Russia had declared war on Japan on August 8, most of the Japanese military hierarchy decided that Japan must continue to fight. Some factions within the Japanese government were urging peace, but three days after Hiroshima, no consensus on surrender had yet been reached.

Nagasaki

Some Japanese military and political officials did not believe that the United States had more than one atomic bomb. In order to convince Japan to surrender, Groves, Truman, and Stimson believed it was essential to drop a second atomic bomb as soon as possible after the first bomb had been dropped on Hiroshima. The timetable for the second atom bomb, Fat Man, was speeded up, and on August 9, it was ready to be dropped.

Bad weather over the primary target of Kokura forced Major Charles W. Sweeney, the pilot of *Bock's Car* which was carrying the atom bomb, to divert to the secondary target of Nagasaki. Nagasaki was also obscured by clouds, but at the last minute, the clouds broke open and the second atom bomb known as Fat Man was dropped on Japan.

Fat Man exploded 1,600 feet above the city with an estimated force of 22,000 tons. The target seen through the clouds was several miles upriver from the original aiming point. Although the damage from the bomb was less severe than the damage at Hiroshima, an estimated 50 percent of the population died from the bomb in the next five years.

Although a third bomb was being prepared to drop on another Japanese city, Truman ordered that atomic bombing be stopped. The idea of killing another 100,000 people was just too horrible, he said, and he could not stand the idea of killing "all those kids."[23]

Surrender

Early in the morning of August 9, the Japanese war council met once again to discuss the possibility of surrender. Although Foreign Minister Shigenori Togo had not yet been informed about the second atomic bomb on Nagasaki, he did know that Japanese troops were faring poorly against an attack by Russian troops in Manchuria. Togo believed Japan was fighting a lost cause and recommended the council accept the terms of surrender as outlined in the Potsdam Declaration. Togo's feelings were not universal, however; Minister of War Korechika Anami and Home Minister Genki Abe did not think the Japanese people would accept a surrender. Reports of the war to the people had always been positive, they said, and so few Japanese knew the true situation. Abe explained their reasoning:

> Because of the Army propaganda that Japan was winning the war, the majority . . . did not realize that Japan was thoroughly defeated. Therefore, if the Potsdam Declaration was

accepted unconditionally, there was the possibility that this would cause considerable confusion and . . . might give rise to assassination of Cabinet ministers by the irate public.[24]

The war council was evenly split over surrender, even after they received news about the bombing of Nagasaki. To resolve the deadlock, Premier Kantaro Suzuki took the unprecedented step of calling in Emperor Hirohito to listen to the arguments and to make the final decision. Although the Japanese people believed Hirohito to be divine, he was mainly a figurehead in the government; all the war decisions had been made by his war council. Finally, at 2 A.M. on August 10, Hirohito announced his decision to his war council:

> I cannot bear to see my innocent people struggle any longer. Ending the war is the only way to restore world peace and to relieve the nation from the terrible distress with which it is burdened.[25]

Thus given a direct order by their emperor, the war council notified the United States that it would surrender provided that the emperor be permitted to retain his throne and authority. The United States agreed, with the stipulation that during the Allied occupation, Hirohito must submit to the authority of the Supreme Commander of the Allied Powers. The surrender was officially accepted on August 14, and the next day was proclaimed V-J (Victory over Japan) Day. The Japanese people heard their emperor's voice for the first time as he announced the news of Japan's surrender over the radio:

> Despite the best that has been done by everyone . . . the war situation has developed not necessarily to Japan's advantage, while the general trends of the world have all turned against her interest. Moreover, the enemy has begun to employ a new and most cruel bomb, the power of which to do damage is indeed incalculable, taking the toll of many innocent lives. . . . This is the reason why We have ordered the acceptance of the provisions of the Joint declaration of the Powers. . . .

The hardships and sufferings to which Our nation is to be subjected hereafter will be certainly great. We are keenly aware of the inmost feelings of all ye, Our subjects. However it is according to the dictate of time and fate that We have resolved to pave the way for a grand peace for all generations to come by enduring the unendurable and suffering what is insufferable.[26]

The war was over.

The Atomic Energy Commission

The destruction of Hiroshima and Nagasaki horrified many of the scientists working on the Manhattan Project, even those who thought the bomb should have been dropped without warning on Japan. They believed using the bombs would lead to a nuclear arms race, as other countries developed their own bombs to prevent the United States from having a monopoly on atomic weapons. But whatever their stance on the use and development of the bomb, most scientists were firmly in favor of removing America's atomic energy policy from the control of the military. They believed civilians should direct America's nuclear policies. With the support of almost everyone involved in the Manhattan Project except Groves and the military, Congress created the Atomic Energy Commission (AEC) in 1946 which placed civilians in control of America's atomic energy policy. Groves formally turned over command of the Manhattan Project to David Lilienthal, the AEC's first chairman, on January 1, 1947.

Espionage

Some scientists and policymakers maintained that civilian control of atomic energy policy was not enough. They argued that only an international panel of atomic energy experts could ensure that safeguards were established to prevent the emergence of a nuclear arms race. Bernard M. Baruch, the American delegate to the United Nations' Atomic Energy Commission, presented a plan to the United Nations in which an international panel would supervise and control all aspects and products of atomic energy, from the production of raw materials to the operation of nuclear reactor plants. In addition, under Baruch's plan, the United States would destroy all its nuclear weapons once a system was installed to verify that no other country was capable of building atomic bombs. The United States believed it was being magnanimous in offering its atomic secrets to the world. However, the Soviets refused to agree to the plan. Teller later explains why the Soviet Union refused to accept the Baruch Plan:

> The plan was a good one. . . . Most Americans could not understand why Russia did not snap at the nuclear cooperation offered by the Baruch Plan . . . to share with the whole world, including Russia, atomic information that we considered secret and valuable. . . . The joke was on us. . . . Russia did not need the Baruch Plan. Russia had Klaus Fuchs.[27]

When the Baruch Plan was presented to the United Nations, Fuchs had been a Russian spy for over five years, since 1941. Everything he had learned about atomic energy from his work with Rudolf Peierls in Birmingham, England, to the Manhattan Project in Los Alamos, New Mexico, had been turned over to the Soviets. Thanks to the information provided by Fuchs, Stalin was aware of the atomic bomb before Truman told him about it at the Potsdam Conference in July 1945. The Russians were also able to test their own version of the atom bomb sometime in August 1949, years before many believed the Soviet Union would be capable of building its own bomb. The Manhattan Project scientists knew that the theory behind the atom bomb was not a secret; but they still believed it would take the Russians at least five years. Groves preferred to think it would be at least ten to twenty years before the Soviets tested a nuclear weapon. However, Fuchs's betrayal advanced the Russian atomic program by at least eighteen months and as much as three years. Fuchs was arrested in 1949 for espionage by Great Britain and was sentenced to fourteen years in prison in 1950. He was released after serving nine years; he then moved to East Germany where he continued to work in atomic research.

The Cold War

Shortly after Truman announced that American satellites had detected radiation in the atmosphere from a Soviet atom bomb, Teller's pet project of a "super" or hydrogen bomb was resurrected. And so began the race to "catch-up and get ahead."[28] The United States tested its first hydrogen bomb, code-named Mike, on November 2, 1952. The bomb had the equivalent yield of 10.4 million tons (megatons) of TNT, a thousand times more explosive than Little Boy. The Soviets responded by testing more atomic bombs and then its own hydrogen bomb in 1955. Columnist Walter Lippman coined the term "Cold War" to describe the tense relations between the United States and the Soviet Union.

During this period of nuclear arms race, atomic energy was also being developed for other, peaceful uses. The first nuclear power plant was built in the United States in 1957. Medical and biological research use radioactive isotopes to diagnose and treat medical conditions. Stimson wrote about the dangers and the promise of atomic energy in 1946:

> The development of atomic energy holds great, but as yet unexploited, promise for the well-being of civilization. Whether this promise will be realized depends on whether the danger of swift and unprecedented destruction can be removed from the earth. Whether it is removed depends on whether we and other nations move firmly, quickly, and with frank transparency of purpose toward the goal of uniting all men of good will against the appalling threat to man's very existence. The focus of the problem does not lie in the atom; it resides in the hearts of men.[29]

The legacy of the atom bomb extends beyond the Cold War and into the present-day. The atom bomb establishes a new balance of power between the countries that have the bomb—the United States, Russia, Great Britain, France, China, Israel, South Africa, India, Pakistan—and those that do not. For example, after India tested its first nuclear weapon in May 1998, Pakistan—refusing to be intimidated by a country with which it has frequent border clashes—

followed with its own nuclear test within a few weeks, despite the financial toll producing and testing such a weapon has on its economy. Combined with the social, economic, and technological factors that followed the discovery of fission, the development of the atom bomb has ushered in a new global era.

Notes

1. Quoted in Richard Rhodes, *The Making of the Atomic Bomb*. New York: Simon and Schuster, 1988, p. 672.

2. Naomi Shohno, *The Legacy of Hiroshima: Its Past, Our Future*. Tokyo: Kosei Publishing, 1986, pp. 31–32.

3. Ibid., pp. 128–29.

4. Quoted in Fletcher Knebel and Charles W. Baile II, *No High Ground*. New York: Harper and Row, 1960, p. i.

5. Quoted in Spencer R. Weart and Gertrud Weiss Szilard, eds., *Leo Szilard: His Version of the Facts: Selected Recollections and Correspondence*. Cambridge, MA: MIT Press, 1978, p. 53.

6. Quoted in Robert Jungk, *Brighter than a Thousand Suns: A Personal History of the Atomic Scientists*. New York: Harcourt, Brace, 1958, p. 112.

7. Ibid., p. 114.

8. Quoted in Rhodes, *The Making of the Atomic Bomb*, p. 512.

9. Ibid., p. 607.

10. Ibid., p. 610.

11. Quoted in Michael B. Stoff, Jonathan F. Fanton, and R. Hal Williams, eds., *The Manhattan Project: A Documentary Introduction to the Atomic Age*. New York: McGraw-Hill, 1991, p. 51.

12. Ibid., p. 53.

13. Quoted in Lansing Lamont, *Day of Trinity*. New York: Atheneum, 1965, p. 180.

14. Don E. Beyer, *The Manhattan Project: America Makes the First Atomic Bomb*. New York: Franklin Watts, 1991, p. 66.

15. Quoted in Rhodes, *The Making of the Atomic Bomb*, p. 675.

16. Laura Fermi, *Atoms in the Family: My Life with Enrico Fermi*. Chicago: University of Chicago Press, 1954, p. 239.

17. Quoted in Rhodes, *The Making of the Atomic Bomb*, p. 675.

18. Harry S. Truman, *Memoirs: Vol. I: Year of Decisions*. Garden City, NY: Doubleday, 1955, p. 416.

19. *Foreign Relations of the United States Diplomatic Papers: The Conference of Berlin (The Potsdam Conference) 1945, Vol. I*. Washington, DC: U.S. Government Printing Office, 1960, p. 894.

20. Quoted in Michael Blow, *The History of the Atomic Bomb*. New York: American Heritage Publishing, 1968, p. 100.

21. Ibid., p. 114.

22. Ibid., p. 115.

23. Quoted in Rhodes, *The Making of the Atomic Bomb*, p. 743.

24. Quoted in Blow, *The History of the Atomic Bomb*, p. 123.

25. Ibid.

26. Quoted in Rhodes, *The Making of the Atomic Bomb*, pp. 745–46.

27. Quoted in Blow, *The History of the Atomic Bomb*, pp. 132–33.

28. Beyer, *The Manhattan Project*, p. 83.

29. Quoted in Blow, *The History of the Atomic Bomb*, p. 145.

Chapter 1

The Development of the Atom Bomb

The Discovery of Fission

C.P. Snow

In the early 1900s, scientists were learning the secrets of the atomic nucleus. Scientists had long known that the atom was comprised of smaller, electrically charged particles, known as electrons and protons. Some even suspected the presence of a third atomic particle with no electrical charge, a particle whose presence was finally confirmed in 1932.

The discovery of the neutron, as the particle was called, was instrumental in the development of the atomic bomb, according to C.P. Snow. Neutrons explained the reason for isotopes, a phenomenon in which atoms of the same element have different atomic weights which was now attributable to an extra neutron or two in their nucleus. Snow notes that some of these isotopes are extremely unstable; by bombarding them with more neutrons, scientists were able to split the atom's nucleus, thus forming two other elements. This process, which became known as fission, also releases a large amount of energy that was later harnessed to fuel a tremendous explosion.

C.P. Snow (1905–1980) was a chemist and physicist in England during the 1930s. He was chief of scientific personnel for the ministry of labor during World War II. He is best known for *Strangers and Brothers*, his series of novels that examines English life and the relationship between scientists and academics between 1920 and 1950.

The year 1932 was one of scientific revelations. British physicist Ernest Rutherford had once predicted, with one of his direct intuitions backed by good firm reasoning, that a third sub-atomic particle must exist. The light-weight, negatively charged electrons were now old friends. The atomic nucleus must contain much heavier, positively charged particles. Physicists called them protons. According to Rutherford, there must exist another particle, as heavy as the proton, but having no electrical charge.

Such a neutral particle would possess great carrying power once it was on the move. With no electrical charge, its motion could not be altered by the electrical charge of an atomic nucleus. It could be stopped only by direct collision. There actually was some evidence from disintegration experiments that such particles existed: but it was necessary to know what one was looking for. In Paris, the great tradition of the Curies continued in the hands of their daughter Irène. [Pierre and Marie Curie, a husband-and-wife team of French physicists, won the Nobel Prize for their work in radioactivity.] She had married the Curies' assistant, Frédéric Joliot, and they combined their names, as they did their research. The Joliot-Curies had evidence for Rutherford's neutral particle in their own experiments, but they had mistakenly interpreted it as a kind of penetrating radiation.

But James Chadwick of Great Britain knew what he was looking for. He calculated just what effects would distinguish a neutral particle from radiation. And then he set up experiments of classical beauty and simplicity to look for these effects. Like the Joliot-Curies, he shot alpha particles at a target of the light metal beryllium; and out came the mysterious 'radiation.' But Chadwick intercepted it with paraffin wax. The 'radiation' hit the nuclei of hydrogen atoms within the paraffin wax, and ejected *them* at high speed. Now the nucleus of hydrogen is none other than a single proton. By his measurements on the ejected protons, Chadwick proved that what was hitting them was not radiation: it was a neutral particle, almost identical in mass to the proton. . . .

The Neutron

The chargeless particle was named the neutron. It was at once clear that it must be a constituent of all atomic nuclei (apart from the single-proton nucleus of hydrogen). At last there was an explanation for the puzzle about atomic weights and atomic numbers. The relative weights of atoms are usually near whole numbers: the carbon atom is twelve times as heavy as the hydrogen atom, so its atomic weight is 12. Since electrons are very light, this means that the carbon nucleus is twelve times as heavy as the hydrogen nucleus which consists of a single proton. So the carbon nucleus is as heavy as twelve protons.

Chemists, however, rank the elements by atomic number, the number of electrons an atom has. It is the electrons which govern an atom's chemical behaviour. But each negatively charged electron 'in orbit' must be balanced by a positively charged proton in the nucleus. The atomic number thus automatically turns out to equal the number of protons in the nucleus. Carbon has an atomic number of 6, it has six protons in the nucleus. With the discovery of the neutron, it became obvious that the difference between its atomic weight of 12 and its atomic number of 6 was made up by six neutrons in the nucleus. They added the mass of six protons to the nucleus without adding any electric charge.

The existence of the neutron also solved at a stroke the problem of isotopes—atoms of the same chemical element, but with different atomic weights. Among a hundred carbon atoms taken at random, ninety-nine have an atomic weight of 12, one is slightly heavier, at 13. Scientists call these isotopes carbon-12 and carbon-13 respectively. Since they have the same chemical properties, each must have six electrons, and a corresponding six protons in the nucleus. The difference in weight must depend on neutrons. Carbon-12 has six neutrons, carbon-13 has seven.

Although the number of neutrons doesn't affect an atom's chemical properties, it—not surprisingly—does change the stability of the nucleus itself. You can add another neutron to carbon-13, to produce carbon-14, with eight neutrons to the six protons. This is too unbalanced. The nucleus is unstable. One of the neutrons spontaneously changes to a proton, emitting a high-speed electron in the process. This radioactive form of carbon is in fact most useful to archaeologists; the gradual decay of carbon-14 atoms enables them to calculate the age of organic remains. The radioactive properties of the different isotopes of the uranium atom were at the end of the decade to have a far more lethal significance. . . .

Experimenting with Neutrons

In Paris, the Joliot-Curies assuaged their chagrin over not recognizing the neutron by producing artificial radioactivity. By bombarding ordinary, stable isotopes of common elements with alpha particles they created new isotopes unknown in nature, and so unstable that they spontaneously broke up and emitted radiation just like the naturally occurring radioactive atoms.

In Rome physicist Enrico Fermi and his school carried that major discovery a decisive step further in 1934. To make isotopes with an unusual number of neutrons, they simply bombarded atoms with neutrons, in the hope that they would stick when they hit the target nucleus. Fermi decided to slow the neutrons down by sending them through paraffin. One of his gifts was inspired common sense, and he explained that the neutrons were more likely to stick in the nucleus they were hitting, the slower they moved. . . .

Later in 1934, Fermi bombarded uranium atoms with his slow neutrons. The results were puzzling. The nuclear scientists couldn't agree on an explanation. An abnormal amount of radiation was being emitted. The natural interpretation was that some uranium nuclei had been collecting neutrons, and had been transmuted into elements unknown to nature—christened trans-uranic elements, for they would have heavier nuclei than uranium, the heaviest naturally present on earth. And these very heavy nuclei should be unstable: their radioactive breakdown could produce the copious radiation that Fermi was picking up. The achievement of new, artificial elements—a misinterpretation as it finally transpired—was actually announced in the Italian press with joyous fanfares. What should the new element or elements be called? Fermi, as usual cool-headed, remained somewhat sceptical about his own discovery, but began to believe in it. So did others. There were more random suggestions than had so far happened in any nuclear research. It was a pity, people thought later, that Rutherford, who had died shortly before, wasn't on the scene. It was just the sort of problem that he might have seen straight through.

One of the best chemists in the world, Otto Hahn, decided to repeat the Fermi experiments at the Kaiser Wilhelm Institute in Berlin. Not surprisingly, since Fermi and his colleagues were first-class experimentors, Hahn obtained the same results. Hahn did some careful chemistry on the end-products. The common isotope of uranium, uranium-238, has 92 protons and 146 neutrons in its nucleus. Transuranic elements would contain more of both, and have new chemical properties. But what Hahn was expecting to find was radium, on the rival interpretation that the neutrons were simply knocking fragments out of the uranium atom. A uranium atom that loses two alpha particles becomes radium-230.

But he found neither. To his own astonishment, and everyone else's, what he did keep on finding was barium. And barium has a very much lighter nucleus. The common isotope has 56 protons and 82 neutrons; a total of 138 particles bound together in the nucleus, as compared to uranium's 238. And all he could detect was barium. An impurity? But Hahn was one of the most meticulous of all chemists, and that was about as likely as if he had absentmindedly slipped in some copper sulphate.

Once more suggestions proliferated, much talk, speculations getting nowhere.

Challenging the Assumption

When Hahn began to repeat the Fermi work, he had a collaborator called Lise Meitner. Lise Meitner was a respected and much loved physicist on the staff of the Kaiser Wilhelm Institute. She was Jewish, but of Austrian nationality and so, by some skilful covering up, had managed to keep her job. Then Hitler's troops marched into Austria; overnight Lise Meitner's nationality changed to German, and it was more than time to quit. Having good fortune, she managed to escape to Sweden, and it was there, in Göteborg, that she entertained her nephew, Otto Frisch, during the Christmas of

1938. Frisch was another high-class physicist and another refugee who had found sanctuary in Copenhagen. He arrived in Göteborg late at night, and didn't see his aunt until the following morning.

Splitting a Liquid Drop

During Christmas 1938, two physicists, Lise Meitner and her nephew Otto Frisch, puzzled over a letter from Meitner's former partner, Otto Hahn. Hahn asked Meitner if she could think of an explanation for why barium was appearing in his neutron experiments with uranium. As Meitner and Frisch studied the problem, they began to envision the uranium nucleus as a liquid drop. The neutron's energy would transform the round nucleus into an elongated nucleus. The electrical charges of the nucleus would force each end of the elongated nucleus farther apart, until the uranium nucleus eventually broke into two roughly equal halves, forming two new elements. This diagram illustrates how a slow-moving neutron could cause uranium-235, an unstable isotope of uranium, to split and form barium and krypton.

Disintegration of Uranium by a Slow Neutron

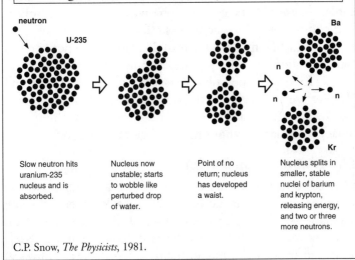

Slow neutron hits uranium-235 nucleus and is absorbed.	Nucleus now unstable; starts to wobble like perturbed drop of water.	Point of no return; nucleus has developed a waist.	Nucleus splits in smaller, stable nuclei of barium and krypton, releasing energy, and two or three more neutrons.

C.P. Snow, *The Physicists*, 1981.

They were an affectionate couple. Both were suffering exile and hardship. Still, the first thing they talked about was her latest letter from Hahn. Why could he detect nothing but barium? Frisch raised the conventional doubts: impurities? carelessness? Impatiently Lise Meitner brushed them aside. She had complete trust in her old chief.

They went for a walk in the winter woods. Each seems to have had the same thought, up to now inadmissible. Like everyone else, they had been living with an assumption. They had all taken for granted that heavy nuclei couldn't be split in two. Could that be wrong?

Nuclei seemed to be stable objects. Although the positively charged protons must repel one another, as all 'like' electric charges do, the presence of the neutrons glues the nucleus firmly together. Scientists had come to accept that there must be a nuclear force, in addition to the two forces then known—of gravitation and electromagnetism. In the big nuclei, the protons are repelling one another so strongly that there must be more neutrons than protons to keep the whole lot glued together. Even so, some nuclei of the really heavyweight kind—like radium—can't contain all that electric force. Small fragments spontaneously break off. These consist of two protons and two neutrons—a bullet carrying off two units of electric charge and leaving the nucleus more stable. These bullets are the alpha particles, which Rutherford had harnessed to such good effect.

So even when nuclei were unstable, all experience showed that they didn't break up. They simply emitted small fragments. Like all other physicists of the 1930s, Frisch and Meitner were carrying that assumption with them unquestioned. Now they alone, of all the physicists in the world, woke up to that assumption, and began to question it.

The Liquid-Drop Model

They sat down. It wasn't comfortable in a Swedish Christmas time, but neither noticed that. Lise Meitner did some calculations. Although the structure of the nucleus was still a mystery, the Danish physicist and Nobel laureate Niels Bohr had proposed a model for it. With his great physical insight, Bohr had ignored all the complications—that nothing was known of the nature of nuclear force, for example. Two decades earlier his brilliantly simple model for the electrons in the hydrogen atom had paved the way for the correct, highly sophisticated quantum mechanical answer. Now he simply likened the nucleus to a drop of water. A water drop is held together by the attraction of the water molecules for each other; a nucleus is held together by the nuclear force between its constituents. The analogy is there. Let us not worry about the nature of the nuclear force. The electrical repulsion between the protons could be simply fitted to this model too.

Meitner carried on calculating, using Bohr's liquid-drop model as her guide. Frisch followed her. In Bohr's model the sums were quite simple. Almost at once they knew they had the answer. A heavy nucleus can indeed break into two halves. Imagine a water drop which is electrically charged to the limit of its extent to hold the charge. Water molecules can evaporate from the surface and carry off the excess charge—this is the equivalent of alpha-particle ejection from radium. Alternatively, the stresses within the drop can split it into two smaller drops. These are more tightly bound than larger drops. In the case of nuclei, the two small nuclei can contain the electric charges that made the parent nucleus unstable.

The neutrons that Fermi, and later Hahn, had fired at uranium nuclei had pushed them over the brink. The uranium nuclei didn't accept the neutrons, to build up heavier, trans-uranic, elements. The neutrons didn't just knock off small fragments. Under neutron bombardment, the uranium nuclei split into two smaller, lighter nuclei. The split need not be exactly half and half. A typical break-up would produce barium (with 56 protons) and the gas krypton (which has 36 protons). Here was the reason for Hahn's strange discovery.

Frisch and Meitner did more sums, to check the release of energy. Those came out right. They had been out in the snow for three hours.

They were cautious, as they had to be. The result, in

terms of pure science, was important but not earthshaking. Heavy nuclei could be disintegrated. It was going to deepen understanding of the nucleus. They had an intimation, though, that the result, in terms of other than the purely scientific, might be momentous.

"What Idiots We All Have Been"

Lise Meitner went back to Stockholm after one of the more remarkable aunt-nephew reunions. Frisch returned to Copenhagen and reported to Bohr. Frisch, not usually an excitable young man, burst into the scientific explanation. Bohr, just about to take a trip to America, accepted the explanation within moments of Frisch beginning to speak. It was then that Bohr made his supreme comment: 'Oh, what idiots we all have been. This is just as it must be.'

It shows the power of a received idea that so many of the best scientific minds in the world had scrabbled about for months, averting themselves from the simplest conclusion. However, they soon made up for lost time. By a loose tongue within Bohr's entourage, the news was leaked as soon as his party arrived in New York. American laboratories repeated the experiment, confirming the results, measuring the energy discharge. Bohr was obliged to ensure that the prime credit went to Meitner-Frisch (whose letter to the science journal *Nature* wasn't, in fact, the first published statement). With his incorruptible sense of justice, he exerted himself in getting the record straight, while he had more imperative matters to think about.

Physicists all over the world were in a ferment. Experiments everywhere. Gossip in newspapers. There were sceptics, but most scientists of sober judgement accepted that the discovery must mean that nuclear energy might sometime be set at large. The obvious thought was that this might lead to explosives of stupendous power.

An Explosive Chain Reaction

Was this realistic? It would be so only if the neutron which split a uranium nucleus could bring about a chain reaction— a scientific term which soon became a common layman's phrase. Each time a uranium nucleus split apart, it released energy as heat. But nuclear energy would never be a reality if one had to keep firing neutrons from some source at the uranium atoms to break them up. If, on the other hand, the uranium atom released neutrons as it split up, then these neutrons could go on and break up other nuclei. The neutrons from these disintegrations would trigger more, producing a chain of reactions that would carry on without outside help, liberating more and more heat, quicker and quicker. So far there was no sign of that. If there had been, Hahn's laboratory, and a good many others, wouldn't have been in a state to report the results: nor would a number of nice comfortable university towns.

Bohr got to work. So did a young colleague of his at Princeton, John Wheeler, a fine and strong-minded scientist who had the distinction of being the only person of Anglo-Saxon descent right at the centre of these first sensations. He and Bohr arrived at the answer with speed and clarity.

Obviously—and fortunately—most of the uranium nuclei were not being split. A small proportion were. These must belong to a particularly susceptible uranium isotope. Nuclear fission—this term for the splitting of a nucleus was just coming into use—happened not in the stable, common nucleus of uranium (uranium-238), but in that of the much rarer isotope uranium-235. Both have 92 protons, but the neutrons number 146 and 143 respectively. Bohr, now feeling his way with certainty among nuclear structures, gave reasons for the nuclei of uranium-235 being fissile. It was a classical piece of scientific thinking. It was absolutely right. At this distance, it jumps to the eye as being right. But it was not immediately accepted. Fermi, who untypically made several misjudgements during this period, didn't believe it. There were weeks of argument. It was March 1939 before the community of physicists were convinced that this uranium isotope could be disintegrated, emit neutrons, and, if accumulated in quantity, might start a chain reaction. Collect enough uranium-235, and there was the chance of an immense explosion.

There the pure science finished.

The First Nuclear Chain Reaction

Laura Fermi

With the discovery of fission—the splitting of an atom's nucleus by bombarding it with slow-moving neutrons—scientists had found a huge potential energy source. The quest then turned to developing a method that would provide a self-sustaining source of nuclear energy. Scientists theorized that a nuclear chain reaction could be achieved if uranium—which produces more free neutrons during fission than are absorbed—was bombarded by neutrons that were slowed down by a carbon-based barrier such as graphite.

In the following article, Laura Fermi describes the steps taken by her husband, Italian physicist Enrico Fermi, to achieve the first controlled nuclear chain reaction. In December 1942 in an abandoned squash court at the University of Chicago, Enrico Fermi built a pile, or nuclear reactor, out of graphite bricks and lumps of uranium to test the theory of a chain reaction. The experiment was a success, and America's program to develop the atom bomb officially began.

Laura Fermi is the author of *Atoms in the Family: My Life with Enrico Fermi.*

The operation of the atomic pile was the result of almost four years of sustained work, which started when discovery of uranium fission became known, arousing enormous interest among physicists.

Experiments at Columbia University and at other universities in the United States had confirmed Enrico Fermi's hypothesis that neutrons would be emitted in the process of fission. Consequently, a chain reaction appeared possible in theory. To achieve it in practice seemed a vague and distant possibility. The odds against it were so great that only the small group of stubborn physicists at Columbia pursued work in that direction. At once they were faced with two sets of difficulties.

Two Difficulties

The first lay in the fact that neutrons emitted in the process of uranium fission were too fast to be effective atomic bullets and to cause fission in uranium. The second difficulty was due to loss of neutrons: under normal circumstances most of the neutrons produced in fission escaped into the air or were absorbed by matter before they had a chance of acting as uranium splitters. Too few produced fission to cause a chain reaction.

Neutrons would have to be slowed down and their losses reduced by a large factor, if a chain reaction was to be achieved. Was this feasible?

To slow down neutrons was an old trick for Enrico, from the time when he and his friends in Rome had recognized the extraordinary action of paraffin and water on neutrons. So the group at Columbia—Leo Szilard, Walter Zinn, Herbert Anderson, and Enrico—undertook the investigation of fission of uranium under water. Water, in the physicists' language, was being used as a moderator.

After many months of research they came to the conclusion that neither water nor any other hydrogenated substance is a suitable moderator. Hydrogen absorbs too many neutrons and makes a chain reaction impossible.

Leo Szilard and Fermi suggested trying carbon for a moderator. They thought that carbon would slow down neutrons sufficiently and absorb fewer of them than water, provided it was of a high degree of purity. Impurities have an astounding capacity for swallowing neutrons.

Graphite

Szilard and Fermi conceived a contrivance that they thought might produce a chain reaction. It would be made of uranium and very pure graphite disposed in layers: layers exclusively of graphite would alternate with layers in which uranium chunks would be imbedded in graphite. In other words, it would be a "pile."

An atomic pile is, of necessity, a bulky object. If it were too small, neutrons would escape into the surrounding air before they had a chance to hit a uranium atom, and they would be lost to fission and chain reaction. How large the pile ought to be, nobody knew.

Did it matter whether the scientists did not know the size of the pile? All they had to do, one might think, was to put blocks of graphite over blocks of graphite, alternating them with lumps of uranium, and keep on at it until they had reached the critical size, at which a chain reaction would occur. They could also give the pile different shapes—cubical, pyramidal, oval, spherical—and determine which worked best.

It was not so simple. Only a few grams of metallic uranium were available in the United States, and no commercial graphite came close to the requirements of purity.

The 1951 edition of Webster's *New Collegiate Dictionary* states that graphite is "soft, black, native carbon of metallic luster; often called *plumbago* or *black lead*. It is used for lead pencils, crucibles, lubricants, etc. . . ." The atomic pile built in 1942, clearly included in the "etc.," was to use as much graphite as would go into making a pencil for each inhabitant of the earth, man, woman, and child. Moreover, graphite for a pile must be of a state of purity absolutely inconceivable for any other purpose. Scientists would have to be patient. . . .

More Space Is Needed

The experiments proceeded slowly for lack of materials, and Fermi would have liked to speed up his work. Besides, he was convinced that from the behavior of a small pile he would obtain much information pertinent to building a larger pile. Fermi and his group were able to start work on the "small pile" by the spring of 1941. They demolished their column of graphite bricks and laid them down again, placing lumps of uranium among them. Slowly, as more graphite arrived at Columbia, a black wall grew up. The black wall reached the ceiling; but it was still far from being a chain-reacting pile: too many neutrons escaped from it or were absorbed inside it, and too few remained to produce fission.

It became evident that the experiment could not be pursued to final success in that same laboratory. A larger room, with higher ceiling, was needed. No such room was available at Columbia, and somebody would have to look for one elsewhere. Fermi was absorbed in his research. His work was too important to be interrupted. So Herbert Anderson took off his overalls, put on a suit coat and a hat, and went scouting New York City and its suburbs in search of a loft that could house a pile. He spotted several possibilities and began some bargaining aimed at the best deal.

Before Herbert could take a final choice, Enrico learned that he, his group, his equipment, and the materials he had gathered would have to move to Chicago. It was the very end of 1941.

A few days previously, on December 6, Vannevar Bush, who was at the head of the Uranium Project, had announced that an all-out effort would be made to speed up atomic research. He had then assigned the various responsibilities to different top men and had placed Professor Arthur H. Compton, of the University of Chicago, in charge of fundamental physical studies of the chain reaction. Soon afterward Compton had resolved to bring all work under him to Chicago. . . .

The Squash Court

The best place Compton had been able to find for work on the pile was a squash court under the West Stands of Stagg Field, the University of Chicago stadium. [University] President [Robert] Hutchins had banned football from the Chicago campus, and Stagg Field was used for odd purposes. To the west, on Ellis Avenue, the stadium is closed by a tall gray-stone structure in the guise of a medieval castle. Through a heavy portal is the entrance to the space beneath the West Stands. The Squash Court was part of this space. It was 30 feet wide, twice as long, and over 26 feet high.

The physicists would have liked more space, but places better suited for the pile, which Professor Compton had hoped he could have, had been requisitioned by the expanding armed forces stationed in Chicago. The physicists were to be contented with the Squash Court, and there Herbert Anderson had started assembling piles. They were still "small piles," because material flowed to the West Stands at a very slow, if steady, pace. . . .

The pile never reached the ceiling. It was planned as a sphere 26 feet in diameter, but the last layers were never put into place. The sphere remained flattened at the top. . . . The critical size of the pile was attained sooner than was anticipated.

Only six weeks had passed from the laying of the first graphite brick, and it was the morning of December 2, 1942. . . .

The Day Arrives

There is no record of what were the feelings of the three young men who crouched on top of the pile, under the ceiling of the square balloon. They were called the "suicide squad." It was a joke, but perhaps they were asking themselves whether the joke held some truth. They were like firemen alerted to the possibility of a fire, ready to extinguish it. If something unexpected were to happen, if the pile should get out of control, they would "extinguish" it by flooding it was a cadmium solution. Cadmium absorbs neutrons and prevents a chain reaction.

A sense of apprehension was in the air. Everyone felt it, but outwardly, at least, they were all calm and composed.

Getting DuPont Interested

Among the persons who gathered in the Squash Court on that morning, one was not connected with the Met. Lab.— Mr. Crawford H. Greenewalt of E.I. duPont de Nemours, who later became the president of the company. Arthur Compton had led him there out of a near-by room where, on that day, he and other men from his company happened to be holding talks with top Army officers.

Mr. Greenewalt and the duPont people were in a difficult position, and they did not know how to reach a decision. The Army had taken over the Uranium Project on the previous August and renamed it Manhattan District. In September General Leslie R. Groves was placed in charge of it. General Groves must have been of a trusting nature: before a chain reaction was achieved, he was already urging the duPont de Nemours Company to build and operate piles on a production scale.

In a pile, Mr. Greenewalt was told, a new element, plutonium, is created during uranium fission. Plutonium would probably be suited for making atomic bombs. So Greenewalt and his group had been taken to Berkeley to see the work done on plutonium, and then flown to Chicago for more negotiations with the Army.

Mr. Greenewalt was hesitant. Of course his company would like to help win the war! But piles and plutonium!

With the Army's insistent voice in his ears, Compton, who had attended the conference, decided to break the rules and take Mr. Greenewalt to witness the first operation of a pile.

The Show Begins

They all climbed onto the balcony at the north end of the Squash Court; all, except the three boys perched on top of the pile and except a young physicist, George Weil, who stood alone on the floor by a cadmium rod that he was to pull out of the pile when so instructed.

And so the show began.

There was utter silence in the audience, and only Fermi spoke. His gray eyes betrayed his intense thinking, and his hands moved along with his thoughts.

"The pile is not performing now because inside it there are rods of cadmium which absorb neutrons. One single rod is sufficient to prevent a chain reaction. So our first step will be to pull out of the pile all control rods, but the one that George Weil will man." As he spoke others acted. Each chore had been assigned in advance and rehearsed. So Fermi went on speaking, and his hands pointed out the things he mentioned.

"This rod, that we have pulled out with the others, is automatically controlled. Should the intensity of the reaction become greater than a pre-set limit, this rod would go back inside the pile by itself.

"This pen will trace a line indicating the intensity of the radiation. When the pile chain-reacts, the pen will trace a line that will go up and up and that will not tend to level off. In other words, it will be an exponential line.

"Presently we shall begin our experiment. George will pull out his rod a little at a time. We shall take measurements and verify that the pile will keep on acting as we have calculated.

"Weil will first set the rod at thirteen feet. This means that thirteen feet of the rod will still be inside the pile. The counters will click faster and the pen will move up to this point, and then its trace will level off. Go ahead, George!"

Eyes turned to the graph pen. Breathing was suspended. Fermi grinned with confidence. The counters stepped up their clicking; the pen went up and then stopped where Fermi had said it would. Greenewalt gasped audibly. Fermi continued to grin.

He gave more orders. Each time Weil pulled the rod out some more, the counters increased the rate of their clicking, the pen raised to the point that Fermi predicted, then it leveled off.

The morning went by. Fermi was conscious that a new experiment of this kind, carried out in the heart of a big city, might become a potential hazard unless all precautions were taken to make sure that at all times the operation of the pile conformed closely with the results of the calculations. In his mind he was sure that if George Weil's rod had been pulled out all at once, the pile would have started reacting at a leisurely rate and could have been stopped at will be reinserting one of the rods. He chose, however, to take his time and be certain that no unforeseen phenomenon would disturb the experiment.

It is impossible to say how great a danger this unforeseen element constituted or what consequences it might have brought about. According to the theory, an explosion was out of the question. The release of lethal amounts of radiation through an uncontrolled reaction was improbable. Yet the men in the Squash Court were working with the unknown. They could not claim to know the answers to all the questions that were in their minds. Caution was welcome. Caution was essential. It would have been reckless to dispense with caution.

So it was lunch time, and, although nobody else had given signs of being hungry, Fermi, who was a man of habits, pronounced the now historical sentence:

"Let's go to lunch."

The Fission Chain Reaction

An artist's diagram depicts the fission chain reaction that produces an atomic explosion. At left, a neutron fired into a U-235 nucleus forms the unstable U-236, which splits into two new elements, in this case, strontium and xenon. Neutrons released in fission are slowed by a moderator so they can be captured by additional U-235 nuclei to initiate a chain reaction.

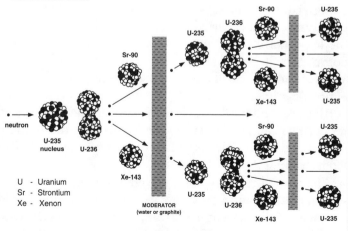

Michael Blow, *The History of the Atomic Bomb*, 1968.

After lunch they all resumed their places, and now Mr. Greenewalt was decidedly excited, almost impatient.

But again the experiment proceeded by small steps, until it was 3:20.

The Pile Chain-Reacts

Once more Fermi said to Weil:

"Pull it out another foot"; but this time he added, turning to the anxious group in the balcony: "This will do it. Now the pile will chain-react."

The counters stepped up; the pen started its upward rise. It showed no tendency to level off. A chain reaction was taking place in the pile.

In the back of everyone's mind was one unavoidable question: "When do we become scared?"

Under the ceiling of the balloon the suicide squad was alert, ready with their liquid cadmium: this was the moment. But nothing much happened. The group watched the recording instruments for 28 minutes. The pile behaved as it should, as they all had hoped it would, as they had feared it would not.

The Celebration

The rest of the story is well known. Eugene Wigner, the Hungarian-born physicist who in 1939 with Szilard and Albert Einstein had alerted President Franklin Roosevelt to the importance of uranium fission, presented Fermi with a bottle of Chianti. According to an improbable legend, Wigner had concealed the bottle behind his back during the entire experiment.

All those present drank. From paper cups, in silence, with no toast. Then all signed the straw cover on the bottle of Chianti. It is the only record of the persons in the Squash Court on that day.

The group broke up. Some stayed to round up their measurements and put in order the data gathered from their instruments. Others went to duties elsewhere. Mr. Greenewalt hastened to the room where his colleagues were still in conference with the military. He announced, all in one breath, that Yes, it would be quite all right for their company to go along with the Army's request and start to build piles. Piles were wonderful objects that performed with the precision of a Swiss watch, and, provided that the advice of such competent scientists as Fermi and his group were available, the duPont company was certainly taking no undue risk.

Arthur Compton placed a long-distance call to Mr. Arthur Conant of the Office of Scientific Research and Development at Harvard.

"The Italian Navigator has reached the New World," said Compton as soon as he got Conant on the line.

"And how did he find the natives?"

"Very friendly."

The Sequel

Here the official story ends, but there is a sequel to it, which started on that same afternoon when a young physicist, Al Wattemberg, picked up the empty Chianti bottle from which all had drunk. With the signatures on its cover, it would make a nice souvenir. In subsequent years Al Wattemberg did his share of traveling, like any other physicist, and the bottle followed him. When big celebrations for the pile's tenth anniversary were planned at the University of Chicago, the bottle and Al Wattemberg were both in Cambridge, Massachusetts. Both, Al promised, would be in Chicago on December 2, 1952.

It so happened, however, that a little Wattemberg decided to come into this world at about that time, and Al could not attend the celebrations. So he shipped his bottle, and, because he wanted to make doubly sure that it would not be broken, he insured it for a thousand dollars. It is not often that an empty bottle is considered worth so much money, and newspaper men on the lookout for sensation gave the story a prominent position in the press.

A couple of months later the Fermis and a few other physicists received a present: a case of Chianti wine. An importer had wished to acknowledge his gratitude for the free advertisement that Chianti had received.

The Race to Make the Atom Bomb

Robert C. Batchelder

When Adolf Hitler began his rise to power in the early 1930s, he also began his persecution of the Jews. As a result of his policies, many scientists left Europe for the safety of the United States. This intellectual emigration took place at the same time as physicists on both sides of the Atlantic were discovering the secrets of the atom.

Robert C. Batchelder writes that those involved in the U.S. atom bomb program believed that Germany's scientists were much farther along in their atomic research than U.S. scientists were. To prevent the Germans from learning about U.S. efforts to develop an atom bomb, he reports that the American scientists shrouded their research in an unusual cloak of secrecy. Batchelder also explains how the Americans intensified their efforts to ensure that they were the first to create the atom bomb. The scientists behind the world's first atom bomb created it not because they wanted to destroy the world, he argues, but because they were afraid of what would happen if Hitler's physicists built it first.

Robert C. Batchelder is the author of *The Irreversible Decision: 1939–1950.*

One of the fateful ironies of the twentieth century is that the crescendo of discovery in nuclear physics and the crescendo of Adolf Hitler's ambitions in Europe reached the point of climax at the same time. The years from 1932 to 1939 witnessed the scaling of one of the highest pinnacles of human intellectual achievement in the discovery of the key for releasing the unlimited energy hitherto locked within the nucleus of the atom. The same years witnessed the swift rise of Hitler to military dominance, the fall of Austria and Czechoslovakia, and the rising tension that brought Europe to the brink of world war. The development of nuclear physics not only paralleled the development of Hitler's power but was significantly influenced by it.

The Refugee Scientists

The key piece to the puzzle of the atom's nucleus was revealed in 1932 when Sir James Chadwick discovered a new subatomic particle which he called the neutron. Within a few months of this discovery, Hitler gained power in Germany. Both events had important repercussions in the scientific world. Hitler's coming to power vitally affected the lives of many of the most brilliant scientists of Europe. Barely a month passed before seven professors, including Max Born and Nobel Prize winner James Franck, were forced to leave their posts in the Natural Science Faculty at the University of Göttingen. Many eastern Europeans studying in Germany, including physicists Edward Teller, Leo Szilard, and Eugene Wigner, were subjected to abuse and persecution because of their Jewish ancestry; they departed the country and sought refuge in Denmark, England, and the United States. In the autumn of 1933, Albert Einstein, whose theory of relativity had been denounced as "Jewish physics," left Berlin for the Institute of Advanced Studies at Princeton. . . .

In November 1938 Enrico Fermi left Italy, ostensibly to go to Stockholm to receive a Nobel Prize in recognition of his 1934 experiments. However, he had quietly determined not to return to Italy, where Mussolini's aping of Hitler's anti-Semitism had created difficulties for Fermi's wife, who was Jewish. From Stockholm, the Fermis sailed to New York, where he became professor of physics at Columbia University in January 1939. . . .

The Point of Climax

The discovery of atomic fission came three months after the Munich agreement. [The Munich agreement was an attempt by England's prime minister Neville Chamberlain to appease Hitler by allowing him to annex Czechoslovakia to Germany.] Both events were hailed as achievements of great promise for the future, yet both events raised haunting questions. While the world wondered whether Hitler would abide by his solemn agreements, the scientists wondered whether nuclear fission would be restricted only to isolated atoms in laboratories, or whether the fission of one atom might lead to fission of many, thus releasing energy in usable amounts. The question of whether significant amounts of energy could be produced by fission of the uranium atom depended upon the answer to another question: Does the breakup of the uranium atom, caused by its being hit by a neutron, produce more neutrons? If so, then these neutrons might in turn serve as bullets to hit other uranium atoms, and the fission process might become a self-sustaining chain reaction.

Within another three months both the scientific and the political questions had been answered. Szilard and Fermi, working independently in New York, undertook experiments which showed that on the average each uranium atom, as it fissions, releases from one to three neutrons; thus the release of nuclear energy by a chain reaction was seen to be theoretically possible. And, on March 15, 1939, German troops marched into Prague in arrogant violation of the Munich pact—less than six months after Hitler had solemnly agreed to it. Hitler's ambitions and ruthlessness were now clear to all.

The point of climax had been reached, both in physics and in international relations. The impact of the one upon the other had resulted in the gathering together in the United States of a small group of men having in common a unique combination of characteristics and experience. Born in Europe, trained in science at German universities, all had experienced persecution (or the threat of it) under Nazi and Fascist regimes, and had left their homes rather than live under totalitarianism—and they also knew the secret of the atom and its energy. As scientists they exulted over the discoveries that promised to unlock the unlimited energy of the atom for the benefit of mankind. Yet, as the oppressive summer of 1939 wore on, they found that their exhilarating hopes for the future were being invaded by fears of what this new energy would mean in the hands of a fanatical and ruthless dictator whose thirst for power was insatiable. The unique combination of their experience, their knowledge, and their fears was destined to give them a decisive role to play in the wartime affairs of their adopted country.

Keeping Atomic Research Secret

The vision of Hitler in possession of an atomic bomb filled with alarm the group of refugee scientists, which centered on Leo Szilard, and included Eugene Wigner, Edward Teller, Enrico Fermi, and Victor Weisskopf. Early in 1939 they took the initiative. Even before his experiments which showed that a chain reaction was theoretically possible, Szilard attempted to persuade his fellow scientists to refrain from publishing the results of their research in the nuclear field, out of fear that the publication of encouraging results might lead to the development of atomic bombs that would be exceedingly dangerous "in the hands of certain governments." This attempt at voluntary censorship was undercut when Frédéric Joliot-Curie, working in Paris, independently discovered the possibility of a chain reaction and published his findings. This setback, combined with the objections of many American scientists, temporarily frustrated Szilard's efforts. Agreement was not reached until a year later on a mechanism for restricting publication of articles in the fission field which had military importance.

This secrecy undoubtedly hid from the Nazis the progress in uranium research being made by American scientists—but it also hid information from their American fellow scientists. The attempt of each university to keep its research secret for security reasons meant the retarding of fission studies elsewhere in the country, for research had to be duplicated in several places, and vital cross-fertilization of ideas was hampered. Arthur H. Compton reports that during the summer of 1940, while Fermi was visiting lecturer at the

University of Chicago, the atmosphere of secrecy was so prevalent that despite the vital interest of both men in uranium research and "almost daily contacts neither he nor I once raised the question of how the atomic chain reaction might be made to work."

Mere secrecy among scientists, however, was not enough without more positive action. Steps should be taken to alert the government to both the dangers and the possibilities inherent in the discovery of nuclear fission. On March 16, 1939, the day after Hitler marched into Prague (and only ten weeks after arrival in the United States), Enrico Fermi traveled to Washington to bring to the attention of the United States Navy the tremendous implications of the possibility that "uranium might be used as an explosive that

Why the Germans Failed to Develop the Atom Bomb

Allied fears about the German atom bomb program turned out to be groundless. While the United States and Germany made simultaneous discoveries about the atom in the 1930s, by 1942 the German effort had stalled. Werner Heisenberg, the director of the German atom bomb project, discusses why Germany fell so far behind the United States in its atomic energy research in this excerpt from an article he wrote after the war.

In the United States, the final decision was taken to go for the production of atomic bombs with an outlay that must have amounted to a considerable fraction of the total American war expenditure; in Germany an attempt was made to solve the problem of the prime mover driven by nuclear energy, with an outlay of perhaps a thousandth part of the American. We have often been asked, not only by Germans but also by Britons and Americans, why Germany made no attempt to produce atomic bombs. The simplest answer one can give to this question is this: because the project could not have succeeded under German war conditions. It could not have succeeded on technical grounds alone: for even in America, with its much greater resources in scientific men, technicians and industrial potential, would liberate a million times as much energy per pound as any known explosive." The Navy's response was less than enthusiastic. As an attempt to stimulate active government support of expanded nuclear research, Fermi's venture failed.

As the summer of 1939 wore on, evidence began to accumulate indicating that the Germans were actively engaged in atomic energy research. Shortly after Hitler took over Czechoslovakia—which possessed one of the world's three major uranium deposits—exports of uranium ore from that country were cut off. Reports were received that at the Kaiser Wilhelm Institute in Berlin (where Hahn had discovered nuclear fission), nuclear physicists had been meeting together under the auspices of the German Army. Appar-

and with an economy undisturbed by enemy action, the bomb was not ready until after the conclusion of the war with Germany. In particular, a German atomic bomb project could not have succeeded because of the military situation. In 1942, German industry was already stretched to the limit, the German Army had suffered serious reverses in Russia in the winter of 1941–42, and enemy air superiority was beginning to make itself felt. The immediate production of armaments could be robbed neither of personnel nor of raw materials, nor could the enormous plants required have been effectively protected against air attack. Finally—and this is a most important fact—the undertaking could not even be initiated against the psychological background of the men responsible for German war policy. These men expected an early decision of the War, even in 1942, and any major project which did not promise quick returns was specifically forbidden. To obtain the necessary support, the experts would have been obliged to promise early results, knowing that these promises could not be kept. Faced with this situation, the experts did not attempt to advocate with the supreme command a great industrial effort for the production of atomic bombs.

Werner Heisenberg, *Nature*, August 16, 1947.

ently Hitler was actively pursuing research in atomic energy for military purposes.

Persuading the President

Reports such as these increased the anxiety of men like Szilard, and stimulated their determination to awaken the government to the real danger of an atomic bomb in the hands of Germany. Wracking their brains for a method of accomplishing this, Szilard and his friends brought their problem to Dr. Alexander Sachs, an economist who had gained President Franklin D. Roosevelt's confidence and had access to the White House. Together they finally hit on the idea of getting Albert Einstein, whose reputation would surely carry weight, to write a letter direct to the President of the United States. Szilard and Wigner, in consultation with Dr. Einstein, drafted the famous letter to the President, which Einstein signed on August 2. The letter pointed out that the possibility of a chain reaction implied the possibility of constructing "extremely powerful bombs," which, if exploded in a port, "might very well destroy the whole port together with some of the surrounding territory." Einstein also reported the signs of German activity, and urged quick action by the government to speed up experimental work on uranium and to secure a supply of uranium ore for the United States.

Sachs was entrusted with the letter, but before he could bring it personally to the attention of the President war broke out in Europe with Hitler's invasion of Poland on September 1, 1939. During the next hectic weeks Roosevelt was preoccupied with the campaign to repeal the arms embargo provisions of the Neutrality Act. It was not until October 11 that Sachs managed to secure an appointment and to present the letter from Einstein. Although Roosevelt was impressed, he was not at first convinced that substantial government action was called for. However, Sachs was persistent, and raised the subject again at breakfast the next morning. Finally Roosevelt said, "Alex, what you are after is to see that the Nazis don't blow us up." Sachs replied, "Precisely." The President then called in his military aide and told him, "This requires action."

German Activity

Further new evidence continued to point to increasing German activity in the field of fission research. The Dutch-born chemist Peter Debye was forced to leave his position as Director of the Kaiser Wilhelm Institute for Physics in Berlin; upon his arrival in the United States, he reported that his former laboratory was being turned over to research on uranium. After Germany had occupied Norway, British intelligence units began to receive reports that the Germans had ordered the Norsk Hydro plant, the world's largest producer of heavy water, to increase its output sharply. The fact that heavy water is the most efficient moderator for a controlled nuclear chain reaction, combined with the fact that German scientists had publicly announced in 1939 that heavy water might become vitally important to Germany's war effort, pointed to German development of atomic energy for war purposes. This seemed to be confirmed by the fact that Germany, despite wartime stress, was continuing the operation of Joliot-Curie's cyclotron in occupied Paris.

The U.S. Government Gets Involved

In the fall of 1941, government officials at the highest level were for the first time brought together formally to advise the President on the future of the atomic energy project. This Top Policy Group included Vice-President Henry Wallace, Secretary of War Henry L. Stimson, Army Chief of Staff George C. Marshall, and inevitably, James B. Conant and Vannevar Bush. In November 1941 Compton's review committee submitted to the Top Policy Group a highly favorable report—the first report to the government focusing primarily on the possibility of a U-235 bomb—estimating that bombs could be made "within three or four years." At last, firm action was taken. On December 6, 1941, the day before Pearl Harbor, the crucial decision was approved by the President. The possibility of obtaining atomic bombs for use in the present war was deemed good enough to justify throwing the full support of the government, both financial and technical, behind the project, which should be reorganized for an all-out effort. If the atomic bomb could be made at all, the United States was now officially committed to making it first. . . .

The Scientists' Motives for Developing the Bomb

We have seen that the imagination and enthusiasm of a small group of nuclear physicists, centered about Enrico Fermi and Leo Szilard, were the primary factors leading to the decision to make an atomic bomb. These men did much more than simply give willing obedience to orders given them by the government. Although outside the government, they repeatedly took the initiative in urging government officials to take the possibility of an atomic bomb seriously. Official skepticism, inertia, and the countless administrative and technical obstacles that blocked the road to the release of atomic energy were finally overcome almost entirely by their determination and persistence. They instituted a precedent-breaking system of censorship of their own research; they dragged many of their American colleagues out of the isolation of their private research into the campaign to produce a weapon of mass destruction.

What were the motives which lay beneath their sense of urgency? What moral claim did they feel which led them to drop their own research projects and give up the cherished scientific tradition of free exchange of ideas in the conviction that they were obeying the call of a higher duty?

Evidence is abundant that the primary force driving Szilard's group, and finally gaining the support of the American scientists and government, was the fear of Hitler's prior achievement of the atomic bomb. Even before the possibility of a nuclear chain reaction was confirmed, Szilard, in a letter to Joliot-Curie urging him to withhold publication of his research, justified his request by a thinly veiled reference to the extreme danger of fission bombs in the hands of "certain governments." Einstein's letters specifically mentioned Germany's activities. Arthur Compton reports that Wigner's "lively fear that the Nazis would make the bomb first" caused him to plead with Compton "almost with tears" to establish an active bomb project in the United States. What finally convinced Compton, Conant, and Ernest O. Lawrence of the urgency of our making the bomb was, according to Compton, "the evidence that the Nazis were making a major effort" to do so. "We just could not afford to let the Nazis beat us to the making of atomic weapons. This would be inviting disaster."

It was this same fear of Hitler that motivated the government's support of the atomic bomb project. President Roosevelt's initial understanding was that government action was necessary to make sure that "the Nazis don't blow us up." Secretary of War Stimson, who was "directly connected with all major decisions of policy on the development and use of atomic energy" during the war, describes the continuing motive behind government action thus:

> The policy adopted and steadily pursued by President Roosevelt and his advisers was a simple one. It was to spare no effort in securing the earliest possible successful development of an atomic weapon. The reasons for this policy were equally simple. The original experimental achievement of atomic fission had occurred in Germany in 1938, and it was known that the Germans had continued their experiments. In 1941 and 1942 they were believed to be ahead of us, and it was vital that they should not be the first to bring atomic weapons into the field of battle.

The scientists' sense of urgency did not grow out of the positive desire to obtain nuclear weapons, or a thirst for military power. On the contrary, it grew out of fear of what might happen to the civilized world if Hitler were the first to achieve such weapons. These men had experienced Hitler and his devices at first hand, and had become refugees rather than submit to him. They were convinced that the German leader had no scruples whatsoever, and would not hesitate to use an atomic bomb in his quest for world domination. It was to prevent the nightmarish possibility that Hitler might at some point in the future have a monopoly of atomic bombs that these scientists undertook their campaign. Many indeed hoped against hope that in the course of their investigations they would stumble upon a wrinkle of nature that would make a chain reaction, and hence a nuclear explosion, inherently impossible, both for Hitler and for them. However, they could not rest comfortably in the *mere hope* that an atomic bomb would prove to be impossible. They had to push forward with their experiments either until it was proved to be impossible, or until they had created the bomb themselves. "If such a weapon is going to be made, we must do it first. We can't afford not to."

The Manhattan Project

Ferenc Morton Szasz

In 1941, a coalition of physicists persuaded the U.S. government to support research on and construction of an atom bomb. A year later, the army was given the responsibility of supervising the atomic research program. Under the army's direction, a bomb-building laboratory and the supporting physical plants needed for the design and creation of the bomb were built from scratch and were soon operational. The best scientists in the United States were convinced to join the atom bomb program, code-named the Manhattan Project.

Ferenc Morton Szasz describes how the building of the bomb was kept secret, even from the tens of thousands of workers who were essential to the bomb's development. However, he writes, the scientists working on the bomb were free to discuss the project's problems and the potential solutions to them, a process that was essential to the success of the Manhattan Project. This free exchange of ideas, Szasz contends, led to the development of the modern-day implosion-type atom bomb.

Ferenc Morton Szasz is a history professor at the University of New Mexico and the author of *The Day the Sun Rose Twice: The Story of the Trinity Site Nuclear Explosion July 16, 1945*.

After the Japanese attack on Pearl Harbor, . . . America's atomic program began to expand more rapidly. There now existed the possibility for direct military application of the new discoveries. Shortly afterwards, Franklin D. Roosevelt set up a National Defense Research Committee (NDRC), to mobilize science for war, and later, the Office of Scientific

Excerpted from *The Day the Sun Rose Twice: The Story of the Trinity Site Nuclear Explosion, July 16, 1945*, by Ferenc Morton Szasz. Copyright © 1984 by the University of New Mexico Press. Reprinted with permission from the University of New Mexico Press.

Research and Development (OSRD). The former was headed by physicist Vannevar Bush and the latter by Harvard President James B. Conant. The discovery of plutonium in 1940—an alternative route to a nuclear reaction—plus a series of optimistic reports from the British scientists, led by physicist Rudolph Peierls, strengthened the fledgling American efforts. By late 1941, the British were confident that a U-235 bomb could be developed before the hostilities were over.

The Army Takes Over

The most important step, however, occurred in June of 1942, when the nuclear program was turned over to the army. On September 17, 1942, Major General Leslie R. Groves, the man who had helped supervise the building of the Pentagon, was placed in charge of the Manhattan Engineer District. (The code name was chosen because the original headquarters were in New York.) Although Groves did not have the academic brilliance or technical training to match the people he had to oversee, he possessed an uncanny ability to learn from the discussions. Over the years he proved his worth as an excellent, no-nonsense administrator. His lively, albeit somewhat biased, account of the project can be found in *Now It Can Be Told* (1963). Although his blunt personality and rotund shape made him a convenient scapegoat for numerous personal gripes, it is doubtful that the Manhattan Project could have succeeded as well as it did without him. Brusque and abrasive though he was, Leslie Groves could get things done. . . .

Under the combined efforts of the army, industry, and labor, gigantic facilities were established at Oak Ridge, Tennessee, and Hanford, Washington. Their tasks were to produce sufficient quantities of the fissionable U-235 and of plutonium for the bombs. At the time the operations began, these materials existed only in microscopic quantities.

The technical problems involved were enormous. The fissionable isotope of uranium (U-235) is relatively rare, occurring in uranium at a ratio of 1 to 139. In other words, in every 140 pounds of uranium, one pound of U-235 exists, but it is scattered throughout so that initially the scientists found it virtually impossible to separate the two. In 1940, it was estimated that it would take twelve million years, at the then rate, to extract a pound of U-235. The creation of plutonium by bombarding uranium 238 with neutrons proved only slightly less complex. That several pounds of each fissionable material were delivered in less than two years is a testimony to the genius of American technological and industrial efforts.

After the war, Groves praised the production efforts at Oak Ridge and Hanford in the highest terms. He stated that the hardest part of the project was producing a sufficient quantity of the fissionable material. Groves likened the task to a "manufacturer who tried to build an automobile full of watch machinery, with the precision that was required of watchmaking, and the knowledge that the failure of a single part would mean complete failure of the whole project." The Los Alamos dimension of the work, he implied, was actually secondary.

Groves, obviously, was exaggerating for effect. What went on at Los Alamos (or Site Y, as it was officially known) proved the cogwheel of the entire program. The secret atomic city in the mountains of northern New Mexico contained the *crème de la crème* of the Manhattan Project.

The Creation of Los Alamos

The Los Alamos site was created for two main reasons. First, the project needed a special weapons laboratory that would put the bomb together. Second, and probably more important, Groves found himself caught in his own massive security regulations. From the beginning, he had insisted that the people involved with the various aspects of the Manhattan Project know only enough to carry out their own jobs effectively. This "compartmentalization" of tasks lay at the heart of all Manhattan Project security. It proved so effective that no information ever reached German hands. It might have succeeded with the Soviet Union, too, had not a member of the British delegation to Los Alamos, Klaus Fuchs, passed along inside secrets to Soviet couriers.

Essential as compartmentalization might have been for security purposes, it was a hindrance on the purely scientific level. The constant exchange of ideas and information became vital to the scientists as they encountered problem after problem, all of which were interconnected. Moreover, as the project grew, the logistics of getting the proper people to the proper places proved cumbersome. After the war, Leo Szilard complained bitterly that Groves's insistence on compartmentalization actually hindered the development of the bomb by eighteen months. Groves, however, always defended his position.

In early 1942, Groves decided that the project needed to create a new isolated site where the scientists could all come together and talk openly. So, in the summer of 1942, after a brief search, Groves, Major John Dudley, and the newly appointed head of this installation, California physicist J. Robert Oppenheimer, selected the region of Los Alamos, New Mexico. Oppenheimer had known and loved this area for years, for his family had had a ranch in the nearby Pecos Mountains. Here he was able to combine his two great loves—physics and New Mexico. Moving swiftly, the government took over the facilities of an exclusive boys' preparatory school and the lands of about twenty-six other area inhabitants. Much was already government owned and soon a total of about 9,000 acres was acquired for the war effort. Oppenheimer assumed that facilities would be needed to house perhaps thirty scientists and their families. The "realists" of the time argued that they would need room for at least 500. At the end of the war, close to 6,500 people were living on the Hill. . . .

A Collection of Brilliant Minds

Oppenheimer recruited many of the top personnel himself. His job was made easier by the fact that the scientists knew they would be applying their talents for the benefit of their country. They also knew that if they succeeded, they would become a part of history. The chief "rival" of the Los Alamos operation lay in the Radiation Laboratory of the Massachusetts Institute of Technology (MIT). But by the middle of

1943, all of the major types of radar had been fairly well developed, and this freed a number of MIT scientists to go to Los Alamos. After some initial hesitation, recruitment snowballed, and by 1944 virtually every American physicist of importance was involved in the project. Some, however, were drawn into the work more by fate than by enthusiasm. "I worked on the bomb," one physicist confessed later, "because everybody I knew was doing it."

Even those at Los Alamos who knew little about the activities behind the fenced-in "Tech Area," knew that they were producing something "that would help end the war." When the scientists returned from the Trinity explosion, a custodian rushed up to physicist Fred Reines, grabbed his hand, and said, "Well, we did it, didn't we." "Yes," said Reines, "we sure did." This commitment pervaded all levels of society.

One must add that the men and women of Los Alamos were then young. The average age was around twenty-seven. Mathematician Stan M. Ulam worried because he was all of thirty-four. Physicist Kenneth T. Bainbridge was almost an elder statesman at forty. Many couples began their families while living on the mesa. Nearly one thousand babies were born in that small community from 1943 to 1949; those 208 born during the war had birth certificates listing the place as simply Box 1663, Sandoval County, Rural.

It is probably safe to say that never before in the history of the human race have so many brilliant minds been gathered together in one place. Visitors walking through the spacious Fuller Lodge at lunch might see four to five Nobel Prize winners dining at the same time. If they had been able to divine the future, they would have known that seven other men would also become Nobel laureates. . . .

"The Best Kept Secret of the War"

When one considers how many people worked at Los Alamos itself, let alone the Manhattan Project in general, the army's success in concealing its purpose was phenomenal. It became, indeed, "the best kept secret of the war." The list of people who were heavily involved, yet knew nothing, proved a lengthy one. Neither the R.E. McKee nor the M.M. Sundt companies, which built most of the town of Los Alamos, nor the Ted Brown Company, which built Trinity Site, knew what their projects were for. With few exceptions, most of the Los Alamos wives were uncertain what their husbands were doing in the Tech Area. (Groves had insisted that the wives not be told.) Los Alamos housewife Lilli Marjon recalled the shocked looks when a newly arrived wife asked innocently, "And what does your husband do?" She was not invited back. Bernice Brode, Ruth Marshack, and Laura Fermi all confessed that they really understood the project only after the dropping of the bomb on Hiroshima.

But security also worked the other way around. From 1941 to late 1944, American intelligence was unable to gather a clear picture of the German atomic effort either. All that was known was that Germany had forbidden all exports of Czechoslovakian uranium and had enlisted about two hundred top physicists, chemists, and engineers for their project. Rumors from newly arrived refugees rushed in to fill the gaps, and many of their predictions were decidedly gloomy. One émigré estimated that the Nazis would have the bomb by early 1944. Since many of the Los Alamos scientists were Jewish, they had no illusions of what they could expect from a Nazi victory. It was from them that the others learned firsthand of the suffering of relatives and friends in the Old World.

Racing the Germans

Los Alamos thus found itself engaged in an all-out race with the Germans, and the stakes were high. In December 1941, right after Pearl Harbor, James B. Conant told his friend Harvey H. Bundy that the Germans could never win the war—unless they were ahead of America in the development of the atomic bomb. Many of the scientists had taken their degrees from German universities, and even those who had not maintained respect for German science. "The pronouncement by Hitler that Nazi Germany would rule the world for the next thousand years strongly affected my resolution," noted Kenneth Bainbridge, "as it did so many others." Vannevar Bush felt the same way. An ironic aspect of this can be seen in the incident where a young Los Alamos WAC was instructed to request over the newly installed public address system that "Werner Heisenberg" please report to the office. After two days, somebody took pity on her and explained that Nobel Prize winner Heisenberg was in Berlin heading the German atomic program.

Yet, curiously, the military seemed to have little sense of the political motivation of the scientists. As far as they were concerned, their only task was to build an atomic bomb in the shortest possible time.

The fate of the German atomic quest lay unknown until the Allied invasion of the continent on June 6, 1944. One component of the D-Day landing party was the secret "Alsos" (Greek for "Groves") mission, headed by Major Boris T. Pash. Dutch-born physicist Samuel Goudsmit accompanied Pash. This contingent had the specific task of discovering just how far the Germans had progressed in their atomic research. As the advancing troops overran university towns and captured Nazi scientists, Goudsmit combed through their documents and interviewed the prisoners—his "enemy colleagues," as he graciously called them. By December 1944, Goudsmit had given the War Department all his information. He concluded that the Germans did not have anything like an atomic bomb. Hitler, who never realized its significance, concentrated on the development of the V-1 and V-2 rockets. Moreover, along the way the Germans had made a series of political and theoretical wrong turns in their search for atomic power. The heavy pounding of cities and industrial plants by Allied bombers also played a role in disrupting the German program. Werner Heisenberg argued later that the reluctance of the numerous pro-German but anti-Nazi physicists to pursue the project proved significant. At any rate, in December 1944, the Germans were found to be at least two years behind the Americans. The German atomic bomb program was a failure.

Ironically, however, when this information arrived at Los Alamos, it had almost no effect on the project. The surrender on May 8, 1945, had even less. In fact, Oppenheimer recalled that "I don't think there was any time when we worked harder at the speed-up than in the period after the German surrender and the actual combat use of the bomb." By early 1945, the scientists were totally involved with the plans for a test of the almost-completed atomic device somewhere in the United States.

The Two Types of Atomic Bombs

There were two separate types of atomic weapons in preparation. The first utilized the rare isotope U-235. It was originally nicknamed "Thin Man" (after Roosevelt), but later renamed "Little Boy" (for nobody) when technical changes shortened the proposed gun barrel. The second utilized plutonium and was nicknamed "Fat Man" (after Winston Churchill) from the beginning. The scientists were much more confident about the former than the latter. In the uranium bomb, one subcritical mass of U-235 is fired at another subcritical mass. When the two join, they become supercritical and ignite in a nuclear reaction. The scientists were so confident about their theories on the uranium bomb that they planned no field test for it. Indeed, this was the first bomb dropped on Hiroshima. By July of 1944, however, the scientists had also concluded that this relatively simple "gun assembly" method would not work for the plutonium bomb. The two subcritical pieces of plutonium could not be brought together fast enough to prevent a premature detonation.

Led by physicist Seth Neddermeyer and mathematician John von Neumann, the solution to the dilemma emerged as the theory of "implosion." Here a subcritical sphere of plutonium was surrounded by charges of heavy explosives, all carefully shaped as "lenses." When these were detonated, they focused the blast wave so as to compress the plutonium instantly into a super-critical mass. This was a much more complicated procedure, however, and many people expressed considerable doubt that it would work as planned.

From May to November 1944, there was a fierce debate at Los Alamos as to whether the scientists should field test the plutonium bomb before actually dropping it. Harvard explosives expert George B. Kistiakowsky and Oppenheimer both argued for such a test, but initially Groves was opposed. He was afraid that if the test failed, the precious plutonium would be scattered all across the countryside by the detonation of the shaped explosive lenses. He lived in constant fear of facing congressional investigating committees if the Manhattan Project did not succeed in time to help end the war.

Eventually Groves was persuaded. The plutonium production at Hanford was increasing at such a rate that a field test would cause little delay in time. Besides, he was told, if the untested plutonium bomb were dropped and did not perform as expected, the enemy would find themselves owners of a "gift" atomic weapon. Finally, as the ultimate compromise, a gigantic, 214-ton, cylinder-shaped tank (called "Jumbo") would be created to house the bomb. If a nuclear explosion occurred, Jumbo would be vaporized. If only the conventional explosives detonated, the vessel would be strong enough to contain the plutonium for yet another try. With this as the agreement, the search for a test site began in earnest.

The Trinity Test

Leslie R. Groves

On July 16, 1945, at 5:30 A.M. at the Trinity Test Site on the Alamogordo Air Base, New Mexico, the world's first atom bomb was exploded. The first bomb of its kind, it was an implosion-type bomb that used plutonium to fuel its nuclear explosion. The scientists working on it had no idea of its destructive capability or if it would work at all.

The following article, which was written by Leslie R. Groves two days after the explosion, is a report on the test to the U.S. secretary of war, Henry L. Stimson. Groves describes the explosion, noting that the bomb was more destructive than anyone had anticipated. Groves concludes that everyone who witnessed the explosion was in awe over what they had created.

Leslie R. Groves was a lieutenant general when he retired in 1948 from the U.S. Army Corps of Engineers. When he was a colonel, he oversaw the construction of the Pentagon in Arlington, Virginia. As a brigadier general, he headed the Manhattan Project—the code name for the development of the atomic bomb—and directed the building and operation of all the plants needed for the bomb's construction.

1. This is not a concise, formal military report but an attempt to recite what I would have told you if you had been here on my return from New Mexico.

2. At 0530, 16 July 1945, in a remote section of the Alamogordo Air Base, New Mexico, the first full scale test was made of the implosion type atomic fission bomb. For the first time in history there was a nuclear explosion. And what an explosion! . . . The bomb was not dropped from an air-

Excerpted from Leslie R. Groves's memo to Henry L. Stimson, July 18, 1945, National Archives.

plane but was exploded on a platform on top of a 100-foot high steel tower.

A Tremendous Success

3. The test was successful beyond the most optimistic expectations of anyone. Based on the data which it has been possible to work up to date, I estimate the energy generated to be in excess of the equivalent of 15,000 to 20,000 tons of TNT; and this is a conservative estimate. Data based on measurements which we have not yet been able to reconcile would make the energy release several times the conservative figure. There were tremendous blast effects. For a brief period there was a lighting effect within a radius of 20 miles equal to several suns in midday; a huge ball of fire was formed which lasted for several seconds. This ball mushroomed and rose to a height of over ten thousand feet before it dimmed. The light from the explosion was seen clearly at Albuquerque, Santa Fe, Silver City, El Paso and other points generally to about 180 miles away. The sound was heard to the same distance in a few instances but generally to about 100 miles. Only a few windows were broken although one was some 125 miles away. A massive cloud was formed which surged and billowed upward with tremendous power, reaching the substratosphere at an elevation of 41,000 feet, 36,000 feet above the ground, in about five minutes, breaking without interruption through a temperature inversion at 17,000 feet which most of the scientists thought would stop it. Two supplementary explosions occurred in the cloud shortly after the main explosion. The cloud contained several thousand tons of dust picked up from the ground and a considerable amount of iron in the gaseous form. Our present thought is that this iron ignited when it mixed with the oxygen in the air to cause these supplementary explosions. Huge concentrations of highly radioactive materials resulted from the fission and were contained in this cloud.

4. A crater from which all vegetation had vanished, with a diameter of 1200 feet and a slight slope toward the center, was formed. In the center was a shallow bowl 130 feet in diameter and 6 feet in depth. The material within the crater

was deeply pulverized dirt. The material within the outer circle is greenish and can be distinctly seen from as much as 5 miles away. The steel from the tower was evaporated. 1500 feet away there was a four-inch iron pipe 16 feet high set in concrete and strongly guyed. It disappeared completely.

5.   One-half mile from the explosion there was a massive steel test cylinder weighing 220 tons. The base of the cylinder was solidly encased in concrete. Surrounding the cylinder was a strong steel tower 70 feet high, firmly anchored to concrete foundations. This tower is comparable to a steel building bay that would be found in typical 15 or 20 story skyscraper or in warehouse construction. Forty tons of steel were used to fabricate the tower which was 70 feet high, the height of a six story building. The cross bracing was much stronger than that normally used in ordinary steel construction. The absence of the solid walls of a building gave the blast a much less effective surface to push against. The blast tore the tower from its foundations, twisted it, ripped it apart and left it flat on the ground. The effects on the tower indicate that, at that distance, unshielded permanent steel and masonry buildings would have been destroyed. I no longer consider the Pentagon a safe shelter from such a bomb. Enclosed are a sketch showing the tower before the explosion and a telephotograph showing what it looked like afterwards. None of us had expected it to be damaged.

Radioactive Effects

6. The cloud traveled to a great height first in the form of a ball, then mushroomed, then changed into a long trailing chimney-shaped column and finally was sent in several directions by the variable winds at the different elevations. It deposited its dust and radioactive materials over a wide area. It was followed and monitored by medical doctors and scientists with instruments to check its radioactive effects. While here and there the activity on the ground was fairly high, at no place did it reach a concentration which required evacuation of the population. Radioactive material in small quantities was located as much as 120 miles away. The measurements are being continued in order to have adequate

data with which to protect the Government's interests in case of future claims. For a few hours I was none too comfortable about the situation.

7. For distances as much as 200 miles away, observers were stationed to check on blast effects, property damage, radioactivity and reactions of the population. While complete reports have not yet been received, I now know that no persons were injured nor was there any real property damage outside our Government area. As soon as all the voluminous data can be checked and correlated, full technical studies will be possible.

The Weather

8. Our long range weather predictions had indicated that we could expect weather favorable for our tests beginning on the morning of the 17th and continuing for four days. This was almost a certainty if we were to believe our long range forecasters. The prediction for the morning of the 16th was not so certain but there was about an 80% chance of the conditions being suitable. During the night there were thunder storms with lightning flashes all over the area. The test had been originally set for 0400 hours and all the night through, because of the bad weather, there were urgings from many of the scientists to postpone the test. Such a delay might well have had crippling results due to mechanical difficulties in our complicated test set-up. Fortunately, we disregarded the urgings. We held firm and waited the night through hoping for suitable weather. We had to delay an hour and a half, to 0530, before we could fire. This was 30 minutes before sunrise.

9. Because of bad weather, our two B-20 observation airplanes were unable to take off as scheduled from Kirtland Field at Albuquerque and when they finally did get off, they found it impossible to get over the target because of the heavy clouds and the thunder storms. Certain desired observations could not be made and while the people in the airplanes saw the explosion from a distance, they were not as close as they will be in action. We still have no reason to anticipate the loss of our plane in an actual operation although

we cannot guarantee safety.

10. Just before 1100 the news stories from all over the state started to flow into the Albuquerque Associated Press. I then directed the issuance by the Commanding Officer, Alamogordo Air Base of a news release as shown on the inclosure. With the assistance of the Office of Censorship we were able to limit the news stories to the approved release supplemented in the local papers by brief stories from the many eyewitnesses not connected with our project. One of these was a blind woman who saw the light.

Other Impressions

11. Brigadier General Thomas F. Farrell was at the control shelter located 10,000 yards south of the point of explosion. His impressions are given below:

> The scene inside the shelter was dramatic beyond words. In and around the shelter were some twenty-odd people concerned with last minute arrangements prior to firing the shot. Included were: Dr. [J. Robert] Oppenheimer, the Director who had borne the great scientific burden of developing the weapon from the raw materials made in Tennessee and Washington and a dozen of his key assistants—Dr. [George B.] Kistiakowsky, who developed the highly speical explosives; Dr. [Kenneth] Bainbridge, who supervised all the detailed arrangements for the test; Dr. [Jack M.] Hubbard, the weather expert, and several others. Besides these, there were a handful of soldiers, two or three Army officers and one Naval officer. The shelter was cluttered with a great variety of instruments and radios.

> For some hectic two hours preceding the blast, General Groves stayed with the Director, walking with him and steadying his tense excitement. Every time the Director would be about to explode because of some untoward happening, General Groves would take him off and walk with him in the rain, counselling with him and reassuring him that everything would be all right. At twenty minutes before zero hour, General Groves left for his station at the base camp, first because it provided a better observation point

and second, because of our rule that he and I must not be together in situations where there is an element of danger, which existed at both points.

Just after General Groves left, announcements began to be broadcast of the interval remaining before the blast. They were sent by radio to the other groups participating in and observing the test. As the time interval grew smaller and changed from minutes to seconds, the tension increased by leaps and bounds. Everyone in that room knew the awful potentialities of the thing that they thought was about to happen. The scientists felt that their figuring must be right and that the bomb had to go off but there was in everyone's mind a strong measure of doubt. The feeling of many could be expressed by "Lord, I believe; help Thou mine unbelief." We were reaching into the unknown and we did not know what might come of it. It can be safely said that most of those present—Christian, Jew and Atheist—were praying and praying harder than they had ever prayed before. If the shot were successful, it was a justification of the several years of intensive effort of tens of thousands of people—statesmen, scientists, engineers, manufacturers, soldiers, and many others in every walk of life.

In that brief instant in the remote New Mexico desert the tremendous effort of the brains and brawn of all these people came suddenly and startingly to the fullest fruition. Dr. Oppenheimer, on whom had rested a very heavy burden, grew tenser as the last seconds ticked off. He scarcely breathed. He held on to a post to steady himself. For the last few seconds, he stared directly ahead and then when the announcer shouted "Now!" and there came this tremendous burst of light followed shortly thereafter by the deep growling roar of the explosion, his face relaxed into an expression of tremendous relief. Several of the observers standing back of the shelter to watch the lighting effects were knocked flat by the blast.

The tension in the room let up and all started congratulating each other. Everyone sensed "This is it!" No matter what might happen now all knew that the impossible scientific job had been done. Atomic fission would no longer be hidden in the cloisters of the theoretical physicists' dreams. It was almost full grown at birth. It was a great new force to be used for good or for evil. There was a feeling in that shelter that those concerned with its nativity should dedicate their lives to the mission that it would always be used for good and never for evil.

Dr. Kistiakowsky, the impulsive Russian, threw his arms around Dr. Oppenheimer and embraced him with shouts of glee. Others were equally enthusiastic. All the pent-up emotions were released in those few minutes and all seemed to sense immediately that the explosion had far exceeded the most optimistic expectations and wildest hopes of the scientists. All seemed to feel that they had been present at the birth of a new age—The Age of Atomic Energy—and felt their profound responsibility to help in guiding into right channels the tremendous forces which had been unlocked for the first time in history.

As to the present war, there was a feeling that no matter what else might happen, we now had the means to insure its speedy conclusion and save thousands of American lives. As to the future, there had been brought into being something big and something new that would prove to be immeasurably more important than the discovery of electricity or any of the other great discoveries which have so affected our existence.

The effects could well be called unprecedented, magnificent, beautiful, stupendous and terrifying. No man-made phenomenon of such tremendous power had ever occurred before. The lighting effects beggared description. The whole country was lighted by a searing light with the intensity many times that of the midday sun. It was golden, purple, violet, gray and blue. It lighted every peak, crevasse and ridge of the nearby mountain range with a clarity and beauty that cannot be described but must be seen to be imagined. It was that beauty the great poets dream about but describe most poorly and inadequately. Thirty seconds after the explosion came first, the air blast pressing hard against the people and things, to be followed almost immediately by the strong, sustained, awesome roar which warned of doomsday and made us feel that we puny things were blasphemous to dare tamper with the forces heretofore reserved to The Almighty. Words are inadequate tools for the job of acquainting those not present with the physical, mental and psychological effects. It had to be witnessed to be realized.

The Night's High Points

12. My impressions of the night's high points follow:

After about an hour's sleep I got up at 0100 and from that time on until about five I was with Dr. Oppenheimer constantly. Naturally he was nervous, although his mind was working at its usual extraordinary efficiency. I devoted my entire attention to shielding him from the excited and generally faulty advice of his assistants who were more than disturbed by their excitement and the uncertain weather conditions. By 0330 we decided that we could probably fire at 0530. By 0400 the rain had stopped but the sky was heavily overcast. Our decision became firmer as time went on. During most of these hours the two of us journeyed from the control house out into the darkness to look at the stars and to assure each other that the one or two visible stars were becoming brighter. At 0510 I left Dr. Oppenheimer and returned to the main observation point which was 17,000 yards from the point of explosion. In accordance with our orders I found all personnel not otherwise occupied massed on a bit of high ground.

At about two minutes of the scheduled firing time all persons lay face down with their feet pointing towards the explosion. As the remaining time was called from the loud speaker from the 10,000 yard control station there was complete silence. Dr. James B. Conant said he had never imagined seconds could be so long. Most of the individuals in accordance with orders shielded their eyes in one way or another. There was then this burst of light of a brilliance beyond any comparison. We all rolled over and looked through dark glasses at the ball of fire. About forty seconds later came the shock wave followed by the sound, neither of which seemed startling after our complete astonishment at the extraordinary lighting intensity. Dr. Conant reached over and we shook hands in mutual congratulations. Dr. Vannevar Bush, who was on the other side of me, did likewise. The feeling of the entire assembly was similar to that described by General Farrell, with even the uninitiated feeling profound awe. Drs. Conant and Bush and myself were struck by an even stronger feeling that the faith of those who had been responsible for the initiation and the carrying on of this Herculean project had been justified. I personally thought of Charles Blondin crossing Niagara Falls on his tight rope, only to me this tight rope had lasted for almost three years and of my repeated confident-appearing assurances that such a thing was possible and that we would do it.

13. A large group of observers were stationed at a point about 27 miles north of the point of explosion. Attached is a memorandum written shortly after the explosion by Dr. E.O. Lawrence which may be of interest.

14. While General Farrell was waiting about midnight for a commercial airplane to Washington at Albuquerque—120 miles away from the site—he overheard several airport employees discussing their reaction to the blast. One said that he was out on the parking apron; it was quite dark; then the whole southern sky was lighted as though by a bright sun; the light lasted several seconds. Another remarked that if a few exploding bombs could have such an effect, it must be terrible to have them drop on a city.

A Blinding Flash of Light

15. My liaison officer at the Alamogordo Air Base, 60 miles away, made the following report:

> There was a blinding flash of light that lighted the entire northwestern sky. In the center of the flash, there appeared to be a huge billow of smoke. The original flash lasted approximately 10 to 15 seconds. As the first flash died down, there arose in the approximate center of where the original flash had occurred an enormous ball of what appeared to be fire and closely resembled a rising sun that was three-fourths above a mountain. The ball of fire lasted approximately 15

seconds, then died down and the sky resumed an almost normal appearance.

Almost immediately, a third, but much smaller, flash and billow of smoke of a whitish-orange color appeared in the sky, again lighting the sky for approximately 4 seconds. At the time of the original flash, the field was lighted well enough so that a newspaper could easily have been read. The second and third flashes were of much lesser intensity.

We were in a glass-enclosed control tower some 70 feet above the ground and felt no concussion or air compression. There was no noticeable earth tremor although reports overheard at the Field during the following 24 hours indicated that some believed that they had both heard the explosion and felt some earth tremor.

16. I have not written a separate report for General George C. Marshall as I feel you will want to show this to him. I have informed the necessary people here of our results. Lord Edward Halifax after discussion with Mr. George L. Harrison and myself stated that he was not sending a full report to his government at this time. I informed him that I was sending this to you and that you might wish to show it to the proper British representatives.

17. We are all fully conscious that our real goal is still before us. The battle test is what counts in the war with Japan.

18. May I express my deep personal appreciation for your congratulatory cable to us and for the support and confidence which I have received from you ever since I have had this work under my charge.

Chapter 2

The Decision to Drop the Atom Bomb

Turning Points

IN WORLD HISTORY

It Was Always Assumed the Bomb Would Be Used

Alan Cranston

The United States dropped the world's first atomic bomb on the Japanese city of Hiroshima on August 6, 1945, and a second bomb on Nagasaki three days later. Ever since then, policy analysts, commentators, and those involved in the making and dropping of the bomb have debated the necessity and morality of using such a weapon of mass destruction.

According to Alan Cranston, there was no actual decision made about whether or not the atom bomb should be used. Cranston contends that it was simply assumed from the time Harry S. Truman became president that the bomb would be utilized when it was ready. He maintains that despite the project's scientists' concerns about the morality of deploying such a destructive weapon, there was no discussion in the Truman administration about the ethics of using the bomb. The mass killing of civilians had become acceptable after years of war, Cranston argues, and it was merely hoped that the use of the atom bomb would speed the war's end. He concludes that it will never be known if another policy might have ended the war since none was ever considered.

Alan Cranston was a California senator from 1969 to 1993.

Hiroshima's fiftieth anniversary has set loose a torrent of magazine covers, TV specials and newspaper pull-out sections re-examining the decision to drop the atomic bomb on Japan. Many have dwelled upon the morality, strategic ne-

Excerpted from "The Non-Event," by Alan Cranston, *The New Republic*, August 21–28, 1995. Copyright © 1995 by The New Republic, Inc. Reprinted with permission from *The New Republic*.

cessity and wisdom of the decision. But, whatever the merits of those arguments, it is a simple but startling historical fact, still virtually unknown even after a half a century, that there was never any "decision," as such. The Truman administration simply assumed that the bomb would be used as soon as it became available. The president and his advisers discussed where, when and how to drop it, but the profound moral and ethical implications of this monstrous new weapon, which bedevil scholars and statesmen to this day, escaped scrutiny.

"The Decision That Was Not a Decision"

Franklin Roosevelt and Winston Churchill had agreed in a secret memorandum on September 18, 1944, that "when a 'bomb' is finally available it might perhaps, after mature deliberation, be used against the Japanese. . . ." But no "mature deliberation" occurred. On September 22 Roosevelt asked Vannevar Bush, head of the Office of Scientific Research and Development, whether he thought the bomb should be used against Japan or employed only as a threat. No decision was made, and they agreed to table to issue temporarily. By the time we got the bomb, FDR was dead, and the memorandum, having been misfiled at the White House, was not available to Harry Truman. Truman's role, according to General Leslie R. Groves, the head of the Manhattan Project, was "one of non-interference—basically a decision not to interfere with existing plans." David McCullough's *Truman* quotes Churchill on "the decision that was not a decision."

When some of the scientists behind the Manhattan Project tried to tell Truman they thought dropping the bomb was immoral and would set off a dangerous nuclear arms race, they were shunted off to former senator and future Secretary of State James F. Byrnes, who gave their views short shrift in his own advice to Truman. The closest Truman's top officials and advisers ever came to questioning the bomb's use was the consideration given to publicly demonstrating its capacity as a warning to Japan. Yet even this brief discussion focused on the pros and cons—mostly cons—of a demonstration; it did not fundamentally question the bombing of Japan itself.

Military planning advanced unquestioned, with cold precision, in the highest secrecy. The U.S. Air Force began to practice dropping atomic bombs in the late summer of 1944. A Target Committee was established in 1945 to consider what to bomb in Japan. Truman later said, "Let there be no mistake about it. I regarded the bomb as a military weapon and never had any doubt that it should be used."

Years of war had dulled moral sensitivities toward civilian slaughter, allowing policymakers to view the terrible new weapon in purely military terms. Back in 1939, before the U.S. entered the war, Roosevelt had urged both sides to avoid the "barbarism" of civilian bombings. But the Nazi Luftwaffe and the British Royal Air Force were soon engaged in bloody tit-for-tat bombings of London, Berlin and other cities, and by early 1945 the U.S. Air Force was itself participating in incendiary assaults on Dresden and Tokyo. The atomic bombing of Hiroshima and Nagasaki was seen as a logical next step rather than a leap into a new realm. Sparing innocents was a principle long since abandoned.

Truman recollected in later years that he made "the" decision to use the bomb on his way home from the Potsdam conference after Japan had rejected the Allies' demand for "unconditional surrender." He claimed to remember calling a high-level meeting at Potsdam with Byrnes, Secretary of War Henry L. Stimson, Admiral William Leahy, Generals George C. Marshall and Dwight D. Eisenhower, Navy Secretary James C. Forrestal "and some others to discuss what should be done with this awful weapon." But, in archival records and other resources, historians have been unable to find any evidence that such a "meeting" ever took place.

Obliteration and Devastation

On August 6 and 9, 1945, it was as if portions of the sun suddenly plummeted down on Hiroshima and Nagasaki. The world, which had known nothing of the weapon, was stunned by the instant obliteration of tens of thousands of human beings. Most Americans were jubilant, convinced that with the long war over, the lives of American troops in the Pacific could be spared. Japan did surrender a few days after Hiroshima. It will never be known whether an alternative policy could have ended the war, for none was ever considered. About this time I met Albert Einstein, who warned me, as he did others, that all-out use of nuclear weapons might extinguish all life on Earth. Truman, who stoutly defended use of the bomb to the end of his days, was nevertheless aghast at the sheer and previously unimaginable human suffering and physical devastation it wrought.

The nuclear chain of events had assumed a life of its own that dwarfed the processes that gave it birth. In Stimson's words, it forever changed "the relationship of man to the universe"—without a "decision" to do so ever having been made. All of this leads to a question for today's world: How confident are we about the processes designed to deal with the nuclear dilemmas that will arise slowly, or more likely suddenly, in the days and decades to come?

The Government Was Justified in Using the Atom Bomb

Henry L. Stimson

Shortly after two atomic bombs were dropped on the Japanese cities of Hiroshima and Nagasaki in August 1945, the euphoria that the American public felt over the end of the war began to be tinged with doubts over the morality of the mass killing of civilians. Several newspaper and magazine editorials argued that the use of the atomic bomb was both immoral and unjustified.

To counter such criticisms, Henry L. Stimson, secretary of war from 1940 to 1945, defends the decision to drop two atomic bombs on Japan in an article published in *Harper's Magazine* in February 1947. The atomic bomb was regarded by policymakers as a legitimate weapon, he asserts, and the decision to use it was carefully considered by a committee of military, scientific, and political advisers. Furthermore, Stimson argues, the atomic bomb presented the fastest and best policy of ensuring the complete surrender of Japan with as little danger to American lives as possible.

Henry L. Stimson served as secretary of state under William H. Taft from 1911 to 1913, secretary of state under Herbert Hoover in the 1930s, and secretary of war under Franklin D. Roosevelt and Harry S. Truman. Stimson was directly involved in the production of the first atomic bomb. He was also the chairman of a special committee of scientists and military and government officials that discussed policy implications of the atomic bomb, and that ultimately recommended the bomb be used against Japan.

In recent months there has been much comment about the decision to use atomic bombs in attacks on the Japanese cities of Hiroshima and Nagasaki. This decision was one of the gravest made by our government in recent years, and it is entirely proper that it should be widely discussed. I have therefore decided to record for all who may be interested my understanding of the events which led up to the attack on Hiroshima on August 6, 1945, on Nagasaki on August 9, and the Japanese decision to surrender, on August 10. No single individual can hope to know exactly what took place in the minds of all of those who had a share in these events, but what follows is an exact description of our thoughts and actions as I find them in the records and in my clear recollection. . . .

No Effort Was Spared

The policy adopted and steadily pursued by President Franklin D. Roosevelt and his advisers was a simple one. It was to spare no effort in securing the earliest possible successful development of an atomic weapon. The reasons for this policy were equally simple. The original experimental achievement of atomic fission had occurred in Germany in 1938, and it was known that the Germans had continued their experiments. In 1941 and 1942 they were believed to be ahead of us, and it was vital that they should not be the first to bring atomic weapons into the field of battle. Furthermore, if we should be the first to develop the weapon, we should have a great new instrument for shortening the war and minimizing destruction. At no time, from 1941 to 1945, did I ever hear it suggested by the President, or by any other responsible member of the government, that atomic energy should not be used in the war. All of us of course understood the terrible responsibility involved in our attempt to unlock the doors to such a devastating weapon; President Roosevelt particularly spoke to me many times of his own awareness of the catastrophic potentialities of our work. but we were at war, and the work must be done. I therefore emphasize that it was our common objective, throughout the war, to be the first to produce an atomic weapon and use it.

The possible atomic weapon was considered to be a new and tremendously powerful explosive, as legitimate as any other of the deadly explosive weapons of modern war. The entire purpose was the production of a military weapon; on no other ground could the wartime expenditure of so much time and money have been justified. The exact circumstances in which that weapon might be used were unknown to any of us until the middle of 1945, and when that time came, as we shall presently see, the military use of atomic energy was connected with larger questions of national policy.

The extraordinary story of the successful development of the atomic bomb has been well told elsewhere. As time went on it became clear that the weapon would not be available in time for use in the European Theater, and the war against Germany was successfully ended by the use of what are now called conventional means. But in the spring of 1945 it became evident that the climax of our prolonged atomic effort was at hand. By the nature of atomic chain reactions, it was impossible to state with certainty that we had succeeded until a bomb had actually exploded in a full-scale experiment; nevertheless it was considered exceedingly probable that we should by midsummer have successfully detonated the first atomic bomb. This was to be done at the Alamogordo Reservation in New Mexico. It was thus time for detailed consideration of our future plans. What had begun as a well-founded hope was now developing into a reality. . . .

The Interim Committee

The next step in our preparations was the appointment of . . . the Interim Committee [which] was charged with the function of advising the President on the various questions raised by our apparently imminent success in developing an atomic weapon. I was its chairman. . . .

The discussions of the committee ranged over the whole field of atomic energy, in its political, military, and scientific aspects. That part of its work which particularly concerns us here relates to its recommendations for the use of atomic energy against Japan, but it should be borne in mind that these recommendations were not made in a vacuum. The committee's work included the drafting of the statements which were published immediately after the first bombs were dropped, the drafting of a bill for the domestic control of atomic energy, and recommendations looking toward the international control of atomic energy. The Interim Committee was assisted in its work by a Scientific Panel whose members were the following: Dr. A.H. Compton, Dr. Enrico Fermi, Dr. E.O. Lawrence, and Dr. J.R. Oppenheimer. All four were nuclear physicists of the first rank; all four had held positions of great importance in the atomic project from its inception. At a meeting with the Interim Committee and the Scientific Panel on May 31, 1945, I urged all those present to feel free to express themselves on any phase of the subject, scientific or political. Both General George C. Marshall and I at this meeting expressed the view that atomic energy could not be considered simply in terms of military weapons but must also be considered in terms of a new relationship of man to the universe.

Recommendations

On June 1, after its discussions with the Scientific Panel, the Interim Committee unanimously adopted the following recommendations:

1. The bomb should be used against Japan as soon as possible.
2. It should be used on a dual target—that is, a military installation or war plant surrounded by or adjacent to houses and other buildings most susceptible to damage, and
3. It should be used without prior warning [of the nature of the weapon]. One member of the committee, Mr. Ralph A. Bard, later changed his view and dissented from recommendation.

In reaching these conclusions the Interim Committee carefully considered such alternatives as a detailed advance warning or a demonstration in some uninhabited area. Both of these suggestions were discarded as impractical. They were not regarded as likely to be effective in compelling a surrender of Japan, and both of them involved serious risks.

Even the New Mexico test would not give final proof that any given bomb was certain to explode when dropped from an airplane. Quite apart from the generally unfamiliar nature of atomic explosives, there was the whole problem of exploding a bomb at a predetermined height in the air by a complicated mechanism which could not be tested in the static test of New Mexico. Nothing would have been more damaging to our effort to obtain surrender than a warning or a demonstration followed by a dud—and this was a real possibility. Furthermore, we had no bombs to waste. It was vital that a sufficient effect be quickly obtained with the few we had. . . .

U.S. Policy Toward Japan in July 1945

The principal political, social, and military objective of the United States in the summer of 1945 was the prompt and complete surrender of Japan. Only the complete destruction of her military power could open the way to lasting peace.

Japan, in July 1945, had been seriously weakened by our increasingly violent attacks. It was known to us that she had gone so far as to make tentative proposals to the Soviet government, hoping to use the Russians as mediators in a negotiated peace. These vague proposals contemplated the retention by Japan of important conquered areas and were therefore not considered seriously. There was as yet no indication of any weakening in the Japanese determination to fight rather than accept unconditional surrender. If she should persist in her fight to the end, she had still a great military force.

Japanese Military Strength

In the middle of July 1945, the intelligence section of the War Department General Staff estimated Japanese military strength as follows: in the home islands, slightly under 2,000,000; in Korea, Manchuria, China proper, and Formosa, slightly over 2,000,000; in French Indochina, Thailand, and Burma, over 200,000; in the East Indies area, including the Philippines, over 500,000; in the by-passed Pacific Islands, over 100,000. The total strength of the

Japanese Army was estimated at about 5,000,000 men. These estimates later proved to be in very close agreement with official Japanese figures.

The Japanese Army was in much better condition than the Japanese Navy and Air Force. The Navy had practically ceased to exist except as a harrying force against an invasion fleet. The Air Force had been reduced mainly to reliance upon Kamikaze, or suicide, attacks. These latter, however, had already inflicted serious damage on our seagoing forces, and their possible effectiveness in a last ditch fight was a matter of real concern to our naval leaders.

As we understood it in July, there was a very strong possibility that the Japanese government might determine upon resistance to the end, in all the areas of the Far East under its control. In such an event the Allies would be faced with the enormous task of destroying an armed force of five million men and five thousand suicide aircraft, belonging to a race which had already amply demonstrated its ability to fight literally to the death.

The Allied Forces

The strategic plans of our armed forces for the defeat of Japan, as they stood in July, had been prepared without reliance upon the atomic bomb, which had not yet been tested in New Mexico. We were planning an intensified sea and air blockade, and greatly intensified strategic air bombing, through the summer and early fall, to be followed on November 1 by an invasion of the southern island of Kyushu. This would be followed in turn by an invasion of the main island of Honshu in the spring of 1946. The total U.S. military and naval force involved in this grand design was of the order of 5,000,000 men; if all those indirectly concerned are included, it was larger still.

We estimated that if we should be forced to carry this plan to its conclusion, the major fighting would not end until the latter part of 1946, at the earliest. I was informed that such operations might be expected to cost over a million casualties, to American forces alone. Additional large losses might be expected among our allies, and, of course, if our campaign were successful and if we could judge by previous experience, enemy casualties would be much larger than our own.

It was already clear in July that even before the invasion we should be able to inflict enormously severe damage on the Japanese homeland by the combined application of "conventional" sea and air power. The critical question was whether this kind of action would induce surrender. It therefore became necessary to consider very carefully the probable state of mind of the enemy, and to assess with accuracy the line of conduct which might end his will to resist. . . .

The Use of the Bomb

I find that I stated in my diary, as early as June 19, that "the last chance warning . . . must be given before an actual landing of the ground forces in Japan, and fortunately the plans provide for enough time to bring in the sanctions to our warning in the shape of heavy ordinary bombing attack and an attack of S-1." S-1 was a code name for the atomic bomb.

There was much discussion in Washington about the timing of the warning to Japan. The controlling factor in the end was the date already set for the Potsdam meeting of the Big Three. It was President Harry S. Truman's decision that such a warning should be solemnly issued by the U.S. and the U.K. from this meeting, with the concurrence of the head of the Chinese government, so that it would be plain that *all* of Japan's principal enemies were in entire unity. This was done, in the Potsdam ultimatum of July 26. . . .

On July 28 the Premier of Japan, Kantaro Suzuki, rejected the Potsdam ultimatum by announcing that it was "unworthy of public notice." In the face of this rejection we could only proceed to demonstrate that the ultimatum had meant exactly what it said when it stated that if the Japanese continued the war, "the full application of our military power, backed by our resolve, will mean the inevitable and complete destruction of the Japanese armed forces and just as inevitably the utter devastation of the Japanese homeland."

For such a purpose the atomic bomb was an eminently suitable weapon. The New Mexico test occurred while we were at Potsdam, on July 16. It was immediately clear that the power of the bomb measured up to our highest estimates. We had developed a weapon of such a revolutionary character that its use against the enemy might well be expected to produce exactly the kind of shock on the Japanese ruling oligarchy which we desired, strengthening the position of those who wished peace, and weakening that of the military party.

The Targets Are Selected

Because of the importance of the atomic mission against Japan, the detailed plans were brought to me by the military staff for approval. With President Truman's warm support I struck off the list of suggested targets the city of Kyoto. Although it was a target of considerable military importance, it had been the ancient capital of Japan and was a shrine of Japanese art and culture. We determined that it should be spared. I approved four other targets including the cities of Hiroshima and Nagasaki.

Hiroshima was bombed on August 6, and Nagasaki on August 9. These two cities were active working parts of the Japanese war effort. One was an army center; the other was naval and industrial. Hiroshima was the headquarters of the Japanese Army defending southern Japan and was a major military storage and assembly point. Nagasaki was a major seaport and it contained several large industrial plants of great wartime importance. We believed that our attacks had struck cities which must certainly be important to the Japanese military leaders, both Army and Navy, and we waited for a result. We waited one day.

Many accounts have been written about the Japanese surrender. After a prolonged Japanese cabinet session in which the deadlock was broken by the Emperor himself, the offer to surrender was made on August 10. It was based on the Potsdam terms, with a reservation concerning the sovereignty of the Emperor. While the Allied reply made no promises other than those already given, it implicitly recognized the Emperor's position by prescribing that his power must be subject to the orders of the Allied Supreme Commander. These terms were accepted on August 14 by the

Japanese, and the instrument of surrender was formally signed on September 2, in Tokyo Bay. Our great objective was thus achieved, and all the evidence I have seen indicates that the controlling factor in the final Japanese decision to accept our terms of surrender was the atomic bomb.

A Psychological Weapon

The two atomic bombs which we had dropped were the only ones we had ready, and our rate of production at the time was very small. Had the war continued until the projected

No Doubts About the Bomb

Harry S. Truman was not informed about the top-secret development of the atomic bomb until after he became president in April 1945. In July, he gave the order directing that atomic bombs be used against Japan as soon as the bombs were ready. The first bomb was dropped on Hiroshima on August 6, and the second bomb on Nagasaki on August 9. The following excerpt is from Truman's Memoirs *in which he explains his decision to use this new weapon.*

I had realized, of course, that an atomic bomb explosion would inflict damage and casualties beyond imagination. On the other hand, the scientific advisers of the committee reported "We can propose no technical demonstration likely to bring an end to the war; we see no acceptance alternative to direct military use." It was their conclusion that no technical demonstration they might propose, such as over a deserted island, would be likely to bring the war to an end. It had to be used against an enemy target.

The final decision of where and when to use the atomic bomb was up to me. Let there be no mistake about it. I regarded the bomb as a military weapon and never had any doubt that it should be used. The top military advisers to the President recommended its use, and when I talked to Churchill he unhesitatingly told me that he favored the use of the atomic bomb if it might aid to end the war.

Harry S. Truman, *Memoirs*, 1955.

invasion on November 1, additional fire raids of B-29's would have been more destructive of life and property than the very limited number of atomic raids which we could have executed in the same period. But the atomic bomb was more than a weapon of terrible destruction; it was a psychological weapon. In March 1945 our Air Force had launched its first great incendiary raid on the Tokyo area. In this raid more damage was done and more casualties were inflicted than was the case at Hiroshima. Hundreds of bombers took part and hundreds of tons of incendiaries were dropped. Similar successive raids burned out a great part of the urban area of Japan, but the Japanese fought on. On August 6 one B-29 dropped a single atomic bomb on Hiroshima. Three days later a second bomb was dropped on Nagasaki and the war was over. So far as the Japanese could know, our ability to execute atomic attacks, if necessary by many planes at a time, was unlimited. As Dr. Karl Compton has said, "it was not one atomic bomb, or two, which brought surrender; it was the experience of what an atomic bomb will *actually do to a community*, plus the dread of many more, that was effective."

The bomb thus served exactly the purpose we intended. The peace party was able to take the path of surrender, and the whole weight of the Emperor's prestige was exerted in favor of peace. When the Emperor ordered surrender, and the small but dangerous group of fanatics who opposed him were brought under control, the Japanese became so subdued that the great undertaking of occupation and disarmament was completed with unprecedented ease.

A Personal Summary

In the foregoing pages I have tried to give an accurate account of my own personal observations of the circumstances which led up to the use of the atomic bomb and the reasons which underlay our use of it. To me they have always seemed compelling and clear, and I cannot see how any person vested with such responsibilities as mine could have taken any other course or given any other advice to his chiefs.

Two great nations were approaching contact in a fight to a finish which would begin on November 1, 1945. Our enemy, Japan, commanded forces of somewhat over 5,000,000 armed men. Men of these armies had already inflicted upon us, in our breakthrough of the outer perimeter of their defenses, over 300,000 battle casualties. Enemy armies still unbeaten had the strength to cost us a million more. *As long as the Japanese government refused to surrender,* we should be forced to take and hold the ground, and smash the Japanese ground armies, by close-in fighting of the same desperate and costly kind that we had faced in the Pacific islands for nearly four years.

In the light of the formidable problem which thus confronted us, I felt that every possible step should be taken to compel a surrender of the homelands, and a withdrawal of all Japanese troops from the Asiatic mainland and from other positions, before we had commenced an invasion. We held two cards to assist us in such an effort. One was the traditional veneration in which the Japanese Emperor was held by his subjects and the power which was thus vested in him over his loyal troops. It was for this reason that I suggested . . . that his dynasty should be continued. The second card was the use of the atomic bomb in the manner best calculated to persuade that Emperor and the counselors about him to submit to our demand for what was essentially unconditional surrender, placing his immense power over his people and his troops subject to our orders.

In order to end the war in the shortest possible time and to avoid the enormous losses of human life which otherwise confronted us, I felt that we must use the Emperor as our instrument to command and compel his people to cease fighting and subject themselves to our authority through him, and that to accomplish this we must give him and his controlling advisers a compelling reason to accede to our demands. This reason furthermore must be of such a nature that his people could understand his decision. The bomb seemed to me to furnish a unique instrument for that purpose.

My chief purpose was to end the war in victory with the least possible cost in the lives of the men in the armies which I had helped to raise. In the light of the alternatives which, on a fair estimate, were open to us I believe that no man, in our position and subject to our responsibilities, holding in his hands a weapon of such possibilities for accomplishing this purpose and saving those lives, could have failed to use it and afterwards looked his countrymen in the face.

War Is Death

As I read over what I have written, I am aware that much of it, in this year of peace, may have a harsh and unfeeling sound. It would perhaps be possible to say the same things and say them more gently. But I do not think it would be wise. As I look back over the five years of my service as Secretary of War, I see too many stern and heartrending decisions to be willing to pretend that war is anything else than what it is. The face of war is the face of death; death is an inevitable part of every order that a wartime leader gives. The decision to use the atomic bomb was a decision that brought death to over a hundred thousand Japanese. No explanation can change that fact and I do not wish to gloss it over. But this deliberate, premeditated destruction was our least abhorrent choice. The destruction of Hiroshima and Nagasaki put an end to the Japanese war. It stopped the fire raids, and the strangling blockade; it ended the ghastly specter of a clash of great land armies.

In this last great action of the Second World War we were given final proof that war is death. War in the twentieth century has grown steadily more barbarous, more destructive, more debased in all its aspects. Now, with the release of atomic energy, man's ability to destroy himself is very nearly complete. The bombs dropped on Hiroshima and Nagasaki ended a war. They also made it wholly clear that we must never have another war. This is the lesson men and leaders everywhere must learn, and I believe that when they learn it they will find a way to lasting peace. There is no other choice.

Using the Atom Bomb Was Unnecessary and Immoral

Hanson W. Baldwin

After Henry L. Stimson published his reasons for using the atom bomb against Japan, Hanson W. Baldwin, military analyst for the *New York Times* and author of numerous books on war, critiqued Stimson's defense in two articles in the *Atlantic Monthly* that were later published as a book.

Baldwin contends that the atomic bomb had no effect on hastening the defeat of Japan. Japan was already in a severely weakened state, he maintains, and was in fact attempting to negotiate a peace settlement when the atomic bombs were dropped on two of its cities. A Japanese surrender was inevitable, he argues, and was merely a short time away from becoming reality. Baldwin concludes that the atomic bomb is a new and horrible weapon to the world; by using it against their enemies, Americans are no better than other notorious war criminals.

Hanson W. Baldwin was the military analyst for the *New York Times* and is the author of numerous books on war, including *Great Mistakes of the War*.

The utilization of the atomic bomb against a prostrate and defeated Japan in the closing days of the war exemplifies— even more graphically than any of the mistakes previously recounted—the narrow, astigmatic concentration of our planners upon one goal, and one alone: victory.

Nowhere in all of Mr. Henry L. Stimson's forceful and eloquent apologia for the leveling of Hiroshima and Nagasaki is there any evidence of an ulterior vision; indeed, the

Excerpted from *Great Mistakes of the War,* by Hanson W. Baldwin (Harper & Brothers, 1949, 1950). Copyright © 1950 by Hanson W. Baldwin. Reprinted with permission from Curtis Brown, Ltd.

entire effort of his famous *Harper's* article, reprinted and rearranged in his book, *On Active Service* is focused on proving that the bomb hastened the end of the war. But at what cost!

To accept the Stimson thesis that the atomic bomb should have been used as it was used, it is necessary first to accept the contention that the atomic bomb achieved or hastened victory, and second, and more important, that it helped to consolidate the peace or to further the political aims for which the war was fought.

History can accept neither contention.

Japan Was Already Defeated

Let us examine the first. The atomic bomb was dropped in August 1945. Long before that month started our forces were securely based in Okinawa, the Marianas and Iwo Jima; Germany had been defeated; our fleet had been cruising off the Japanese coast with impunity bombarding the shoreline; our submarines were operating in the Sea of Japan; even inter-island ferries had been attacked and sunk. Bombing, which started slowly in June, 1944, from China bases and from the Marianas in November, 1944, had been increased materially in 1945, and by August, 1945, more than 16,000 tons of bombs had ravaged Japanese cities. Food was short; mines and submarines and surface vessels and planes clamped an iron blockade around the main islands; raw materials were scarce. Blockade, bombing, and unsuccessful attempts at dispersion had reduced Japanese production capacity from 20 to 60 per cent. The enemy, in a military sense, was in a hopeless strategic position by the time the Potsdam demand for unconditional surrender was made on July 26.

Such, then, was the situation when we wiped out Hiroshima and Nagasaki.

Need we have done it? No one can, of course, be positive, but the answer is almost certainly negative.

The invasion of Japan, which Admiral Leahy had opposed as too wasteful of American blood, and in any case unnecessary, was scheduled (for the southern island of Kyushu) for Nov. 1, 1945, to be followed if necessary, in the spring of

1946, by a major landing on the main island of Honshu. We dropped the two atomic bombs in early August, almost two months before our first D-Day. The decision to drop them, after the Japanese rejection of the Potsdam ultimatum, was a pretty hasty one. It followed the recommendations of Secretary Stimson and an "Interim Committee" of distinguished officials and scientists, who had found "no acceptable alternative to direct military use."

No Alternatives Were Tried

But the weakness of this statement is inherent, for none was tried and "military use" of the bomb was undertaken despite strong opposition to this course by numerous scientists and Japanese experts, including former Ambassador Joseph Grew. Not only was the Potsdam ultimatum merely a restatement of the politically impossible—unconditional surrender—but it could hardly be construed as a direct warning of the atomic bomb and was not taken as such by anyone who did not know the bomb had been created. A technical demonstration of the bomb's power may well have been unfeasible, but certainly far more definite warning could have been given; and it is hard to believe that a target objective in Japan with but sparse population could not have been found. The truth is we did not try; we gave no specific warning. There were almost two months before our scheduled invasion of Kyushu, in which American ingenuity could have found ways to bring home to the Japanese the impossibility of their position and the horrors of the weapon being held over them; yet we rushed to use the bomb as soon as unconditional surrender was rejected. Had we devised some demonstration or given a more specific warning than the Potsdam ultimatum, and had the Japanese still persisted in continued resistance after some weeks of our psychological offensive, we should perhaps have been justified in the bomb's use; at least, our hands would have been more clean.

But, in fact, our only warning to a Japan already militarily defeated, and in a hopeless situation, was the Potsdam demand for unconditional surrender issued on July 26, when we knew Japanese surrender attempts had started. Yet when the Japanese surrender was negotiated about two weeks later, after the bomb was dropped, our unconditional surrender demand was made conditional and we agreed, as Stimson had originally proposed we should do, to continuation of the Emperor upon his imperial throne.

Twice Guilty

We were, therefore, twice guilty. We dropped the bomb at a time when Japan already was negotiating for an end of the war but before those negotiations could come to fruition. We demanded unconditional surrender, then dropped the bomb and accepted conditional surrender, a sequence which indicates pretty clearly that the Japanese would have surrendered, even if the bomb had not been dropped, had the Potsdam Declaration included our promise to permit the Emperor to remain on his imperial throne.

What we now know of the condition of Japan, and of the days preceding her final surrender on Aug. 15, verifies these conclusions. It is clear, in retrospect, (and was understood by some, notably Admiral Leahy, at the time) that Japan was militarily on her last legs. Yet our intelligence estimates greatly overstated her strength.

The background for surrender had been sketched in fully, well before the bombs were dropped, and the Strategic Bombing Survey declares that "interrogation of the highest Japanese officials, following V-J Day, indicated that Japan would have surrendered . . . even . . . if the atomic bombs had not been dropped." The survey also notes, "Even before the large-scale bombing of Japan was initiated, the raw material base of Japanese industry was effectively undermined. An accelerated decline of armament production was inevitable."

Hastening the Inevitable

Admiral Chester W. Nimitz, in a talk to the National Geographic Society on January 25, 1946, declared:

> I am convinced that the complete impunity with which the Pacific Fleet pounded Japan at point-blank range was the decisive factor in forcing the Japanese to ask the Russians to ap-

proach us for peace proposals in July.

Meanwhile, aircraft from our new fields in the Okinawa group were daily shuttling back and forth over Kyushu and Shokoku and B-29's of the Twentieth Air Force were fire-bombing major Japanese cities. The pace and the fury were mounting and the government of Japan, as its official spokesmen have now admitted, were looking for a way to end the war. At this point the Potsdam Ultimatum was delivered and the Japanese knew their choice.

They were debating that choice when the atomic bomb fell on Hiroshima. They were debating that choice when our ships shelled installations within less than 100 miles of Tokyo. . . .

The atomic bomb merely hastened a process already reaching an inevitable conclusion. . . .

There can be no doubt that this conclusion of Admiral Nimitz will be the verdict of history. Militarily, we "killed" Japan in many different ways: by crushing defeats at sea and on land; by the strangulation of the blockade of which the principal instrument was the submarine; by bombing with conventional bombs. After the seizure of Okinawa—probably even before that—the blockade alone could have defeated Japan; was, indeed, defeating her. Admiral Leahy was right; invasion was not necessary. . . .

The Atomic Bomb Was Not Necessary

In the words of a well known Japanese correspondent, Masuo Kato, who was in Washington for the Domei News Agency when the war started: "The thunderous arrival of the first atomic bomb at Hiroshima was only a *coup de grâce* for an empire already struggling in particularly agonizing death throes. The world's newest and most devastating of weapons had floated out of the summer sky to destroy a city at a stroke, but its arrival had small effect on the outcome of the war between Japan and the United Nations."

It is therefore clear today—and was clear to many even as early as the spring of 1945—that the military defeat of Japan was certain; the atomic bomb was not needed.

But if the bomb did not procure victory, did it hasten it?

This question cannot be answered with equal precision, particularly since the full story of the Japanese surrender attempts has not been compiled. But a brief chronology of known events indicates that the atomic bomb may have shortened the war by a few days—not more.

Japanese Talk About Surrender

The day before Christmas, 1944 (two months *before* the Yalta conference), U.S. intelligence authorities in Washington received a report from a confidential agent in Japan that a peace party was emerging and that the Koiso cabinet would soon be succeeded by a cabinet headed by Admiral Baron Suzuki who would initiate surrender proceedings.

The Koiso cabinet *was* succeeded by a new government headed by Suzuki in early April, 1945, but even prior to this significant change, the Japanese—in February, 1945—had approached the Russians with a request that they act as intermediary in arranging a peace with the Western powers. The Russian Ambassador, Malik, in Tokyo, was the channel of the approach. The Russians, however, set their price of mediation so high that the Japanese temporarily dropped the matter. The United States was not officially informed of this approach until after the end of the war.

Prior to, coincident with, and after this February attempt, ill-defined peace approaches were made through the Japanese Ambassadors in Stockholm and Moscow, particularly Moscow. These approaches were so informal, and to some extent represented to such a degree the personal initiative of the two Ambassadors concerned, that they never came to a head.

But after a meeting with Stalin in Moscow on May 27, before the trial A-bomb was even tested in New Mexico, Harry Hopkins cabled President Truman that:

"1.   Japan is doomed and the Japanese know it.

"2.   Peace feelers are being put out by certain elements in Japan. . . ."

In April, 1945, as the United States was establishing a

foothold on Okinawa, the Russians in effect denounced their neutrality agreement with Japan, and from then until July 12, the new cabinet was moving rapidly toward surrender attempts.

On July 12, fourteen days before we issued the Potsdam Proclamation, these attempts reached a clearly defined point. Prince Konoye was received by the Emperor on that day and ordered to Moscow as a peace plenipotentiary to "secure peace at any price." On July 13, Moscow was notified officially by the Japanese foreign office that the "Emperor was desirous of peace."

It was hoped that Moscow would inform the United States and Britain at the Potsdam conference of Japan's desire to discuss peace. But instead of an answer from the "Big Three," Ambassador Sato in Moscow was told by [foreign minister Vyacheslav] Molotov on August 8 of Russia's entry into the war against Japan, effective immediately.

However, since early May—well before this disappointing denouement to the most definite peace attempts the Japanese had yet made—the six-man Supreme War Direction Council in Japan had been discussing peace. On June 20, the Emperor told the (Supreme War Direction) Council that it "was necessary to have a plan to close the war at once as well as a plan to defend the home islands."

The *Gozenkaigi*

The Council was deadlocked three to three, and Premier Suzuki, to break the deadlock, had decided to summon a *Gozenkaigi* (a meeting of "Elder Statesmen," summoned only in hours of crises) at which the Emperor himself could make the decision for peace or further war. Suzuki knew his Emperor's mind; Hirohito had been convinced for some weeks that peace was the only answer to Japan's ordeal.

The first atomic bomb was dropped on Hiroshima on August 6; Russia entered the war on August 8; and the second atomic bomb was dropped on Nagasaki on August 9. The dropping of the first bomb, and the Russian entry into the war, gave Suzuki additional arguments for again putting the issue before the Supreme War Direction Council, and, on

August 9, he won their approval for the *Gozenkaigi*. But neither the people of Japan nor their leaders were as impressed with the atomic bomb as were we. The public did not know until after the war what had happened to Hiroshima; and even so, they had endured fire raids against Tokyo which had caused more casualties than the atomic bomb and had devastated a greater area than that destroyed at Hiroshima. The Supreme War Direction Council was initially told that a fragment of the Hiroshima bomb indicated that it was made in Germany (!), that it appeared to be a conventional explosive of great power, and that there was only one bomb available. When the *Gozenkaigi* actually was held on August 14, five days after the second bomb was dropped, War Minister Anami and the chiefs of the Army and Navy General Staff—three members of the War Council who had been adamant for continuation of the war—were still in favor of continuing it; those who had wanted peace still wanted it. In other words, the bomb changed no opinions; the Emperor himself, who had already favored peace, broke the deadlock.

"If nobody else has any opinion to express," Hirohito said, "we would express our own. We demand that you will agree to it. We see only one way left for Japan to save herself. That is the reason we have made this determination to endure the unendurable and suffer the insufferable."

The Bomb as an Excuse

In the words of Harry F. Kern, managing editor of *Newsweek*, who had made a special study, with the assistance of *Newsweek* correspondents, of the events surrounding the Japanese surrender:

> I think it's fair to say that the principal effect of the atom bomb on the Japanese surrender was to provide Suzuki with the immediate excuse for setting in motion the chain of events which resulted in the surrender. (An "excuse" was necessary—as the attempted military coup, following the *Gozenkaigi* of August 14, showed—if the leaders of the "peace party" were to avoid assassination at the hands of the

rabid militarists of the "war party.")

However, I think it is also a reasonable surmise that the Russian declaration of war would have served the same purpose, and that the dropping of the bomb was therefore unnecessary. In no case was the dropping of the bomb the reason for the Japanese surrender, and I don't think we can say that it acted as anything more than a catalyst in advancing the plans of Suzuki and his supporters.

Or, as the Strategic Bombing Survey puts it, "it is the Survey's opinion that certainly prior to December 31, 1945, and in all probability prior to November 1, 1945, Japan would have surrendered even if the atomic bombs had not been dropped, even if Russia had not entered the war, and even if no invasion had been planned or contemplated.

An Expensive Peace

This seems, in the light of history, a reasonable judgment, and, in view of our available intelligence estimates, one that we could have then made. It is quite possible that the atomic bombs shortened the war by a day, a week, or a month or two—not more.

But at what a price! For whether or not the atomic bomb hastened victory, it is quite clear it has not won the peace.

Some may point to the comparative tranquility of Japan under MacArthur in the postwar period as due in part to the terror of American arms created by the bomb. This is scarcely so; Japan's seeming tranquility is a surface one which has been furthered by a single occupation authority and the nature of the Japanese people. But I venture to estimate that those who suffered at Hiroshima and Nagasaki will never forget it, and that we sowed there a whirlwind of hate which we shall someday reap.

In estimating the effect of the use of the bomb upon the peace, we must remember, first, that we used the bomb for one purpose, and one only: not to secure a more equable peace, but to hasten victory. By using the bomb we have become identified, rightfully or wrongly, as inheritors of the mantle of Genghis Khan and all those of past history who have justified the use of utter ruthlessness in war.

It may well be argued, of course, that war—least of all modern war—knows no humanity, no rules, and no limitations, and that death by the atomic bomb is no worse than death by fire bombs or high explosives or gas or flame throwers. It is, of course, true that the atomic bomb is no worse qualitatively than other lethal weapons; it is merely quantitatively more powerful; other weapons cause death in fearful ways; the atomic bomb caused more deaths. We already had utilized fire raids, mass bombardment of cities, and flame throwers in the name of expediency and victory prior to August 6, even though many of our people had recoiled from such practices. . . .

Americans Do Not Have a Clean Record

Americans, in their own eyes, are a naively idealistic people, with none of the crass ruthlessness so often exhibited by other nations. Yet in the eyes of others our record is very far from clean, nor can objective history palliate it. Rarely have we been found on the side of restricting horror; too often we have failed to support the feeble hands of those who would limit war. We did not ratify the Hague convention of 1899, outlawing the use of dumdum (expanding) bullets in war. We never ratified the Geneva Protocol of 1925, outlawing the use of biological agents and gas in war. At the time the war in the Pacific ended, pressure for the use of gas against Japanese island positions had reached the open discussion stage, and rationalization was leading surely to justification, an expedient justification since we had air superiority and the means to deluge the enemy with gas, while he had no similar way to reply. We condemned the Japanese for their alleged use of biological agents against the Chinese, yet in July and August, 1945, a shipload of U.S. biological agents for use in destruction of the Japanese rice crop was en route to the Marianas. And even before the war, our fundamental theory of air war, like the Trenchard school of Britain, coincided, or stemmed from, the Douchet doctrine of destructiveness: the bombardment of enemy cities and peoples.

Yet surely these methods—particularly the extension of

unrestricted warfare to enemy civilians—defeated any peace aims we might have had, and had little appreciable effect in hastening military victory. For in any totalitarian state, the leaders rather than the peoples must be convinced of defeat, and the indiscriminate use of mass or area weapons, like biological agents and the atomic bomb, strike at the people, not the rulers. We cannot succeed, therefore, by such methods, in drawing that fine line between ruler and ruled that ought to be drawn in every war; we cannot hasten military victory by slaughtering the led; such methods only serve to bind the led closer to their leaders. Moreover, unrestricted warfare can never lay the groundwork for a more stable peace. Its heritage may be the salt-sown fields of Carthage, or the rubble and ruin of a Berlin or Tokyo or Hiroshima; but neither economically nor psychologically can unrestricted warfare—atomic warfare or biological warfare—lead anywhere save to eventual disaster.

During the last conflict we brought new horror to the meaning of war; the ruins of Germany and Japan, the flame-scarred tissues of the war-wounded attest our efficiency. And on August 6, 1945, that blinding flash above Hiroshima wrote a climax to an era of American expediency. On that date we joined the list of those who had introduced new and horrible weapons for the extermination of man; we joined the Germans who had first utilized gas, the Japanese with their biological agents, the Huns and the Mongols who had made destruction a fine art.

It is my contention that in the eyes of the world the atomic bomb has cost us dearly; we have lost morally; we no longer are the world's moral leader as in the days of the Wilsonian Fourteen Points. It is my contention that the unlimited destruction caused by our unlimited methods of waging war has caused us heavy economic losses in the forms of American tax subsidies to Germany and Japan. It is my contention that unrestricted warfare and unlimited aims cost us politically the winning of the peace.

But it is not only—and perhaps not chiefly—in public opinion or in the public pocketbook or even in public stability that we have suffered, but in our own souls. The American public is tending to accept the nefarious doctrine that the ends justify the means, the doctrine of exigency. . . .

The Moral Position Is Lost

The use of the atomic bomb, therefore, cost us dearly; we are now branded with the mark of the beast. Its use may have hastened victory—though by very little—but it has cost us in peace the pre-eminent moral position we once occupied. Japan's economic troubles are in some degree the result of unnecessary devastation. We have embarked upon Total War with a vengeance; we have done our best to make it far more total. If we do not soon reverse this trend, if we do not cast about for means to limit and control war, if we do not abandon the doctrine of expediency, of unconditional surrender, of total victory, we shall someday ourselves become the victims of our own theories and practices.

The Atom Bomb Was Used to Intimidate the Soviets

Gar Alperovitz

In the years following the dropping of the atomic bomb on Hiroshima and Nagasaki, some historians and analysts began to argue that the bomb was not used for military reasons but for foreign policy reasons. This "revisionist" theory continues to be hotly debated more than fifty years after the bombs were dropped.

Gar Alperovitz argues in the following essay that Japan was already defeated when the bombs were dropped on Hiroshima and Nagasaki. It was just a matter of time, therefore, before Japan surrendered to the United States, he claims. Furthermore, Alperovitz asserts, Harry S. Truman and his advisers were well aware of Japan's intention to surrender and, despite readily available alternatives to ending the war, chose to drop the bomb anyway. The real reason Truman deployed the atom bomb, Alperovitz maintains, was to impress the Soviet Union with America's military strength, which would give the United States the upper hand in postwar diplomatic relations.

Gar Alperovitz, a political economist and historian, is one of the best well-known revisionist authors. He is a senior research scientist in the department of government and politics at the University of Maryland, a fellow of the Institute for Policy Studies, and president of the National Center for Economic Alternatives. Alperovitz is the author of several revisionist articles and books, including *Cold War Essays, Atomic Diplomacy: Hiroshima and Potsdam* and *The Decision to Use the Atomic Bomb and the Architecture of an American Myth.*

Excerpted from "Hiroshima: Historians Reassess," by Gar Alperovitz, *Foreign Policy*, vol. 99, Summer 1995. Copyright © 1995 by the Carnegie Endowment for International Peace. Reprinted with permission from *Foreign Policy*.

Any serious attempt to understand the depth of feeling the story of the atomic bomb still arouses must confront two critical realities. First, there is a rapidly expanding gap between what the expert scholarly community now knows and what the public has been taught. Second, a steady narrowing of the questions in dispute in the most sophisticated studies has sharpened some of the truly controversial issues in the historical debate.

Consider the following assessment:

> Careful scholarly treatment of the records and manuscripts opened over the past few years has greatly enhanced our understanding of why the Truman administration used atomic weapons against Japan. Experts continue to disagree on some issues, but critical questions have been answered. The consensus among scholars is that the bomb was not needed to avoid an invasion of Japan and to end the war within a relatively short time. *It is clear that alternatives to the bomb existed and that Truman and his advisers knew it.* [Emphasis added.]

The author of that statement is not a revisionist; he is J. Samuel Walker, chief historian of the U.S. Nuclear Regulatory Commission. Nor is he alone in that opinion. Walker is summarizing the findings of modern specialists in his literature review in the Winter 1990 issue of *Diplomatic History*. Another expert review, by University of Illinois historian Robert Messer, concludes that recently discovered documents have been "devastating" to the traditional idea that using the bomb was the only way to avoid an invasion of Japan that might have cost many more lives.

Divided Opinions

Even allowing for continuing areas of dispute, these judgments are so far from the conventional wisdom that there is obviously something strange going on. One source of the divide between expert research and public understanding stems from a common feature of all serious scholarship: As in many areas of specialized research, perhaps a dozen truly knowledgeable experts are at the forefront of modern studies of the decision to use the atomic bomb. A second circle of generalists—historians concerned, for instance, with the Truman administration, with World War II in general, or even with the history of air power—depends heavily on the archival digging and analysis of the first circle. Beyond this second group are authors of general textbooks and articles and, still further out, journalists and other popular writers.

One can, of course, find many historians who still believe that the atomic bomb was needed to avoid an invasion. Among the inner circle of experts, however, conclusions that are at odds with this official rationale have long been commonplace. Indeed, as early as 1946 the U.S. Strategic Bombing Survey, in its report *Japan's Struggle to End the War*, concluded that "certainly prior to 31 December 1945, and in all probability prior to 1 November 1945, Japan would have surrendered even if the atomic bombs had not been dropped, even if Russia had not entered the war, and even if no invasion had been planned or contemplated."

Similarly, a top-secret April 1946 War Department study, *Use of Atomic Bomb on Japan*, declassified during the 1970s but brought to broad public attention only in 1989, found that "the Japanese leaders had decided to surrender and were merely looking for sufficient pretext to convince the diehard Army Group that Japan had lost the war and must capitulate to the Allies." This official document judged that Russia's early-August entry into the war "would almost certainly have furnished this pretext, and would have been sufficient to convince all responsible leaders that surrender was unavoidable." The study concluded that even an initial November 1945 landing on the southern Japanese island of Kyushu would have been only a "remote" possibility and that the full invasion of Japan in the spring of 1946 would not have occurred.

The Military View

Military specialists who have examined Japanese decision-making have added to expert understanding that the bombing was unnecessary. For instance, political scientist Robert Pape's study, "Why Japan Surrendered," which appeared in the Fall 1993 issue of *International Security*, details Japan's military vulnerability, particularly its shortages of everything from ammunition and fuel to trained personnel: "Japan's military position was so poor that its leaders would likely have surrendered before invasion, and at roughly the same time in August 1945, even if the United States had not employed strategic bombing or the atomic bomb." In this situation, Pape stresses, "The Soviet invasion of Manchuria on August 9 raised Japan's military vulnerability to a very high level. The Soviet offensive ruptured Japanese lines immediately, and rapidly penetrated deep into the rear. Since the Kwantung Army was thought to be Japan's premier fighting force, this had a devastating effect on Japanese calculations of the prospects for home island defense." Pape adds, "If their best forces were so easily sliced to pieces, the unavoidable implication was that the less well-equipped and trained forces assembled for [the last decisive home island battle] had no chance of success against American forces that were even more capable than the Soviets."

Whether the use of the atomic bomb was in fact necessary is, of course, a different question from whether it was believed to be necessary at the time. Walker's summary of the expert literature is important because it underscores the availability of the alternatives to using the bomb, and because it documents that "Truman and his advisers knew" of the alternatives. . . .

The "Preferred" Options

Martin Sherwin has suggested that the atomic bomb was used because it was "preferred" to the other options. Although it is sometimes thought that sheer momentum carried the day, there is no doubt that it was, in fact, an active choice. When Truman and Byrnes cut the critical assurances to the emperor out of paragraph 12 of the draft Potsdam Proclamation, they did so against the recommendation of virtually the entire top American and British leadership. Truman and Byrnes had to reverse the thrust of a near-unanimous judgment that the terms should be clarified. Truman's journal also indicates that he understood that the proclamation in final form—without the key passage—was not likely to be accepted by Japan.

If the Soviet option for ending the war was shelved for political and diplomatic reasons—and if the political reasons for not modifying the surrender formula no longer look so solid—is there any other explanation for why the Japanese were not told their emperor would not be harmed, that he could stay on the throne in some innocuous position like that of the king of England? Some historians, of course, continue to hold that the bomb's use was militarily necessary—or perhaps inevitable because of the inherited technological, bureaucratic, and military momentum that built up during the war. Others suggest that because huge sums had been spent developing the weapon, political leaders found it impossible not to use it. Still others have probed the intricacies of decision-making through an analysis of bureaucratic dynamics.

Of greatest interest, perhaps, is another factor. The traditional argument has been that solely military considerations were involved in the decision to use the bomb; increasingly, however, the once controversial idea that diplomatic issues—especially the hope of strengthening the West against the Soviet Union—played a significant role in the decision has gained widespread scholarly acceptance. Although analysts still debate exactly how much weight to accord such factors, that they were involved is not well established for most experts.

Atomic Diplomacy

Modern research findings, for instance, clearly demonstrate that from April 1945 on, top American officials calculated that using the atomic bomb would enormously bolster U.S. diplomacy vis-à-vis the Soviet Union in negotiations over postwar Europe and the Far East. The atomic bomb was not, in fact, initially brought to Truman's attention because of its relationship to the war against Japan, but because of its likely impact on diplomacy. In late April, in the midst of an explosive confrontation with Stalin over the Polish issue, Secretary of War Henry L. Stimson urged discussion of the bomb because, as he told Truman, it had "such a bearing on our present foreign relations and . . . such an important effect upon all my thinking in this field."

Stimson, for his part, regarded the atomic bomb as what he called the "master card" of diplomacy toward Russia. However, he believed that sparring with the Soviet Union in the early spring, before the weapon was demonstrated, would be counterproductive. Before a mid-May meeting of a cabinet-level committee considering Far Eastern issues, Stimson observed that "the questions cut very deep and [were] powerfully connected with our success with S-1 [the atomic bomb]." Two days later, he noted in his diary that

> I tried to point out the difficulties which existed and I thought it premature to ask those questions; at least we were not yet in a position to answer them. . . . It may be necessary to have it out with Russia on her relations to Manchuria and Port Arthur and various other parts of North China, and also the relations of China to us. Over any such tangled wave of problems the [atomic bomb] secret would be dominant and yet we will not know until after that time probably . . . whether this is a weapon in our hands or not. We think it will be shortly afterwards, but it seems a terrible thing to gamble with such big stakes in diplomacy without having your master card in your hand.

Stimson's argument for delaying diplomatic fights with the Soviet Union was also described in another mid-May diary entry after a conversation with Assistant Secretary of War John McCloy:

> The time now and the method now to deal with Russia was to keep our mouths shut and let our actions speak for words. The Russians will understand them better than anything else. It is a case where we have got to regain the lead and perhaps do it in a pretty tough and realistic way. . . . This [is] a place where we really held all the cards. I called it a royal straight flush and we mustn't be a fool about the way we play it. They can't get along without our help and industries and we have coming into action a weapon which will be unique. Now the thing is not to get into unnecessary quarrels by talking too much and not to indicate any weakness by talking too much; let our actions speak for themselves.

The Meeting Is Postponed

Stimson's files indicate that Truman had come to similar conclusions roughly a month after taking office. Quite specifically—and against the advice of Churchill, who wanted an early meeting with Stalin before American troops were withdrawn from Europe—the president postponed his only diplomatic encounter with the Soviet leader because he first wanted to know for certain that the still-untested atomic bomb actually worked. Stimson's papers indicate the president's view was that he would have "more cards" later. In a 1949 interview, Truman recalled telling a close associate before the test, "If it explodes as I think it will I'll certainly have a hammer on those boys" (meaning, it seemed clear, the Russians as well as the Japanese). After another May 1945 meeting with Truman, Ambassador Joseph Davies's diaries also record that

> to my surprise, he said he did not want it [the heads-of-government meeting] until July. The reason which I could assign was that he had his budget on his hands. . . . "But," said he, "I have another reason . . . which I have not told anybody."
>
> He told me of the atomic bomb. The final test had been set for June, but now had been postponed until July. I was startled, shocked and amazed.

Evidence in the Stimson diaries suggests that the broad strategy was probably secretly explained to Ambassador Averell Harriman and British foreign minister Anthony Eden at this time. Scientists in the field also got an inkling that there was a link between the Potsdam meeting with Stalin and the atomic test. J. Robert Oppenheimer, for instance, later testified before the U.S. Atomic Energy Commission that "I don't think there was any time where we worked harder at the speedup than in the period after the German surrender."

Changed Attitudes

The timing was perfect. The first successful atomic test occurred on July 16, 1945, and Truman sat down for discussions with Stalin the very next day. Stimson's diary includes this entry after a full report of the test results was received:

> [Churchill] told me that he had noticed at the meeting of the [Big] Three yesterday that Truman was evidently much fortified by something that had happened and that he stood up to the Russians in a most emphatic and decisive manner, telling them as to certain demands that they absolutely could not have and that the United States was entirely against them. He said "Now I know what happened to Truman yesterday. I couldn't understand it. When he got to the meeting after having read this report he was a changed man. He told the Russians just where they got on and off and generally bossed the whole meeting."

The July 23, 1945, diary entry of Lord Alanbrooke, chairman of the U.K. Chiefs of Staff Committee, provides a description of both Churchill's own reaction and further indirect evidence of the atomic bomb's impact on American attitudes:

> [The prime minister] had absorbed all the minor American exaggerations and, as a result, was completely carried away. . . . We now had something in our hands which would redress the balance with the Russians. The secret of this explosive and the power to use it would completely alter the diplomatic equilibrium which was adrift since the defeat of Germany. Now we had a new value which redressed our position (pushing out his chin and scowling); now we could say, "If you insist on doing this or that, well. . . . And then where are the Russians!"

Refusing to Face the Past

There is no longer much dispute that ending the war with Japan before the Soviet Union entered it played a role in the thinking of those responsible for using the atomic bomb. There is also evidence that impressing the Russians was a consideration. Scholarly discussion of this controversial point has been heated, and even carefully qualified judgments that such a motive is "strongly suggested" by the available documents have often been twisted and distorted into extreme claims. It is, nevertheless, impossible to ignore the considerable range of evidence that now points in this direction.

First, there are the diaries and other sources indicating that the president and his top advisers appear from late April on to have based their diplomatic strategy on the assumption that the new weapon, once demonstrated, would strengthen the U.S. position against the Soviet Union. A number of historians now agree that Truman, Stimson, and Byrnes were influenced, consciously or unconsciously, by this fact when they chose to reject other available options for ending the war. Like the language of others, Stimson's specific words to describe the new "master card" of diplomacy are also difficult to ignore:

> *Let our actions speak for words.* The Russians will understand them better than anything else. . . . We have got to regain the lead and perhaps do it in a pretty rough and realistic way. . . . *We have coming into action a weapon which will be unique. Now the thing is not . . . to indicate any weakness by talking too much; let our actions speak for themselves.* [Emphasis added.]

Particularly important has been research illuminating the role played by Byrnes. Although it was once believed that Stimson was the most important presidential adviser on atomic matters, historians increasingly understand that Byrnes had the president's ear. Indeed, in the judgment of many experts, he fairly dominated Truman during the first five or six months of Truman's presidency.

Byrnes, in fact, had been one of Truman's mentors when the young unknown from Missouri first came to the Senate. In selecting the highly influential former Supreme Court justice as secretary of state, Truman put him in direct line of succession to the presidency. By also choosing Byrnes as his personal representative on the high-level Interim Committee—which made recommendations concerning the new weapon—Truman arranged to secure primary counsel on both foreign policy and the atomic bomb from a single trusted adviser.

A More Manageable Russia

There is not much doubt about Byrnes's general view. In one of their very first meetings, Byrnes told Truman that "in his belief the atomic bomb might well put us in a position to dictate our own terms at the end of the war." Again, at the end of May, Byrnes met, at White House request, with atomic scientist Leo Szilard. In his 1949 *A Personal History of the Atomic Bomb*, Szilard recalled that

> Mr. Byrnes did not argue that it was necessary to use the bomb against the cities of Japan in order to win the war. . . . Mr. Byrnes's . . . view [was] that our possessing and demonstrating the bomb would make Russia more manageable in Europe.

In a 1968 article in *Perspectives in American History*, Szilard wrote that "Russian troops had moved into Hungary and Rumania; Byrnes thought . . . that Russia might be more manageable if impressed by American military might."

Another excerpt from Ambassador Joseph Davies's diary records that at Potsdam

> [Byrnes] was still having a hard time. . . . The details as to the success of the Atomic Bomb, which he had just received, gave him confidence that the Soviets would agree.

> Byrnes' attitude that the atomic bomb assured ultimate success in negotiations disturbed me. . . . I told him the threat wouldn't work, and might do irreparable harm.

Stimson's friend Herbert Feis judged a quarter century ago that the desire to "impress" the Soviets almost certainly played a role in the decision to use the atomic bomb. On the basis of currently available information it is impossible to prove precisely to what extent Byrnes and the president were influenced by this consideration. Nevertheless, just as the discovery of new documents has led to greater recognition of the role of diplomatic factors in the decision, research on Byrnes's role—and the consistency of his attitude throughout this period—has clarified our understanding of this motive. Writing in the August 18, 1985, *New York Times*, Yale historian Gaddis Smith summarized this point: "It has been demonstrated that the decision to bomb Japan was centrally connected to Truman's confrontational approach to the Soviet Union."

Careless Reporting

Quite apart from the basic judgment as to the necessity of and reasons for the bomb's uses the issue of why the public is generally ignorant of so many of the basic facts discussed in the expert literature remains. For one thing, the modern press has been careless in its reporting. During the *Enola Gay* controversy at the Smithsonian, few reporters bothered to seriously consult specialist literature, or to present the range of specific issues in contention among the experts. [Many war veterans and historians were angered over the proposed atomic bomb exhibit's commentary which portrayed the United States as the aggressor taking revenge on the innocent Japanese.] Instead, historians who still remain unqualified defenders of the decision as dictated solely by military necessity were often cited as unquestioned authoritative sources. Many reporters repeated as fact the myth that "over a million" Americans would have perished or been wounded in an invasion of Japan. Only a handful wrote that among the many historians who criticized the Smithsonian for its "cleansing" of history were conservatives and others who disagreed about the specific issue, but begged for an honest discussion of the questions involved.

Emotional Issues

Emotional issues were also at work. Time and again, the question of whether dropping the atomic bomb was militarily necessary has become entangled with the separate issue of anger at Japan's sneak attack and the brutality of its military. The Japanese people have an ugly history to confront, including not only Pearl Harbor but also the bombing of Shanghai, the rape of Nanking, the forced prostitution of Korean women, the horror of the Bataan death march, and the systematic torture and murder of American and other prisoners of war. Even so, the question of Hiroshima persists.

Americans also have often allowed themselves to confuse the discussion of research findings on Hiroshima with criticism of American servicemen. This is certainly unjustified. The Americans serving in the Pacific in 1945 were prepared to risk their lives for their nation; by this most fundamental test, they can only be called heroes. This is neither the first nor the last time, however, that those in the field were not informed of what was going on at higher levels.

Finally, we Americans clearly do not like to see our nation as vulnerable to the same moral failings as others. To raise questions about Hiroshima is to raise doubts, it seems to some, about the moral integrity of the country and its leaders. It is also to raise the most profound questions about the legitimacy of nuclear weapons in general. America's continued unwillingness to confront the fundamental questions about Hiroshima may well be at the root of the quiet acceptance that has characterized so many other dangerous developments in the nuclear era that began in 1945.

Chapter 3

Aftermath

A Hiroshima Survivor's Tale

Atsuko Tsujioka

At 8:15 A.M. on August 6, 1945, Hiroshima was destroyed by an atom bomb that exploded approximately two thousand feet above the city center. Over one-third of Hiroshima's residents were killed, injured, or missing after the blast, and more than half became homeless. Two-thirds of the city's buildings were completely flattened by the bomb's explosion and another quarter were damaged.

Atsuko Tsujioka, nicknamed At-chan, was a teenager when the atom bomb was dropped on Hiroshima in 1945. She wrote this account of her experiences as part of a school assignment six years later when she was in junior college. Tsujioka's injuries were typical of many of the blast's victims. She describes the suffering she and the other victims endured as a result of the atom bomb. Tsujioka argues that science should develop technological advancements to benefit civilization and not develop weapons that can annihilate an entire population.

Ah, that instant! I felt as though I had been struck on the back with something like a big hammer, and thrown into boiling oil. For some time I was unconscious. When I abruptly came to again, everything around me was smothered in black smoke; it was all like a dream or something that didn't make sense. My chest hurt, I could barely breathe, and I thought "This is the end!" I pressed my chest tightly and lay face down on the ground, and ever so many times I called for help:

"Mother!" "Mother!" "Father!" but of course in that place there was no answer from Mother, no answer from Father.

This time I was really resigned to the thought that I was done for, but as I lay quietly face down on the ground, suddenly there drifted into my mind the smiling face of my littlest sister who is dead now. Oh! I recovered my senses. Through a darkness like the bottom of Hell I could hear the voices of the other students calling for their mothers. I could barely sense the fact that the students seemed to be running away from that place. I immediately got up, and without any definite idea of escaping I just frantically ran in the direction they were all taking. As we came close to Tsurumi Bridge a red hot electric wire wrapped itself around both my ankles. I don't know how but I managed to pull it off, and as though I were moving in a dream I reached the end of the bridge. By this time everything had long since changed to white smoke. The place where I had been working was Tanaka-cho, a little more than 600 yards from the center of the explosion. Although I should have been at a place straight in from Tsurumi Bridge, I seem to have been blown a good way to the north, and I felt as though the directions were all changed around.

Injured

At the base of the bridge, inside a big cistern that had been dug out there, was a mother weeping and holding above her head a naked baby that was burned bright red all over its body, and another mother was crying and sobbing as she gave her burned breast to her baby. In the cistern the students stood with only their heads above the water and their two hands, which they clasped as they imploringly cried and screamed, calling their parents. But every single person who passed was wounded, all of them, and there was no one to turn to for help. The singed hair on people's heads was frizzled up and whitish, and covered with dust—from their appearance you couldn't believe that they were human creatures of this world. Looking at these people made me think suddenly "It can't be possible that I—." I looked at my two hands and found them covered with blood, and from my arms something that looked like rags was hanging and inside I could see the healthy-looking flesh with its mingled colors of white, red and black. Shocked, I put my hand into my *mompei* pocket to get out my handkerchief, but there was no handkerchief, nor pocket either. And my *mompei* were also burned off below my hips. I could feel my face gradually swelling up, but there was nothing I could do about it, and when some of my friends suggested that we try to return to our homes in the suburbs, I set out with them. As we walked along, fires were blazing high on both sides of us, and my back was painfully hot. From inside the wreckage of the houses we would hear screaming voices calling "Help!" and then the flames would swallow up everything. A child of about six, all covered with blood, holding a kitchen pot in his arms, was facing a burning house, stamping his feet and screaming something. I was in such a state that I didn't even know what to do about myself, so I could hardly attempt to be much help to him, and there was nothing to do but let him go. I wonder what happened to those people? Those people trapped under the houses? The four of us, simply obsessed with the idea of reaching home at the earliest possible minute, hurried long in just the opposite direction from that of the fleeing townspeople—straight toward the center of the blast area. However when we came to Inarimachi, we found that the iron bridge had collapsed and we could not go any farther. We turned about there and ran toward Futaba Hill. When we were close to the foot of the hill I simply couldn't make my legs carry me another step.

Medical Treatment at Last

"Wait for me. Please wait for me," I said, and practically crawling, I finally reached the foot of the hill. Luckily there were some kind soldiers from a medical unit there, and they carried me up the hill to a place where I could lie down. There they gave me first aid treatment right away. It seemed that I had received a terrific blow on the back of my head, and there were fragments of roof tile left there. They pulled these out and bandaged the wound for me.

"You just lie there quietly. Your teacher will surely be along any minute now to take care of you," they said to comfort me.

But no matter how long I waited, my teacher didn't come. (Our teachers themselves were severely wounded; some of them died on the afternoon of the sixth, and all of them were dead by the next day.)

Finally the soldiers couldn't wait any longer, and they carried us one by one on their backs down to the barracks at the foot of the hill. A Red Cross flag was waving there. They carried us inside and asked the doctors to take care of us right away. But there were so many wounded people that we had to wait a very long time for our turn to come. In the meantime my strength was exhausted and I couldn't even keep myself standing up. At last they gave us treatment, and we spent the night there. The big buildings in the city were burning steadily, bright red against the dark sky. As the night wore on, the barracks gradually filled to overflowing with moaning voices—over in one corner someone shrieking "Bring me a straw mat if there's nothing better," and here a patient rolling about even on top of people too badly burned to move.

The Second Day

The first night came to an end. From earliest morning voices calling "Water, water," came from every side. I too was so thirsty I could hardly bear it. Inside the barracks there was a sink with water in it. Even though I knew that all sorts of things drained into it and the water was dirty, I scooped up some of that milk-coffee-colored water with my shoe and drank it. Maybe it is because I was normally healthy—anyway my mind was perfectly clear even though I had that severe wound, and since I knew there was a stream running right behind the barracks, I got up and took that shoe and went and drank and drank. And after that any number of times I brought water and gave it to the people who were lying near me and to the soldiers who were wounded. My drawers got soaking wet every time but they soon dried in the blazing hot sun. I had only had my burns painted once with mercurochrome, and they had turned black and were all wet. I was trying to get them dried by the sun so they would harden up. My friends, and other people too, could not move after they once lay down. Their backs and arms and legs were all slippery where the skin had peeled off, and even if I wanted to raise them up, there was no place I could take hold of them. From about noon of the second day people began to come in a few at a time. I got a white rice-ball from those people, but since my whole face was burned and I couldn't open my mouth very well, I spilled the grains of rice all around when I tried to eat, and only a little bit of it finally ended up in my mouth. By the third day I too was all swollen up, even around my eyes, and I had to lie there beside my friends unable to move at all. And drawn on by the delirious ravings of my friends, I was talking away at random in a dreamy state between sleeping and waking. All at once—was it a dream?—I had a feeling that my father and big sister had come from the foot of the hill to take me away. I was awfully happy, and I forced my eyes open with my hands and looked all around, but I couldn't see anything in the dim light. All the people who came always kept calling the names of the streets and their family names. My father and four or five of our neighbors were searching around for me day after day and finally on the evening of the third day they discovered me in one corner of the barracks at the foot of Futaba Hill. On my blouse there was sewn a name-tag that my father had written for me; the letters had been burned out just as though that part of the cloth had been eaten away by moths, and it was by this that they were able to find me.

Rescued

"At-chan. This is Father."

When he said that, I was so happy that I couldn't say a word—I could only nod my head. My swollen eyes wouldn't open, so I couldn't see my father's face. This is how I was rescued.

An Inner Beauty

Even now the scars of those wounds remain over my whole body. On my head, my face, my arms, my legs and my chest. As I stroke these blackish-red raised scars on my arms, and every time I look in a mirror at this face of mine which is not like my face, and think that never again will I be able to see my former face and that I have to live my life forever in this condition, it becomes too sad to bear. At the time I lost hope for the future. And not for a single moment could I get rid of the feeling that I had become a cripple. And naturally, for that reason I hated to meet people. And along with that, I couldn't get out of my mind the thought that so many of my good friends, and the teachers who had taken care of me so lovingly, had died under such pitiable circumstances, and I was continually choked with tears. No matter what I thought about, I was likely to be suspicious, and I took a pessimistic attitude toward everything. And my voice, which until now had been a pleasant one that all my friends liked, was lost all at once and became a hoarse voice without any volume. Every time I think about these things, my chest feels as though a terribly tight band is closing around it. But with human beings, it isn't only a beautiful outward appearance that is good, True beauty, worthy of a human being, takes away an ugly appearance and makes it into a splendid one. When I first realized that, my spirit softened somewhat. At the present time, with a fresh hope for life, and studying earnestly to discipline both my body and spirit, I cannot help seeking the inner sort of beauty which comes from a cultivated mind.

The Mission of Science

Science—what in the world is science? Such an atom bomb is undoubtedly a crystal of scientific progress. But can it really be said that a thing which takes several hundred thousand human lives at one time is true scientific development? No, science ought to be something that to the very last stimulates those advancements of civilization which are beneficial to mankind. Moreover, the mission of science is to raise the standard of living of mankind. It ought never to be such a thing as would annihilate the life of mankind. It is also obvious that the power of the atom, instead of being thus used as a means of making human beings lose their lives, ought to be turned to the advancement of human civilization. It is my hope that in the future such a tragic event as this will never make a second appearance in this world. And I want things to work out so that atomic energy will be the power which will give birth to a peaceful world. I believe there is no necessity for mankind to experience directly such suffering.

Visiting the Devastation of Nagasaki

Charles W. Sweeney, with James A. Antonucci and
Marion K. Antonucci

The United States dropped its second atomic bomb on the
Japanese city of Nagasaki on August 9, 1945, three days
after Hiroshima was destroyed by the first atom bomb. On
August 14, the United States accepted the Japanese offer
to surrender.

Charles W. Sweeney is one of the first Americans to
visit Nagasaki less than a month after the Japanese surrender. He finds a city that was obliterated in an instant by
one bomb. Although the destruction wrought by the atom
bomb is terrible, he feels no remorse about dropping the
bomb. The atom bomb ended the war, he asserts, and
therefore it saved many more lives than it took. Sweeney
notes that the rebuilding of the city and the nation is already underway with the assistance of the United States.

Charles W. Sweeney is the only pilot who flew both
atomic bomb missions in World War II. On August 6,
1945, Sweeney's plane, *The Great Artiste*, carried instruments to record and measure the atomic blast over Hiroshima. Three days later, he piloted *Bock's Car* which
dropped the atomic bomb on Nagasaki. Sweeney was
awarded the Silver Star for his mission. He retired as a
major general from the air force in 1976. James A. Antonucci and Marion K. Antonucci are both lawyers in the
Boston area.

"How would you like to go up to Japan tomorrow?" Paul
Tibbets asked. [Tibbets was the pilot of the *Enola Gay*, the

Excerpted from pp. 246–59 of *War's End: An Eyewitness Account of America's Last
Atomic Mission*, by Charles W. Sweeney, with James A. Antonucci and Marion K.
Antonucci. Copyright © 1997 by James A. Antonucci and Marion K. Antonucci.
Reprinted with the permission of Avon Books, Inc.

plane that dropped the atomic bomb on Hiroshima.] In Tokyo Bay, General Douglas MacArthur was, at that very hour on September 2, accepting the formal surrender of Japan aboard the USS *Missouri.*

It took me all of one second to answer, "I'd love it. Let's go." . . .

The Road to Nagasaki

The road to Nagasaki wound up and over hills and down into valleys dotted with small homes along the sides of the road. The hillsides were green and leafy. A summer breeze whispered through the tall grass and shrubs and stands of trees. Here and there, Japanese families toiled in fields and gardens, paying us no attention. Occasionally a single, un-armed Japanese soldier—never a group of soldiers, always one at a time—would be walking along the road, showing no response to us, as if our presence was as normal and expected as any other everyday occurrence in this beautiful country-side. Two weeks earlier, he and the families along the road probably would have killed us on sight.

On the outskirts of Nagasaki, we came upon a small re-sort inn nestled among ancient trees. It was a charming place, two stories high, with double red-tile pagoda-styled roofs, the second-story roof overhanging a lower roof rim-ming the first story. We decided to spend the night there before pressing on to Nagasaki. Inside on the reception desk lay the register. I wasn't sure if the Japanese knew the names of the crew who had bombed their city. It crossed my mind that perhaps the better part of valor would be to avoid signing in. We were the only Americans on Japanese soil within three hundred miles of this spot. I watched as Paul walked up to the desk, swiveled the register around toward him, and in a clear hand wrote, "Colonel Paul W. Tibbets USAAF." I stepped right up after him and signed "Major Charles W. Sweeney USAAF," and in turn each of our party registered.

An elderly couple were the innkeepers. They were cour-teous and attentive, and they spoke English. Before the war, Nagasaki had been a favorite tourist destination for American and English travelers. That night we sat around the inn relaxing and drinking sake. I still wasn't quite at ease, though, and I did something I had never done before or since: I hung the holster with my loaded weapon on the headrest of my bed, within easy reach.

Entering the City

The next morning we proceeded to Nagasaki. The trucks coughed and gagged up the last set of hills. Over the next ridge was the Urakami Valley. At the crest we could survey the length of the valley where a month before the Mitsubishi war plants had been operating at full capacity producing small arms, torpedoes, and various other munitions for the Japanese armed forces.

The valley floor was a stretch of rubble dotted by grotesquely twisted lumps of steel beams and columns. A brick chimney rose here and there amid the wreckage where the munitions plants had once stood. From a distance, the destroyed armaments plants looked like erector sets a child had twisted and bent and carelessly tossed away. We had driven through the verdant hills to a wasteland. As we descended into the valley, we were the first Americans to set foot in Nagasaki and survey the damage. United States naval personnel were waiting on board vessels anchored in the harbor until scientific survey teams were sent in first to test for radioactivity. We weren't even supposed to be in the area, not to mention driving through the valley.

The trucks came to a stop midway in the valley. I walked alone along a brick sidewalk to a point I estimated was where ground zero would have been on August 9. In the distance ahead of me I could see a solitary Japanese soldier walking away along the same sidewalk, unaware or uncaring that we were here. There were very few people around as I surveyed the surroundings.

I looked straight up into the blue sky where at 1,890 feet the Fat Man [the second atom bomb] had exploded. In an instant on that August day, which oddly seemed so long ago, everything around me that morning had been vaporized in a burst of blistering heat and blast.

Instant Obliteration

I walked to what must have been an intersection of main streets. On one corner I peered down into the cellar of what had been a fire station. It was then that I was struck by the significance of our weapon. In the cellar was a fire truck that had been crushed flat, as if a giant had stepped on it. In fact, the entire infrastructure of the city was flat—no water, no emergency facilities, no firefighters. Everything was gone.

This had not been the conventional slow, incremental destruction of a target, as we had destroyed other Japanese cities. This had been instantaneous obliteration. There had been no time for the people to grow accustomed to the bombing, as other Japanese had done in Kobe, Nagoya, and Osaka. There had been no time to allow the mind to rationalize that you could survive. More Japanese had died during a single fire-bombing of Tokyo on March 9 than at Hiroshima or Nagasaki—97,000 killed, 125,000 wounded, 1,200,000 homeless. For its victims, the firestorms in Tokyo were every bit as horrifying as the nuclear blast. Intense napalm fires incinerated everything. Tornadolike winds whipped through the city as the fires consumed all the oxygen, creating a vacuum that itself suffocated people. Yet the Japanese fought on. But they could not fight on after the second atomic strike.

Nuclear weapons had changed the human response to warfare. No longer would war be seen as simply an extension of national policies by other means, a condition of the human spirit that occasionally broke out of the bounds of civilized conduct. The Japanese military leaders might wish to fight to the death, but it would be their nation that would die.

The casualty figures at Nagasaki were still a matter of some speculation. It would finally be estimated that in the first instant 40,000 people were killed, and that another 30,000 to 35,000 died of their injuries within a few days. Seventy-five thousand more were wounded. As I looked around, I saw no bodies among the rubble, nor would I see any in other parts of the city. Apparently, and with the efficiency for which the Japanese are noted, the survivors had almost immediately started to clean up and care for the wounded.

So Many Deaths

Standing amid the rubble, I felt a sadness that so many had died on both sides, not only there but in all the horrible places where the war had been fought. We would learn that over fifty million people had perished because of Japanese and German aggression—the majority of them unarmed men, women, and children—in Asia, the Pacific, Europe, Africa, the Middle East, and a thousand other places. And millions of soldiers, sailors, marines, and airmen, the best and brightest of an entire generation, would never realize their tomorrows.

I thanked God that it was we who had this weapon and not the Japanese or the Germans. I hoped there would never be another atomic mission.

I took no pride or pleasure then, nor do I take any now, in the brutality of war, whether suffered by my people or those of another nation. Every life is precious. But I felt no remorse or guilt that I had bombed the city where I stood. The suffering evidenced by the destruction around me had been born of the cruelty of the Japanese militaristic culture and a tradition that glorified the conquest of "inferior" races and saw Japan as destined to rule Asia. The true vessel of remorse and guilt belonged to the Japanese nation, which could and should call to account the warlords who so willingly offered up their own people to achieve their visions of greatness.

My crew and I had flown to Nagasaki to end the war, not to inflict suffering. There was no sense of joy among us as we walked the streets there. We were relieved it was over, for us and for them.

Life Goes On

Although the industrial valley and the shipbuilding facilities along the Urakami River had been totally destroyed, the residential and business districts of Nagasaki had been spared. The life of Nagasaki was going on as usual there. Kermit Beahan, Don Albury, and I walked around the city. Businesses were open; the people went about their daily routine. Children lined up in their uniforms to attend school. The mood was different from the mood in Tokyo. There was an air of sullenness, but not of despair. The people on the street were polite to us. Of course, they didn't know who we were, but they didn't seem fazed at the sight of three American servicemen strolling through their city.

The rebuilding was already under way. Unlike the Russians, who had immediately carted off the spoils of victory from Manchuria, dismantling factories, railroad trains, and rolling stock and literally taking every nut, bolt, and brick, the United States, even in the early days of the Occupation, began to assist in feeding, clothing, and housing its former enemy. Soon money and material would flood into Japan to rebuild the economy its leaders had so recklessly destroyed.

A Society Laid Waste

The Committee for the Compilation of Materials on Damage Caused by the Atomic Bombs in Hiroshima and Nagasaki

The Committee for the Compilation of Materials on Damage Caused by the Atomic Bombs in Hiroshima and Nagasaki was established by the cities of Hiroshima and Nagasaki in 1977 to publish in a single book all the available scientific research on the damages caused by the dropping of the atom bombs. According to research collected by the committee, densely populated cities—not enemy armies—were clearly the bombs' targets. Furthermore, the researchers contend, the bomb not only killed tens of thousands of innocent civilians instantly and indiscriminately, but it ruptured community life by obliterating businesses, medical care, and governmental and social services. They maintain that the psychological trauma faced by the survivors due to the horror of the devastation, the loss of family and community, and the destruction of work, school, and other social institutions led to the disintegration of society.

The Committee for the Compilation of Materials on Damage Caused by the Atomic Bombs in Hiroshima and Nagasaki was comprised of three editors who were assisted by thirty-four experts in the fields of physics, medicine, social sciences, and the humanities to compile the book *Hiroshima and Nagasaki: The Physical, Medical, and Social Effects of the Atomic Bombings.*

Excerpted from *Hiroshima and Nagasaki: Physical, Medical and Social Effects of the Atomic Bombings*, compiled by The Committee for the Compilation of Materials on Damage Caused by the Atomic Bombs in Hiroshima and Nagasaki, originally published in Japanese by Iwanami Shoten. Copyright © 1981 by Hiroshima City and Nagasaki City. Reprinted with the permission of Basic Books, a member of Perseus Books, L.L.C.

An atomic bomb, because of the enormous energy it releases in the multiple forms of heat, blast, and radiation, is capable of unprecedented physical destruction, killing, and maiming. It is a weapon of mass slaughter. The first special feature of this bomb, then, is its capability for massive devastation and death.

Besides the awesome physical, medical, and biological threats of the bomb, we are especially concerned that in 1945 it was dropped directly on cities whose people had no way to anticipate, or to protect themselves from, its enormous destructive powers. From the course of events that led to its development and use, it is clear that from the outset this new weapon was not intended for use in war theaters where opposing armies were locked in battle; rather, it was to be dropped on densely populated centers that contained military facilities and industries as well as a high concentration of houses and other buildings. Moreover, the A-bomb attacks were needed not so much against Japan—already on the brink of surrender and no longer capable of mounting an effective counteroffensive—as to establish clearly America's postwar international position and strategic supremacy in the anticipated cold war setting. One tragedy of Hiroshima and Nagasaki is that this historically unprecedented devastation of human society stemmed from essentially experimental and political aims.

The two cities were, indeed, dense with houses and people. They were developed communities with families, neighborhood associations, stores, schools, hospitals, prefectural and municipal offices, courts, banks, companies, and industries—that is, organizations and personnel with many social relations and functions, many life styles and activities, all integrated into traditional corporate societies. The atomic bombs reduced to dismal ruins these centers of human life and livelihood.

Destruction Without Discrimination

The second feature of an atomic bombing is that its massive destruction occurs instantaneously and sweepingly without discrimination—young and old, men and women, combatants and noncombatants, residents and visitors—none is exempt from its death-dealing fury. In Hiroshima and Nagasaki, not just personal lives, families, and neighborhood groups but the entire network of community life, all the social systems, structures, and functional organs built up over many years, were burned and blasted into oblivion. Countless people lost parents, friends, and neighbors; their households and places of work were reduced to rubble; and all human relationships were ruptured as the whole of society was laid waste to its very foundations.

In the overall breakdown of the cities, their administrative organs also were subjected to confusion and collapse. The civil defense and first-aid systems for dealing with air raids and other emergencies were destroyed and, thus, unable to give the aid urgently needed by the seriously injured who barely survived the atomic holocaust. As Hiroshima and Nagasaki were in designated air defense zones, they therefore had special military police garrisons, civil police and civil defense systems, and government-conscripted workers teams, as well as many well-trained local neighborhood associations and relief, first-aid, and sanitation teams, along with emergency hospitals, first-aid stations, and refuge shelters. All townships and factories and firms had emergency evacuation plans; evacuation shelters had food, clothing, and medical supplies; and routes for evacuation by railway, streetcar, and truck had been established. The A-bomb damages, however, far exceeded all levels of preparedness; as both cities were almost totally destroyed, all these agencies were rendered virtually useless. Consequently, countless A-bomb victims huddled in bombed-out buildings and, unable to move due to serious injuries, died in an inferno. Of those who managed somehow to escape the blazing cities, most could not get needed treatment at the evacuation shelters and thus died in harsh circumstances.

Massive Radiation

Most crucial of all was the enormous amount of radioactivity released by the atomic bombs; it penetrated deeply into the victims' bodies and caused a variety of serious diseases.

Massive radiation doubled the gravity of the situation and greatly increased the number of casualties.

People who had been evacuated, or who for other reasons had left the cities, not only lost family members and friends but were also deprived of places to live and work. Dispossessed of all means of livelihood, theirs, too, was a desperate situation.

An atomic bomb's massive destruction and indiscriminate slaughter involves the sweeping breakdown of all order and existence—in a word, the collapse of society itself. The destruction of the social and environmental systems that support human life, combined with the A-bomb victims' own loss of health and resources for living, brought about a "total disintegration of human life," according to Minoru Yuzaki.

Scattered Families

For those Japanese who lived within two kilometers of the atom bomb's blast, there was no time to rescue any of their belongings or money from their destroyed or burning houses. Junko Kayashige, who was a first grader when her house was destroyed, tells how she and her family survived after the bombing:

My house in Hiroshima was a shack, only a six-mat room with a closet. While in bed, I saw stars through a hole in the zinc roof, which leaked badly when it rained. My father and brother first lived in the shack after the bombing, and then I joined them after coming back from my place of refuge. All the neighboring houses were like ours. We lived by asking others to give us water and to lend us rice bowls and chopsticks. We went to a military warehouse at Yokogawa Station and the site of a candle manufacturing plant to look for daily necessities. It was practically thieving. At that time, we were living without tableware, pans, clocks, watches, or electricity. When it grew dark, there was nothing to do but go to bed. It was a primitive life with no communications media such as radio or newspapers, and with no lights.

Naomi Shohno, *The Legacy of Hiroshima: Its Past, Our Future*, 1986.

The problems of atomic destruction were not, of course, confined to Hiroshima and Nagasaki. At the time of the bombings there were in the two cities people from nearby towns and villages, from other prefectures, and even from foreign countries—many of whom were among the dead and injured. Their families, too, experienced great shock and loss. Moreover, persons who came into the two cities immediately after the bombings to look for family members and friends or as part of civil defense and relief teams were subjected to direct or residual radiation, as were people in outlying areas where wind currents carried the radioactive "black rain." The effects of radiation did not, of course, end with the bombings but have continued to plague the A-bomb victims and cause grave anxieties among their children and grandchildren.

Third among the special features of A-bomb damage, in addition to social and economic loss, are the aftereffects of both heat and radiation injuries, which seriously handicapped the A-bomb victims' efforts to restore their health and livelihood. This handicap includes both real impairment and the constant fear of its striking. The damages of conventional war are generally temporary or one-time affairs; A-bomb damages continue indefinitely. The long delay in extending aid to the victims aggravated their initial hardships, and many victims remained in serious difficulty. . . .

A-bomb damage, then, is so complex and extensive that it cannot be reduced to any single characteristic or problem. It must be seen overall, as an interrelated array—massive physical and human loss, social disintegration, and psychological and spiritual shock—that affects all life and society. Only then can one grasp the seriousness of its total impact on the biological systems that sustain life and health, on the social systems that enable people to live and work together, and on the mental functions that hold these two dimensions in integrated unity. The essence of atomic destruction lies in the totality of its impact on man and society and on all the systems that affect their mutual continuation.

The functional breakdown caused by the loss of key household members and by the drastic decline in manpower, the consequent inability of corporate groups (families, relatives, community organizations) to give aid to each other, and the added aggravation of radiation injuries and the constant anxiety over them—these together inflicted great distress on A-bomb victims and their families. The bodily, social, and psychological handicaps have continued to exert heavy pressures that, in time, have led to further loss of livelihood, to disintegration of families, and, worse, to personality breakdown.

No Help from the Government

Despite the desolation of the cities and the sufferings of the A-bomb victims, the response of the Japanese government was exceedingly passive. From the time of the bombings to the end of the war—when the victims' needs were most urgent—the government gave neither any reports on radiation casualties nor the help the people desperately needed. It simply left them to fend for themselves. Afterward, demands were made for surveys of the A-bomb victims, including the dead, and responsible organizations publicly advised the government to conduct surveys, but the government ignored all advice and appeals.

This attitude is not unrelated to the fact that, even to this day, the government has consistently rejected the demand for an "A-bomb Victims Relief Law" that would require it to extend aid to A-bomb victims who suffered bodily injury or loss of livelihood, on the premise that the government should assume responsibility for and give compensation to those victimized by the war and the atomic bombings. The aid extended through the General Plan for Relief to A-bomb Victims by the cities of Hiroshima and Nagasaki has not been able, due to limited financial and political resources, to match what national policies could have achieved. Given this situation, the A-bomb victims have had to grow old and then die in social isolation. Thus, the A-bomb victims' initial suffering has been exacerbated by social and political circumstances ever since.

Out of their own experiences, therefore, the A-bomb victims have persistently appealed for the eradication of all nuclear weapons; and to this end they have compiled countless diaries and testimonies, for they feel strongly that there must never be another victim of an atomic bomb. Their own cruel fate came not, as was claimed soon after the bombings, from the Allies' desire to end the war quickly and restore peace; it came, as we know now, from the United States's expectation of a postwar confrontation with the Soviet Union and its wish to make a show of force by demonstrating the bomb's incredible might. Moreover, the superpowers have continued to escalate their nuclear capabilities, in both mass and might; and the danger of nuclear war mounts daily. All this creates an intolerable spiritual burden for the world's first A-bomb victims.

The Annihilation of Mankind

The total disintegration of society and the unmitigated and indiscriminate killing of people in Hiroshima and Nagasaki cannot be dismissed as just another hazard of war. The magnitude of the killing is, in essence, better termed *genocide*—if not also *sociocide*, *ecocide*, *biocide*, and *earthocide*—for it is a complete negation of human existence. The experience of these two cities was the opening chapter to the possible annihilation of mankind. To all peoples of the world, it poses the crucial question of human existence. With the wide range of modern scientific knowledge and military technology at his disposal, man at last can devise the means for ending all human life. Such is the dilemma of modern civilization: Will we choose the way of self-destruction? Or will we, by abolishing all nuclear weapons, choose to preserve life on this earth? We stand today at the crossroads of that choice.

Chapter 4

America in the Cold War

Turning | Points
IN WORLD HISTORY

U.S. Soldiers Are Exposed to Radiation in Postwar Tests

Michael Uhl and Tod Ensign

After the United States dropped two atom bombs on Japan to end World War II, the U.S. military began to explode atomic weapons in the Nevada desert and in the South Pacific to study the feasibility of fighting and surviving a limited nuclear war. Thousands of U.S. soldiers and sailors were exposed to radioactive fallout between 1945 and 1961 while the Pentagon tried to determine if atomic and hydrogen bombs had any effect on their fighting skills.

Michael Uhl and Tod Ensign recount the experiences of U.S. soldiers who were involved in nuclear bomb tests in the Nevada desert during the 1950s. They maintain that U.S. military commanders showed little interest in protecting their troops from the effects of the blast or from the subsequent radiation. Uhl and Ensign contend that established safety standards were routinely ignored and that troops rarely received proper instructions on how to avoid becoming contaminated from the radioactive fallout. Furthermore, Uhl and Ensign charge that the soldiers were deliberately exposed to excessive amounts of radiation, and when soldiers became sick years later from radiation-induced cancers, the Pentagon and Veterans Administration refused to accept responsibility for their illnesses.

Michael Uhl and Tod Ensign are the authors of *GI Guinea Pigs: How the Pentagon Exposed Our Troops to Dangers More Deadly than War: Agent Orange and Atomic Radiation*.

Excerpted from *GI Guinea Pigs: How the Pentagon Exposed Our Troops to Dangers More Deadly than War: Agent Orange and Atomic Radiation*, by Michael Uhl and Tod Ensign (Playboy Press, 1980). Copyright © 1980 by Michael Uhl and Tod Ensign. Reprinted with permission from Tod Ensign.

Beginning with the very first [atomic] tests [at Camp Desert Rock, Nevada,] in 1951, independent defense contractors were given grants to produce studies on all manner of human response to the blasts. For example, the Human Resources Research Office (HumRRO) of George Washington University was given a military contract to perform elaborate psychological studies of troop attitudes and reactions during nuclear bomb tests. HumRRO divided the GI observers into various categories and "control groups" and subjected them to a barrage of questionnaires, polls, surveys, and even lie-detector tests, before, during, and after each blast. To a typical survey question, "When do you think we'll have war with the Soviet Union?" 64 percent of the troops responded, "Within ten years."

Troop Maneuvers Are Deemed Safe

Desert Rock Reports I, II, and III set the stage for the use of tens of thousands of troops at subsequent tests. At one point the reports conclude that the tests proved "that combat troops can safely cross the area of a nuclear explosion within minutes of the [blast]." According to the reports, "Residual radiological contamination from explosions of this size (21–31 kilotons) is of no *military* significance at distances greater than 1000 yards from ground zero." After studying the bomb's effect on the tethered sheep, it was concluded that "it's *possible* that humans would have been free from serious harm if they were in trenches at least 1000 yards from ground zero [italics ours]." The report noted, however, that because sheep's wool provided unusual protection against some of the effects of radiation, further study was needed. These reports were written within a few weeks after the tests, so long-term effects, such as various types of cancers and genetic birth defects associated with some types of radiation exposure, are not dealt with at all—nor is the possibility of such future effects even taken into account. Because only immediate health effects were deemed to be of "military significance," it was perhaps inevitable that no medical follow-up or monitoring ever was conducted.

The social scientists from HumRRO were equally sanguine about the value of further troop maneuvers at nuclear blasts: "Widespread and thorough indoctrination, careful

Decontamination Measures for Atom Bomb Tests

The September 19, 1952, issue of the Pentagon-produced magazine Armed Forces Talk *includes an article about the atomic bomb tests at Camp Desert Rock in Nevada. The following excerpts address the soldiers' fears about radiation due to the nuclear explosions. Decontamination measures have become much more thorough and extensive than the procedures followed in the 1950s.*

If you are like most of the observers at Desert Rock, you will be a little worried at first about the dangers of radiation. Maybe you have read books in which it is claimed that areas under an atomic blast will be uninhabitable for 20 years, 50 years, a century. This is not true. The radiation from an atomic weapon, when burst in the air, is all gone in a minute and a half. After that time, no signficant radiation exists on the ground. . . .

The radiation for which these [chemical, biological, and radiological] monitors are looking will exist in the form of radioactive dust particles. Dust may be on your shoes, on your clothes or in your hair, so that when you come back, you too are radioactive. These low level radiation dust particles on your clothes and shoes may be removed by brushing off the dust with an ordinary broom. If you get rid of the dust, you get rid of the radiation. . . .

If you are alive and uninjured after being near an A-bomb blast you needn't worry too much about the flash radiation. The decontamination problem is relatively simple, although there is no chemical or medical method of neutralizing the radiation. Just use good old-fashioned soap and water—the hotter the water and the stronger the soap the better. If you get rid of the dirt from yourself and your equipment, you get rid of the radiation.

Howard L. Rosenberg, *Atomic Soldiers: American Victims of Nuclear Experiments*, 1980.

planning, strong leadership, together with [test site] experience will result in a reasonable attitude toward the weapon." Summarizing its interviews with individual soldiers, HumRRO enthused: "It was a memorable experience for the men and much of the superstition and mystery surrounding radiation was removed. They are [now] convinced that the [blast] area can be safely entered after the explosion; that effects decrease rapidly with distance; and, most important, of the life-saving protection of a hole in the ground at any distance [from ground zero]." HumRRO did report that some GIs felt they'd been used as "guinea pigs" and questioned why they had to participate in these maneuvers if the army already knew (as it claimed) what the effects would be. But HumRRO concluded: "Remove the mystery and deemphasize the radiological hazard and the thing is accepted in its proper proportion."

Apparently the social scientists believed that radiation hazards were merely an "attitudinal" problem, which could be overcome if enough indoctrination and training were applied. And evidently the army was pleased with HumRRO's work; they received contracts for similar studies at subsequent tests.

Strategy and Tactics

Turning to the assessment of the impact of nuclear weapons upon strategy and tactics in the future, the field commanders happily reported that an A-bomb of the size used in the tests would not knock out an infantry division (10,000–15,000 men) if the division was well dug in and dispersed. Nevertheless, they argued against using larger bombs against conventional enemy forces, since these bombs "are more difficult to deliver and a portion of the destructive area is wasted due to a lack of profitable targets." Instead, they urged the use of multiple small nuclear weapons which could "saturate critical areas, without creating major dead space." This doctrine would later contribute to the concept of "limited warfare" as a cornerstone of national defense policy.

The joint command made a number of recommendations for future tests. First, they urged that atomic-weapons data be much more widely disseminated within the military. Further, all military personnel should be indoctrinated on the effects of A-bombs so that "widespread misconceptions can be overcome." They also proposed that definite radiation-exposure standards be established.

In a separate report, the Armed Forces Special Weapons Project (AFSWP) attempted to forecast radiation effects on humans by studying test animals and instruments placed at varying distances from ground zero and in various types of fortifications. Perhaps to remove any ambiguity, AFSWP recommended that human volunteers be used at future tests to allow more precise measurement of effects. This recommendation was implemented once the military gained full control over the use of its troops at the site.

The Military Says Safety Restrictions Are Excessive

The commanders were quite unhappy with what they considered "excessive safety restrictions" imposed by the Atomic Energy Commission (AEC). Their report implored the Pentagon to exert pressure at the "highest levels of government" to remedy this annoying problem. They included the report of one of their university contractors who wrote: "Under AEC restrictions . . . it was difficult to make the maneuver realistic. The usual performance requirements . . . were absent. The troops moved across the terrain in single file [behind monitors], a formation . . . vulnerable to enemy fire."

Apparently the Pentagon took these complaints seriously, for the minutes of the December 23, 1951 AEC meeting report that General A. Fields told the commission that the military wanted to make changes at future tests; this would mean the existing standards for radiation exposure would probably be exceeded.

AEC chairman Gordon Dean played Pontius Pilate: "Since the Department of Defense considered it necessary to conduct the exercises in this manner, the AEC was not in a position to recommend that normal limits be observed."

But the commission saw to it that a public statement was

issued by the Department of Defense prior to the tests "clarifying Department of Defense responsibility for the safety of the troops." By the time the Joint Chiefs of Staff had issued a standing order to AFSWP on January 18, 1952, authorizing the use of GIs at future tests, troop maneuvers on the "atomic battlefield" had become an integral part of military life.

The military defined its primary mission for the Desert Rock exercise as "troop indoctrination under nuclear conditions." Effects tests on weapons and equipment were assigned a lower priority than at the previous series.

Nuclear Combat

Troops from the Eighty-second Airborne, the First Armored Division, and other elements were initiated into nuclear combat on April 22, 1952, during the third shot of the series, called "Upshot-Knothole" by the AEC. They watched from trenches four miles away as a 31-kiloton bomb was dropped from a B-29 and detonated over the desert. An hour later, rad-safe monitors reported that it was safe to advance and an Airborne company and some other units moved to within a half-mile of ground zero.

Never comfortable being too far from the action, marines arrived, many directly from duty in Korea, and two battalions participated in their first test on May Day. According to Los Alamos sources, several high-ranking Marine officers were so pleased with this exercise that they asked for a 1-kiloton bomb which they wanted to detonate for training purposes at their El Toro base, adjacent to San Diego. Fortunately for San Diegans, their request was denied.

Tower Shots

On May 25, history was made when an atomic bomb was detonated for the first time from a steel tower in Nevada. Previous bombs had been detonated in the air after being dropped from a B-29, with the exception of two that were touched off at ground level. A 30-kiloton bomb was powerful enough to obliterate the tower totally, except for a small stump at the base.

In a section entitled "Clothing and Equipment for D-Day," the *Camp Desert Rock Information and Guide* stated that "gas masks and film badges will be worn and carried in the forward area." But the standard army masks would offer no protection against the inhalation of microscopic "hot" particles, and we have found only one participant who recalls his unit ever using gas masks. Dr. Edward A. Martell, of the National Center for Atmospheric Research says on the subject of gas masks: "People have to breathe, and fine particles can get through anything that allows air to enter. The fine particles that can be inhaled and deposited deeply in the lungs get through these gas masks. That's one of the misleading things about these protective devices: you'll be inhaling the extremely small particles that can do the most harm."

From the standpoint of safety, these tower shots were the most hazardous form of detonation. Nevertheless, after-action reports contain virtually no discussion of the danger of radioactive particles becoming attached to tiny steel fragments and then being inhaled by maneuvering troops. In a response to a question by the Rogers Subcommittee about this danger, the Pentagon commented: "In a tower shot, much, if not all, of the iron in the tower is vaporized and made radioactive in the same process." Asked if troops entering the fallout area would risk inhalation of these particles, the Pentagon gave a one-word answer: "yes."

Although the towers were several hundred feet high, these blasts were considered "ground shots" since tons of sand from the desert floor were sucked high into the mushroom cloud as it ascended. These "hot" sand particles constituted an added hazard, for, when they fell back to earth, the whirlpoollike winds that buffeted the desert floor dispersed them in every direction. Still, detonating bombs from several hundred feet in the air seemed an improvement over the last two blasts of the previous series. These had been detonated on, or just below, the earth's surface and had so contaminated a large area of the test site that the AEC had had to declare it "off limits" for several days. At least now, it was felt, most of the "prompt" (immediately released) radiation would be propelled skyward into the atmosphere.

The Army Takes Control

By the time the "How" shot brought this series to an end, the army had taken complete control over radiation safety from the AEC. The after-action report for Desert Rock provides a good insight into what the military deemed important. Achievements of the series: "Troops were in trenches at 7000 yards [from ground zero], nearer than any personnel have ever been, excluding Hiroshima and Nagasaki[!]" Other "advances" were: army personnel assuming more responsibility for rad-safety, and troops moving to within 175 yards of ground zero only minutes after a blast. During the last shot, troops advanced immediately after detonation without waiting for AEC clearance.

The 1979 Senate testimony of Eugene Zuckert, the AEC Commissioner, is a good illustration of the pervasive attitude that soldiers are not deserving of the same consideration extended to other citizens. He opined that even today he would vote to permit the military to assume total authority for the safety of troops at the test site. His reasoning: "The responsibility of the AEC was to tell the military what we thought the implications were. We should not have had control over their final decision. They [had] responsibility for training and having been fully informed, I don't think it was our responsibility to try and override them."

Increasing the Radiation Exposure

Once the military succeeded in gaining complete control over the use of troops at the start of the 1953 series, they made several significant changes. First, they doubled the amount of radiation to which soldiers could be exposed from 3 to 6 roentgens, half of which could be from immediate radiation and half from fallout. (AEC site workers, by comparison, were limited to 3.9 rads for an entire test series.) Second, combat units began to be placed routinely in trenches as close as two miles from ground zero. These GIs then conducted maneuvers in and around the blast area just a short time after detonations. Also instituted was an experimental program wherein "volunteer officers" crouched in trenches a mile or so from ground zero during three of the tests. The exposure limits for these volunteers was raised to 10 roentgens per test, as long as only half was "immediate" radiation. This proved to be a wise decision because their exposure at the very first test exceeded the old 6-rad limit. They were allowed 25 rads for three shots. Army reports claim that the men chose the precise location of their trench, based on their own calculations of weather and other factors. Perhaps in this way the military hoped to absolve itself of responsibility for any future effects of radiation on these men.

During the 1952 series, the army's rad-safe monitors had gradually replaced those provided by the AEC. Beginning with the 1953 series, the military also assumed full responsibility for film badging and lab analysis. Unfortunately, the army's photodosimetry unit was not adequately equipped or staffed so that each GI could have a film badge, so the reports state that one or two men in a unit would have a badge.

We interviewed four soldiers who participated in different shots during this first "all-army" series. They confirmed the military's success at finally providing a "realistic" experience on the nuclear battlefield. Two of the four are seriously ill today, suffering from health problems that may be related to radiation exposure.

Guinea Pigs

Stanley Jaffee, age forty-seven, is a pharmacist from River Edge, New Jersey, married, with three teen-age daughters. In November 1977 he underwent emergency surgery for breast cancer. Unfortunately, the cancer had already spread throughout his lymphatic system. He has sued the federal government, charging it with responsibility for his cancer. For his lawsuit, he has testified that he was given no radiation-safety training prior to participating in the test and that at no time did he see anyone wearing a film badge during the exercise. "We were given no special clothing, nor were the trenches lead-lined or designed to keep out radiation," he recalls.

"The explosion itself defied description. After the initial blast, I opened my eyes and saw a fireball which looked like a red sun setting on the desert floor. While I can't be precise about the distance between me and the point of explosion, I don't believe that it was more than two or three thousand yards.

"We felt an incredibly powerful shock wave, followed by another shock wave moving back toward the bomb site. It was this reverse wave that [created] an enormous mushroom cloud. While this was happening we were ordered . . . to march in the direction of the fireball. I don't know how far we were able to [go], but I do recall that the heat was incredibly fierce and that later a number of men were ill on the trucks which removed us from the site."

Ken Watson, fifty, of Tacoma, Washington, was sent to Nevada for the first shot of the 1953 series. Like Jaffee, he states that he received no training or indoctrination prior to the test and he doesn't remember seeing anyone with a film badge at the site.

"They kept stressing that everything was top-secret. They told us that two GIs who'd been at the last test had talked with strangers about Desert Rock and now they were doing long prison terms at Leavenworth. We were warned that FBI agents might buy us drinks in Las Vegas and then try and get us to talk about what we'd seen at the test site."

Watson says he was so frightened by these warnings that when he later underwent surgery for cancer he didn't dare tell his doctors how he might have been exposed to unusual amounts of radiation.

After witnessing a blast from trenches that he estimates were about 2500 yards from ground zero, Watson was shipped back to Fort Carson, from whence he was sent to Korea. It was after he returned from Korea that army doctors removed a football-size tumor from his abdomen. He has been plagued since that time with arterial and vascular problems that have rendered him unable to work.

The Grable Test

Chuck Willmoth and Richard Larzelere, two young draftees from Detroit, became pals while serving in an army unit that was guarding the Soo Locks in northern Michigan.

They and four other GIs were suddenly sent to Chicago

where they boarded a special troop train. Willmoth remembers that the train had many cars and was pulled by several engines. In the dining car they were served what tasted like army food. "They wouldn't tell us where we were going, other than that we should take summer clothes. As I'd just spent a winter on the Canadian Border, that was okay with me," Willmoth reminisces. "Only when the train pulled into Las Vegas did some of the guys begin to guess we were going to the atomic bomb site."

Unlike Jaffee and Watson, both Willmoth and Larzelere remember being given rad-safe briefings and lectures at Desert Rock. They also remember a pleasant afternoon when the GIs were entertained by a variety show from Las Vegas which featured comedian Jan Murray. They confirm, however, that they saw no one wearing a film badge during their time at Desert Rock. The two Detroiters participated in the last shot of the test series—the only time the army got to fire an atomic shell from its 280-millimeter field cannon. The shot was called the "Grable" test, named for the movie star with famed legs.

Now a draftsman with Fisher Body in Detroit, Larzelere recalls: "They placed us in shallow trenches I would guess were about 3000 yards from ground zero. They told us that as soon as we saw the flash we could get up. I did, and got knocked on my butt when the shock wave passed. A few minutes later, we followed rad-safe monitors toward ground zero. For protection, we wore our gas masks during the entire exercise."

Chuck Willmoth, now forty-six and chief of police in Garden City, Michigan, remembers watching, fascinated, as a pickup truck drove right down to where the bomb had just gone off. "A guy jumped out, picked up some sort of instrument, and drove off again."

As the men moved forward, Larzalere remembers seeing sheep on fire. "The closer we got to ground zero, the worse shape they were in." Both men recall being ordered out of the area after they'd gone over half the distance to ground zero. They were taken to a rear area, told to wash and shower, and given new uniforms to wear.

Willmoth shared a bit of Desert Rock scuttlebutt: "We heard that they took alarm clocks and tied them around the necks of rabbits. Supposedly, they were timed to ring so that the rabbits' eyes would be wide open just when the bomb went off."

Atomic Boosterism

The postmortems for the 1953 series again display the brand of atomic boosterism peculiar to the military. Among "advances" claimed for the series was the placing of troops 3500 yards from ground zero, "the nearest any known large body of troops has been deliberately exposed to date." The "volunteers" qualified for an even more impressive entry in the *Guinness Book of World Records*—2000 yards, "the closest any known personnel had been since the atomic bombs were dropped on Japan." The official report argues that by studying the volunteer officers "who accepted larger doses" one could deduce proper radiation-exposure limitation. Finding that the volunteers suffered no apparent ill-effects, the report concluded that the placement of their trenches was "sound and should be used in the future." . . .

The report writers urged that future tests emphasize "tactical operations rather than weapons effects," thus "recommending" even greater radiation exposure for the unfortunate GI participants. Nevertheless, effects tests were anything but devalued. In fact, effects tests were promoted and became the subject of a national spectacle when the armed forces returned to Desert Rock in 1955.

The Continuing Cycle of Fear and Apathy

Paul Boyer

Americans have experienced several cycles of apathy and fear relating to the atomic bomb, according to Paul Boyer. Americans are most fearful of an atomic war during times of nuclear crisis or when nations are testing atomic weapons or expanding their nuclear arsenal, Boyer reports. On the other hand, he writes, anxiety levels tend to decline when the risk of nuclear war appears to diminish due to treaties or disarmament, or when other events, such as the Vietnam War, are foremost in the American consciousness. Boyer concludes that fears of a nuclear war are well-founded; just because the world has managed to avoid a nuclear war so far does not mean that it will continue to do so, he asserts.

Paul Boyer is a history professor at the University of Wisconsin in Madison. He is the author of *By the Bomb's Early Light: American Thought and Culture at the Dawn of the Atomic Age.*

Histories end; history goes on. The early 1950s [is] a moment in our forty-year encounter with the bomb [that was] dramatically different from the immediate postwar period. By 1950, the obsessive post-Hiroshima awareness of the horror of the atomic bomb had given way to an interval of diminished cultural attention and uneasy acquiescence in the goal of maintaining atomic superiority over the Russians.

But the story of this cultural shift is only the prelude to a much longer one. In the decades that followed, two more

Excerpted from *By the Bomb's Early Light: American Thought and Culture at the Dawn of the Atomic Age*, by Paul Boyer. Copyright © 1994 by the University of North Carolina Press. Reprinted with the permission of the publisher.

such cycles of activism and apathy would play themselves out. . . . In order to place the developments of 1945–1950 in perspective and suggest how an understanding of that five-year period can contribute to a deeper understanding of our present situation, one must at least sketch in the contours of what followed.

Fear of Radioactive Fallout

The early 1950s mood of diminished awareness and acqui-escence in the developing nuclear arms race soon gave way to a new and very different stage. In the mid-1950s the issue of nuclear weapons again surged dramatically to the fore-front, once more becoming a central cultural theme. As in 1945–1946, the reason was fear—this time, fear of radioac-tive fallout. As we have seen, such fears had surfaced after the Bikini test of 1946, but when the United States in 1952 and the Russians soon after began atmospheric testing of multimegaton thermonuclear bombs, they increased dra-matically. It was the United States' 1954 test series that re-ally aroused alarm, spreading radioactive ash over seven thousand square miles of the Pacific, forcing the emergency evacuation of nearby islanders, and bringing illness and death to Japanese fishermen eighty miles away. In 1955, ra-dioactive rain fell on Chicago. In 1959, deadly strontium-90 began to show up in milk. The *Saturday Evening Post* ran a feature called "Fallout: The Silent Killer." A new group of scientists and physicians warned of the health hazards of fall-out, including leukemia, bone cancer, and long-term genetic damage. A full-blown fallout scare gripped the nation.

This in turn spawned a national movement against nu-clear testing. Adlai Stevenson raised the issue in the 1956 presidential campaign. Soon it was taken up by such groups as Leo Szilard's Council for a Liveable World; Bernard Lown's Physicians for Social Responsibility; SANE, the Na-tional Committee for a Sane Nuclear Policy, founded in 1957. One memorable SANE ad in the *New York Times* fea-tured the famed pediatrician Benjamin Spock gazing with furrowed brow at a young girl under the caption: DR. SPOCK IS WORRIED.

The revived nuclear anxieties of these years were also fed by a renewed emphasis on civil defense, including radio alerts (remember "CONEL-RAD"?) and wailing warning sirens. In a practice test in 1956, ten thousand Washington government workers scattered to secret relocation centers and President Eisenhower was helicoptered to an underground command post in Maryland. Civil defense hit the big time in 1961 as part of President Kennedy's sparring with the Russians over Berlin. With little advance preparation Kennedy went on television, warned of the danger of nuclear war, and called for a massive fallout-shelter program. Soon, black-and-yellow "Fallout Shelter" signs were adorning schools and public buildings across America. Few homeowners actually built shelters, but a lot of publicity was given to those who did. Schoolchildren hid under their desks in air-raid drills. In one civil-defense film, Bert the Turtle taught schoolchildren to "Duck and Cover." . . .

The Era of the Big Sleep

This second period of nuclear fear and activism ended abruptly in 1963. After the Cuban missile crisis of 1962, when the United States and the Soviets went to the nuclear brink and pulled back, it was widely hoped that they would cooperate to avoid such confrontations in the future. Then in 1963 the United States, the Soviet Union, and Great Britain signed a treaty banning atmospheric nuclear testing. A mood of euphoria swept the country. Almost overnight, the nuclear fear that had been building since the mid-1950s seemed to dissipate. "Writers rarely write about this subject anymore, and people hardly ever talk about it," the columnist Stewart Alsop observed in 1967. "In recent years there has been something like a conspiracy of silence about the threat of nuclear holocaust."

This is not to suggest that nuclear fear ceased to be a significant cultural force in these years. Robert Jay Lifton may well be right in his speculation that the denial of nuclear awareness—like the massive underwater mountain chains that influence ocean currents, marine life, and weather patterns in all kinds of hidden ways—affects a culture as profoundly as acknowledging it does. Psychiatrist John Mack may be correct in suggesting that deep-seated fear of nuclear war is a pervasive constant in children.

What one does see after 1963, however, as in 1947–1954, is a sharp decline in culturally expressed engagement with the issue. With apologies to Raymond Chandler, one might call this the Era of the Big Sleep. Public-opinion data reflect the shift. In 1959, 64 percent of Americans listed nuclear war as the nation's most urgent problem. By 1964, the figure had dropped to 16 percent. Soon it vanished entirely from the surveys. An early 1970s study of the treatment of the nuclear arms race in American educational journals found the subject almost totally ignored. "The atom bomb is a dead issue," concluded a sociologist studying student attitudes in 1973. Soon after, the editor of the *Bulletin of Atomic Scientists* lamented the ubiquitous "public apathy" on the issue. In 1976 a political journalist observed: "Any politician who would now speak, as President Kennedy once did, about the 'nuclear sword of Damocles' poised above our collective head, would be dismissed out of hand as an anachronism. The fear of nuclear war, once so great, has steadily receded."

In the later 1960s, it is true, Pentagon proposals to build a city-based antiballistic missile system aroused a flurry of activism and media attention. Like the atomic obliteration of two cities in 1945 and the fallout of 1954–1963, such talk forced the nuclear danger unavoidably to the forefront of public awareness, as citizens contemplated the prospect of defensive missile systems practically in their backyards. But apart from this issue (which faded with the signing of the ABM Treaty in 1972), the prevailing American stance toward the nuclear war threat from 1963 until well into the 1970s was one of apathy and neglect. . . .

Why the Apathy and Neglect?

Why this sharp decline in cultural attention to the bomb? Why this Big Sleep? The most reassuring explanation would be that the complacency was justified—that the nuclear threat did diminish in these years. Unfortunately, this was not the case. Taking advantage of a gaping loophole in the

1963 test-ban treaty, both sides developed sophisticated techniques of underground testing. The United States tested more nuclear weapons in the five years after the "test ban" treaty than in the five years before. And despite various arms-control agreements culminating in SALT I (1972), the nation's nuclear weapons program went forward at a rapid rate. Despite minor fluctuations as new systems were introduced and old ones retired, the United States' stockpile of nuclear warheads and bombs never fell below twenty-four thousand during the years of the Big Sleep (1963–1980). Indeed, these years brought a number of highly dangerous innovations in nuclear technology, most notably MIRV, the American technological breakout of the 1970s, by which a single missile could carry up to sixteen independently targeted nuclear warheads.

If this long period of nuclear apathy and cultural neglect had so little basis in objective facts, why did it happen? Several reasons might be at least briefly suggested.

First, the *illusion of diminished risk*. The 1963 treaty did not stop nuclear tests, but it did put them underground, out of sight. The various arms-limitation negotiations and treaties of these years did not stop the nuclear arms race, but they gave the appearance that something was being done about the hazard of nuclear war, reassuring a public only too ready to grasp at hopeful straws suggesting that the experts had the problem in hand.

Second, the *loss of immediacy*. With atmospheric tests no longer dominating newspapers and TV screens, the world's massive nuclear arsenals seemed increasingly unreal. As one journalist wrote in 1966: "Familiarity takes the sting out of practically anything, even Armageddon." Nuclear weapons "constitute a danger so theoretical, so remote, as to be almost nonexistent." This loss of immediacy was furthered by an increasingly sanitized, impersonal strategic vocabulary and by the names of doomsday missile systems that evoked comfortable associations with the stars, classical mythology, American history, even popular slang: Polaris, Poseidon, Tomahawk, Pershing, David Crockett, Honest John, Hound Dog. As George Orwell wrote in another context:

"The revolution will be complete when the language is perfect." The nuclear arms race—theoretical, remote, largely invisible—was ill-suited to the insatiable visual demands of television. After 1963, the mushroom-shaped cloud, the corporate logo of the nuclear age, became a tired visual cliché, embalmed in the pages of history textbooks where it had little more emotional impact than the lithographs of shivering soldiers at Valley Forge.

The Promise of Nuclear Power

Third, in the 1960s and early 1970s, *the promise of a world transformed by atomic energy*. Once again, as in the late 1940s, this helped mute concern about nuclear weapons. This time the utopian dream was focused on nuclear power, reinforced by the reality of power plants springing up from Maine to California. By the mid-1970s these plants would become the focus of demonstrations and protest, but initially, thanks to heavy promotion by the nuclear power industry, they were viewed in a hopeful light. Indeed, a kind of psychological balancing act seems to have occurred, with images of the peaceful atom once again counteracting and to a degree neutralizing images of the destroying atom. As nuclear strategist Albert Wohlstetter observed in 1967, "bright hopes for civilian nuclear energy" offered "an emotional counterweight to . . . nuclear destruction." Implicitly, the policy issue was often posed as a kind of zero-sum game: support peaceful development enthusiastically enough, and the destroying atom would somehow wither away. In a 1967 speech entitled "Need We Fear Our Nuclear Future?" the chairman of the Atomic Energy Commission, Glenn T. Seaborg, managed a resounding "no" by the simple expedient of never once mentioning nuclear weapons.

Of course, it was not a zero-sum game. Military and civilian uses of atomic energy were deeply interwoven, as the Reagan administration would later remind the nation with its proposals to recycle plutonium from nuclear power plants for weapons production. But for a time, the delicate psychological balancing act seemed to have worked.

The Deterrence Theory

Fourth, the Big Sleep was linked to the *complexity and comfort of deterrence theory*. In the immediate postwar years, American nuclear strategy, such as it was, involved a simple if chilling premise: if war came, the United States would simply rain all its available atomic bombs upon Russia's urban and military centers. By the 1960s, nuclear strategy had become an esoteric, complex pursuit involving computers, game theory, and a specialized technical vocabulary. This had a chilling effect on public engagement with the issue. It all seemed—and was clearly meant to seem—too arcane for the average citizen. It also seemed, at least superficially, reassuring. As promulgated by Secretary of Defense Robert McNamara in 1967–1968, the basic logic of deterrence theory was seductive: in a nuclear world, security lay in maintaining a retaliatory capacity so powerful and so invulnerable that no nation would dare attack us or our allies. To tinker carelessly with this arsenal, even to diminish it, could heighten rather than reduce the risk of nuclear war.

A fifth and final explanation for the nuclear apathy of these years is perhaps the most obvious of all: in the later 1960s, *the Vietnam War* absorbed nearly every available drop of antiwar energy. From the major escalation of February 1965 to the final helicopter evacuation from Saigon a little over ten years later, Vietnam obsessed the national consciousness. From the first "teach-in" at the University of Michigan in March 1965 through successive "mobilizations" and "moratoriums" to the final convulsive demonstration against the Cambodian invasion of May 1970, the war was *the* focus of activist energy. For radicals, peace activists, many religious leaders, college students facing the draft, and ultimately countless Americans of no strong ideological bent, opposition to a war that was claiming thousands of lives, devastating entire regions, turning hundreds of thousands of peasants into refugees, and draining the national treasury with no sign of "victory" in sight had an urgency that could not be denied.

Even as media events and as the source of powerful television images, the war and the domestic turmoil it engendered had an immediacy the more abstract nuclear weapons issue could not begin to match. "The second round of Strategic Arms Limitation Talks have started in Geneva," the *Wall Street Journal* could report as late as 1973, "though even an attentive newspaper reader would scarcely have noticed amid the distractions of Vietnam hopes and fears." . . .

Nuclear Concerns Are Revived

By the later 1970s, however, the nexus of circumstances that had sustained the Big Sleep for some fifteen years was beginning to break up. India's explosion of a "nuclear device" in 1974, after a decade when the "nuclear club" had held steady at five, revived concerns about proliferation. The arms-control process—never notably successful at best—lost momentum after 1972 and ground to a halt in 1979 when President Jimmy Carter withdrew the SALT II treaty from the Senate after the Soviet invasion of Afghanistan. The Vietnam War faded at last from the spotlight, as did Watergate, OPEC, the Iranian hostage crisis, and the grinding inflation of the Carter years.

Two further developments—one originating abroad and the other in the American heartland—also played a decisive role in the late-1970s revival of nuclear awareness. A vigorous anti-nuclear-weapons movement in Western Europe, focused on the planned NATO deployment of Pershing and cruise missiles, provided both a stimulus and model for Americans growing increasingly uneasy about the bomb.

Simultaneously, without much media attention, opposition to nuclear power had been spreading in grass-roots America. This movement gained massive visibility in 1979 with the release of the Jane Fonda movie *China Syndrome* and the accident at Three Mile Island, but in fact it had been building for several years at the local level. For decades government officials had urged Americans to focus on the peacetime promise of atomic energy as a reassuring alternative to worrying about nuclear war. In the 1970s they succeeded beyond their wildest dreams, but with results far different than they had anticipated. For when people at last did begin to think seriously about the "peaceful" atom—now symbolized by the nuclear power industry—they concluded that it was not reassuring at all, but deeply alarming. Local activists, students, church groups, and concerned citizens began to focus heavy publicity on nuclear power plants that not only were failing in their economic promise but also raising grave doubts about public health and safety.

Unconsciously influenced by the long-standing official insistence that nuclear weapons and nuclear power were two totally distinct realms, these "Anti-Nuke" activists of the 1970s initially paid little attention to the remote and theoretical issue of nuclear war and focused instead on the local, immediate, and highly visible issue of nuclear power. But by the end of the decade, as other developments forced the nuclear weapons issue once again into public awareness, the always unstable distinction between the "peaceful" atom and the "destroying" atom rapidly collapsed, and activists who had been focusing only on nuclear power began to confront the entire issue in its full and disturbing interconnectedness.

The Threat of Nuclear War

By 1980, then, the stage was already set for a return to the oldest item on the agenda: the threat of nuclear war. The accession of Ronald Reagan, with his bellicose rhetoric, his vast military buildup, his elaborate and heavily publicized civil-defense programs, his proposals to push the nuclear arms race into space, and the barely concealed contempt of powerful administration figures for the whole concept of arms control provided the final decisive push back toward antinuclear activism and revived cultural awareness.

By late 1981, a dramatic shift in the nation's political consciousness was beginning to be felt. Town meetings in rural New England passed resolutions calling for a halt to nuclear weapons production. On November 11—Veterans' Day—students on college campuses turned out in unexpectedly large numbers for speeches and panel discussions on the nuclear threat. "After several decades in which scarcely anyone but a few indestructible peaceniks and the limited fraternity of arms-control specialists gave any sustained attention to the peril of nuclear destruction in war," observed the president of the Rockefeller Foundation in March 1982, "it is being written about and talked about on every side." That April, towns and colleges across America observed Ground Zero Week with films, lectures, and such consciousness-raising events as a Race for Life, in which runners set out from the center of a hypothetical nuclear blast and ran out of town, passing successive mile markers describing the destruction at that point. That same month, historian Barbara Tuchman wrote in the *New York Times Magazine* of "the remarkable change in this country from the recent indifference to the new deep and widespread concern." On June 12, 1982, over seven hundred thousand antinuclear demonstrators—the largest such assembly in American history—marched in New York City. In November, voters in eight states overwhelmingly approved a referendum calling for a mutual and verifiable freeze on the production and deployment of nuclear weapons. Moribund organizations dating from the days of the test-ban movement—SANE, Physicians for Social Responsibility, the Council for a Liveable World, the Union of Concerned Scientists—dusted off their mailing lists and reemerged with new vigor and visibility. Aging veterans of the Manhattan Project and the postwar scientists' movement found themselves once more in demand. . . .

Déjà Vu

To the historian immersed in studying the bomb's cultural and intellectual impact in the earliest postwar years, this latest upsurge of awareness brings a powerful sense of *déjà vu*. Once again the possibility of nuclear annihilation looms large in the national consciousness, and once again the agencies of culture and the media both resonate to and amplify that awareness. Indeed, the parallels are striking. Except for a post-holocaust "Nuclear Winter," every theme and image by which we express our nuclear fear today has its counterpart in the immediate post-Hiroshima period. The concentric circles of hypothetical destruction we superimpose upon maps of our cities appeared in American newspapers within hours of August 6, 1945. (On today's maps, of course, there are a great many more circles.) Jonathan Schell's graphic description of what a nuclear attack would do to New York City would have been familiar to any reader of *Life, Collier's*, or *Reader's Digest* in the late 1940s. Even images like Schell's arresting "Republic of Insects and Grass" appeared in newspaper editorials within days of the atomic-bomb announcement. Those critics of the Reagan Strategic Defense Initiative who point out that even if it worked the United States would still be vulnerable to nuclear weapons smuggled into the country are resurrecting one of the major themes of the scientists' campaign of 1945–1947.

And again, as in the later 1940s, voices of reassurance are to be heard. Once more we hear of security through civil defense (crisis relocation in rural hamlets now, rather than fallout shelters or redesigned cities), new missile systems, new modes of defense, new technological marvels. (Just as one turns from the more bizarre civil-defense schemes of the late 1940s, congratulating oneself that at least we're not *that* naïve anymore, NASA scientists seriously consider research on putting large quantities of human bone marrow into orbit, for retrieval after a nuclear war for the treatment of radiation victims!)

A Major Difference

But for all the similarities, there is also a major, and depressing, difference between the current wave of nuclear awareness and that of the late 1940s. The first time around, the images of mass destruction were anticipatory. By a remarkable leap, Americans in the earliest days of the atomic era summoned up vivid scenes of their great cities in smouldering ruins—scenes that would not, in fact, become real possibilities for another twenty years. The holocaust scenarios of the 1980s, by contrast, are only too plausible. Indeed, our stabs at imagining possible nuclear futures are continually outdistanced by actual developments. In the 1940s, imagination raced ahead of reality; in the 1980s, reality races ahead of imagination.

A further discouraging dimension to one's sense of déjà vu is the fact that today's activists have so little awareness of the long history to which they are contributing the latest chapter. We extemporize everything, from strategy and tactics to metaphors and images, as though it had not all been done before—several times, in fact. We debate the wisdom of the scare tactics of a Helen Caldicott [an antinuclear activist] with little apparent awareness that this very issue was the subject of massive discussion—and some bitter lessons—a generation ago.

Ample Reason for Pessimism

Certainly there is in all this ample reason for pessimism. Viewed in historical perspective, this latest upsurge of activism could easily be seen as simply the latest convolution of a long cyclical process—the most recent swing of a pendulum that since 1945 has oscillated several times between political activism and cultural attention on the one hand and political apathy and cultural neglect on the other. More depressing still is the realization that after each of those earlier periods of activism, the nuclear arms race in fact entered a new and more deadly upward spiral. Will the same be true this time? Certainly by mid-decade, activism seemed already distinctly on the wane, and it was not at all clear that a new cycle of nuclear competition, burdening the earth and perhaps even the heavens above with still more horrible instruments of mass death, would not be our long-term fate.

But it would be wrong to conclude that this cyclical pattern must inexorably shape the trajectory of the future. This fallacy could be as potentially dangerous as its opposite: the comforting assumption that since forty years have now passed without a nuclear war, such a war can be avoided indefinitely in the future. Such a view of historical inevitability, based on a projection of past trends into the future, reckons without the factor of human unpredictability. History never repeats itself mechanically, like a stuck record. There are always novel twists, in the interstices of which one may sometimes find reason for hope. Our breathing space may be perilously small, and diminishing day by day, but it still remains. Those who warn of the danger of nuclear war rightly point out how readily unpredictable human factors—whether individual miscalculation or some surge of collective madness—could propel us down the road to holocaust despite all efforts to rationalize the technology of decision-making. Yet this same unpredictable human factor can work in the opposite way as well, introducing new forces for sanity and survival in a situation that seems increasingly structured toward a catastrophic denouement.

The Atom Bomb in Pop Culture

Bryan C. Taylor

At any particular time, popular culture reflects the hopes and fears of the public. It was no different with the media's portrayal of the atom bomb, contends Bryan C. Taylor. According to Taylor, early reports during the 1940s were little more than propaganda directed by the U.S. government to normalize the bomb. As accounts of radioactive fallout and nuclear testing emerged in the 1950s, so, too, did stories of monsters mutated by radiation, Taylor writes. He concludes that as the view of nuclear weapons and technology evolves, popular culture will continue to mirror society's interests and concerns.

Bryan C. Taylor is an associate professor of communications at the University of Colorado in Boulder. He is writing a book about the atom bomb and pop culture.

Although the bomb has been an enduring feature of postwar culture, most Americans have never encountered it directly. Nuclear weapons are manufactured and deployed under the strictest secrecy. They are controlled by experts using technical language and complex reasoning. And the sheer anxiety that such weapons inspire inhibits most citizens from even wanting to learn about them.

Pop Culture Focuses on the Bomb

But even if we have not deliberately sought information on the bomb, we have not stopped thinking about it, and popular culture reflects that. Television programs, mass-marketed fiction, and Hollywood films have repeatedly focused on nuclear weapons. In fact, argues the philosopher Jacques Derrida, it could not have been any other way. Because full-scale nuclear war has not happened, and could not be recorded if it did, stories of the bomb are mostly all that we have—symbols without a "real" referent (we keep hoping). Looking back on these cultural artifacts, we can see the shock, fantasy, regret, denial, and resolve of society as it has struggled with the possibility of nuclear destruction.

That struggle has been going on longer than most Americans might think: extensive storytelling actually anticipated the development of nuclear weapons. Historian Spencer Weart has detailed how early twentieth-century audiences incorporated the discovery of radioactivity into the pre-existing cultural myth of alchemy. Americans were fascinated and horrified by the way in which matter could, through its own destruction, be converted into this strange kind of energy, and they harbored similar feelings toward the scientific elites who possessed such powerful, forbidden secrets. While popular writers of the period conjured utopian visions of inexpensive and unlimited power generated by nuclear fission, entrepreneurs exploited the primordial association between energy rays and sexuality, marketing radioactive tonics for fatigue, baldness, and impotence. But underneath this enthusiasm lay fear. H. G. Wells imagined global nuclear war in his 1914 novel *The World Set Free*, and apocalyptic visionaries of all stripes quickly took up nuclear energy as a potential cause of The End.

The 1945 atomic bombings only heightened the conflict, creating an outburst of both jubilation and anxiety. The bomb decisively concluded a long and bitter war, but according to Weart, it also disrupted "the delicate balance by which people in normal times manage to live with the knowledge of their mortality." It was not simply the scale of damage at Hiroshima and Nagasaki that produced this dread; indeed, as defenders of the bomb argued, the fire-bombings of Dresden and Tokyo produced a greater level of devastation. Rather, what disturbed people was the frightening efficiency of destruction inherent in nuclear-weapons technology—the ability to wipe out whole cities in an instant. As philosophers and religious leaders debated the implications of nuclear weapons—and as defense analysts both predicted their development by other governments and acknowledged the impossibility of defending against them—the nation shuddered.

Eruptions of Fear

The mass media quickly moved to assist Americans in assimilating the bomb, and nuclear technology in general, as a necessary, positive, and "natural" presence. The propagandistic tone of what emerged suggests that government interests had an influence as well. William Laurence of the *New York Times*, for example, described nuclear weapons and test explosions in mythical and supernatural terms—as awesome, "titanic" forces from "the heavens" reflecting "the power of the Almighty"; such descriptions deflected questions about human responsibility that might have leaped out at readers if the writing had been more matter of fact. Curious moviegoers were treated to a spate of melodramatic, pseudo-documentary reenactments of the top-secret Manhattan Project, including *The Beginning or the End*, which featured a young scientist who resolves his moral doubts about working on the bomb through patriotic rationalizations.

As historian Paul Boyer has argued, the campaign to normalize nuclear weapons was not entirely successful, however. The decade between 1953 and 1963 saw an outpouring of works that were anything but reassuring. Writers and filmmakers not wholly preoccupied with reaching a mass audience recovered their artistic voices to evoke the existential dread of postnuclear contamination, as reflected in the novel *On the Beach* and the film of the same name. Popular culture also carried nuclear-psychological freight. Susan Sontag has observed that the "radiated monster" films of this period, such as *The Beast from 20,000 Fathoms*, reflected the public's anxiety about the biological effects of ionizing radiation, the monsters functioning as symbols of a mutated postnuclear humanity. Ironically, these films often showed the monsters created by radiation finally being defeated with nuclear weapons. It was as if the symbolic eruptions of nuclear fear could be disciplined only by the technology that had caused them in the first place.

The surge of nightmarish images declined temporarily after the 1963 signing of the atmospheric test-ban treaty. Antinuclear sentiment, like nuclear testing itself, went underground—only to resurface in the early 1980s in reaction to renewed Cold War tensions during Ronald Reagan's first term. Literature such as Jonathan Schell's *The Fate of the Earth*, television dramas such as *The Day After*, and films such as *Testament* aimed to frighten people into opposing the arms race by depicting a desperate, bleak, and violent post-nuclear landscape.

An Evolving Portrayal

Yet not all pop-culture genres appeared to dread the prospect of such a world. Macho pulp-fiction series like *The Survivalist* portrayed bands of hard men roaming the same landscape and recovering the Cold War, armed combat, and primitive heterosexuality from the ashes of feminism and the liberal welfare state. This fantastic denial of postnuclear realities, argue critics such as William Chaloupka, Robert Mielke, and James William Gibson, reflected the insecurity of the American male warrior—whose traditional battlefield heroism had been supplanted by nuclear weapons.

Still other kinds of works have arrived on the scene since 1989, when the apparent end of the Cold War confused both American foreign policy and popular culture. An emerging impulse toward seeing nuclear history in new ways was displayed in the 1989 film *Fat Man and Little Boy*, which showed Manhattan Project officials at odds with the nuclear scientists in their employ, suppressing ethical dissent among them to produce a weapon whose military effect was redundant. At the same time, ambivalence about the possibility of national security without nuclear weapons was manifested in the 1989 film *The Package*, in which renegade U.S. and Soviet military officers conspire to prevent the signing of an arms-control treaty because they are certain that it will lead to conventional warfare between their nations.

In more recent years, films and novels with scenarios based on destabilized post–Cold War politics have become popular. These newly fashionable thrillers center on the theft of nuclear materials and weapons by various ethnic, nationalist, and separatist groups. The result is either nuclear terrorism and blackmail, as in Steven Seagal's *Under Siege* and Tom Clancy's *Ops Center*, or an accidental or unauthorized use of nuclear might that threatens the fragile post–Cold War peace, as in *Crimson Tide*.

As the post–Cold War world evolves, spawning new concerns, we can count on nuclear popular culture to evolve with it, mirroring those concerns in works that feel both timely and familiar, stocked with predictably heroic characters and well-worn plot devices. If we have made peace with nuclear weapons, it is an uneasy peace at best. The bomb is, in Weart's words, "a symbol for the worst of modernity," and for just that reason it will continue to form a screen onto which we project our assorted and ever-changing conflicts.

Chapter 5

In Retrospect: Scientists Evaluate the Atom Bomb

Turning | Points
IN WORLD HISTORY

A Scientist Leaves the Manhattan Project

Joseph Rotblat

Many of the scientists working on the atom bomb project were European emigrants who escaped to England or the United States to avoid persecution by Nazi Germany. When these scientists were recruited to work on the atom bomb, they were glad to do whatever they could to ensure that the United States developed the bomb before Adolf Hitler did. They believed that if Hitler had the bomb before the United States, he would not hesitate to use it.

Joseph Rotblat is a Polish physicist who originally resisted working in nuclear technology because he believes scientists should work to benefit mankind, not develop weapons of mass destruction. However, he explains, when it appeared that Germany was working on the bomb, he overcame his qualms and joined the effort to help the United States develop the bomb first. Rotblat convinced himself that the bomb would only be a tool of intimidation, a threat that would keep other nations from using atomic weapons for fear of retaliation. When he learned the Americans actually intended to use the bomb, Rotblat contends that he could no longer work with a clear conscience and so he left the Manhattan Project in 1944.

After leaving the Manhattan Project, Joseph Rotblat began working in the field of nuclear medicine. He is currently a professor emeritus at the University of London, St. Bartholomew's Hospital Medical College. He is also a founder of the Pugwash Conference on Science and World Affairs, a symposium of world leaders and academics that meets annually to discuss disarmament. He and the Pugwash Conference shared the Nobel Peace prize in 1995.

Excerpted from "Leaving the Bomb Project," by Joseph Rotblat, *The Bulletin of the Atomic Scientists*, August 1985. Copyright © 1998 by the Educational Foundation for Nuclear Science, 6042 S. Kimbark, Chicago, IL 60637, USA. A one-year subscription is $28. Reprinted with the permission of *The Bulletin of the Atomic Scientists*.

Working on the Manhattan Project was a traumatic experience. It is not often given to one to participate in the birth of a new era. For some the effect has endured throughout their lives; I am one of those.

This essay is not an autobiography; it describes only my involvement in the genesis of the atomic bomb. All extraneous personal elements are left out, but their exclusion does not mean that they are unimportant. Our hopes and fears, our resolutions and actions, are influenced by an infinite number of small events interacting with each other all the time. Because of this, each of us may react differently to the same set of conditions. The experience of every Los Alamite is unique.

Early Experiments

At the beginning of 1939, when the news reached me of the discovery of fission, I was working in the Radiological Laboratory in Warsaw. Its director was Ludwik Wertenstein, a pupil of Marie Curie and a pioneer in the science of radioactivity in Poland. Our source of radiation consisted of 30 milligrams of radium in solution; every few days we pumped the accumulated radon into a tube filled with beryllium powder. With this minute neutron source we managed to carry out much research, even competing with Enrico Fermi's prestigious team, then in Rome, in the discovery of radionuclides. Our main achievement was the direct evidence of the inelastic scattering of neutrons; my doctoral thesis was on that subject.

In the earlier experiments on inelastic scattering we used gold as the scatterer. By the end of 1938 I had begun to experiment with uranium, so when I heard of the fission of uranium, it did not take me long to set up an experiment to see whether neutrons are emitted at fission. I soon found that they are—indeed, that more neutrons are emitted than produce fission. From this discovery it was a fairly simple intellectual exercise to envisage a divergent chain reaction with a vast release of energy. The logical sequel was that if this energy were released in a very short time it would result in an explosion of unprecedented power. Many scientists in other countries, doing this type of research, went through a similar thought process, although not necessarily evoking the same reaction.

In my case, my first reflex was to put the whole thing out of my mind, like a person trying to ignore the first symptom of a fatal disease in the hope that it will go away. But the fear gnaws all the same, and my fear was that someone would put the idea into practice. The thought that I myself would do it did not cross my mind, because it was completely alien to me. I was brought up on humanitarian principles. At that time my life was centered on doing "pure" research work, but I always believed that science should be used in the service of mankind. The notion of utilizing my knowledge to produce an awesome weapon of destruction was abhorrent to me.

Fear of the Germans

In my gnawing fear, the "someone" who might put it into practice was precisely defined: German scientists. I had no doubt that the Nazis would not hesitate to use any device, however inhumane, if it gave their doctrine world domination. If so, should one look into the problem to find out whether the fear had a realistic basis? Wrestling with this question was agonizing, and I was therefore glad that another pressing matter gave me an excuse to put it aside.

This other matter was my move to England, where I was to spend a year with Professor James Chadwick in Liverpool, on a grant to work on the cyclotron which was then being completed there. This was my first trip abroad, and the upheaval kept me busy both before the journey in April 1939 and for some time afterward, because I spoke very little English, and it took me a long time to settle down.

Throughout the spring and summer the gnawing went on relentlessly. It intensified with the increasing signs that Germany was getting ready for war. And it became acute when I read an article by S. Flügge in *Naturwissenschaften* mentioning the possibility of nuclear explosives.

Gradually I worked out a rationale for doing research on the feasibility of the bomb. I convinced myself that the only way to stop the Germans from using it against us would be if we too had the bomb and threatened to retaliate. My scenario never envisaged that we should use it, not even against the Germans. We needed the bomb for the sole purpose of making sure that it would not be used by them: the same argument that is now being used by proponents of the deterrence doctrine.

With the wisdom of hindsight, I can see the folly of the deterrent thesis, quite apart from a few other flaws in my rationalization. For one thing, it would not have worked with a psychopath like Hitler. If he had had the bomb, it is very likely that his last order from the bunker in Berlin would have been to destroy London, even if this were to bring terrible retribution to Germany. Indeed, he would have seen this as a heroic way of going down, in a *Götterdämmerung*.

Overcoming Moral Scruples

My thinking at the time required that the feasibility of the atom bomb be established, one way or the other, with the utmost urgency. Yet I could not overcome my scruples. I felt the need to talk it over with someone, but my English was too halting to discuss such a sensitive issue with my colleagues in Liverpool.

In August 1939, having gone to Poland on a personal matter, I took the opportunity to visit Wertenstein and put my dilemma before him. The idea of a nuclear weapon had not occurred to him, but when I showed him my rough calculations he could not find anything scientifically wrong with them. On the moral issue, however, he was unwilling to advise me. He himself would never engage in this type of work, but he would not try to influence me. It had to be left to my own conscience.

The war broke out two days after I returned to Liverpool. Within a few weeks Poland was overrun. The stories that Hitler's military strength was all bluff, that his tanks were painted cardboard, turned out to be wishful thinking. The might of Germany stood revealed, and the whole of our civilization was in mortal peril. My scruples were finally overcome.

Research on the Bomb's Feasibility

By November 1939 my English was good enough for me to give a course of lectures on nuclear physics to the Honors School at Liverpool University, but by then the department's senior research staff had disappeared: they had gone to work on radar and other war projects. I had, therefore, to approach Chadwick directly with an outline of my plan for research on the feasibility of the atom bomb. His response was typically Chadwickian: he just grunted, without letting on whether he had already thought of such a plan. Later I learned that other scientists in the United Kingdom did have the same idea, some of them with similar motivation.

A few days later Chadwick told me to go ahead and gave me two young assistants. One of them presented a problem. He was a Quaker and as such had refused to do war work. He was therefore sent to Liverpool University for academic duties—but was diverted to work with me on the atom bomb! I was not allowed to reveal to him the nature of our research, and I had qualms of conscience about using him in such an unethical way.

The main idea which I put to Chadwick was that for the atom bomb the chain reaction would have to be propagated by fast neutrons; otherwise it would not differ much from a chemical explosive. It was therefore important to measure the fission cross-section for fast neutrons, the energy distribution of fission neutrons, their inelastic scattering, and the proportion of those captured without producing fission. It was also relevant to find out whether stray neutrons might cause a premature start of the reaction, which meant determining the probability of spontaneous fission of uranium.

We built up a small team of young but devoted physicists and used the cyclotron to tackle some of these problems. Later we were joined by Otto Frisch who measured the fast neutron fission cross-section for uranium-235. I had the idea of using plutonium, but we had no means of making it.

As a result of these investigations, we were able to establish that the atom bomb was feasible from the scientific point of view. However, it also became clear that in order to make the bomb a vast technological effort would be required, far exceeding the manpower and industrial potential of wartime Britain. A top-level decision was reached to collaborate with the Americans. And so I found myself eventually in the "wondrous strange" place, Los Alamos.

Betrayal

In March 1944 I experienced a disagreeable shock. At that time I was living with the Chadwicks in their house on the Mesa, before moving later to the "Big House," the quarters for single scientists. General Leslie Groves, when visiting Los Alamos, frequently came to the Chadwicks for dinner and relaxed palaver. During one such conversation Groves said that, of course, the real purpose in making the bomb was to subdue the Soviets. (Whatever his exact words, his real meaning was clear.) Although I had no illusions about the Stalin regime—after all, it was his pact with Hitler that enabled the latter to invade Poland—I felt deeply the sense of betrayal of an ally. Remember, this was said at a time when thousands of Russians were dying every day on the Eastern Front, tying down the Germans and giving the Allies time to prepare for the landing on the continent of Europe. Until then I had thought that our work was to prevent a Nazi victory, and now I was told that the weapon we were preparing was intended for use against the people who were making extreme sacrifices for that very aim.

My concern about the purpose of our work gained substance from conversations with Niels Bohr. He used to come to my room at eight in the morning to listen to the BBC news bulletin. Like myself, he could not stand the U.S. bulletins which urged us every few seconds to purchase a certain laxative! I owned a special radio on which I could receive the BBC World Service. Sometimes Bohr stayed on and talked to me about the social and political implications of the discovery of nuclear energy and of his worry about the dire consequences of a nuclear arms race between East and West which he foresaw.

All this, and the growing evidence that the war in Europe would be over before the bomb project was completed, made my participation in it pointless. If it took the Americans such a long time, then my fear of the Germans being first was groundless.

When it became evident, toward the end of 1944, that the Germans had abandoned their bomb project, the whole purpose of my being in Los Alamos ceased to be, and I asked for permission to leave and return to Britain.

Why Others Stayed

Why did other scientists not make the same decision? Obviously, one would not expect General Groves to wind up the project as soon as Germany was defeated, but there were many scientists for whom the German factor was the main motivation. Why did they not quit when this factor ceased to be?

I was not allowed to discuss this issue with anybody after I declared my intention to leave Los Alamos, but earlier conversations, as well as much later ones, elicited several reasons.

The most frequent reason given was pure and simple scientific curiosity—the strong urge to find out whether the theoretical calculations and predictions would come true. These scientists felt that only after the test at Alamogordo should they enter into the debate about the use of the bomb.

Others were prepared to put the matter off even longer, persuaded by the argument that many American lives would be saved if the bomb brought a rapid end to the war with Japan. Only when peace was restored would they take a hand in efforts to ensure that the bomb would not be used again.

Still others, while agreeing that the project should have been stopped when the German factor ceased to operate, were not willing to take an individual stand because they feared it would adversely affect their future career.

The groups I have just described—scientists with a social conscience—were a minority in the scientific community. The majority were not bothered by moral scruples; they were quite content to leave it to others to decide how their work would be used. Much the same situation exists now in many countries in relation to work on military projects. But it is the morality issue at a time of war that perplexes and worries me most.

Recently I came across a document released under the Freedom of Information Act. It is a letter, dated May 25, 1943, from Robert Oppenheimer to Enrico Fermi, on the military use of radioactive materials, specifically, the poisoning of food with radioactive strontium. The Smyth Report mentions such use as a possible German threat, but Oppenheimer apparently thought the idea worthy of consideration, and asked Fermi whether he could produce the strontium without letting too many people into the secret. He went on: "I think we should not attempt a plan unless we can poison food sufficient to kill a half a million men." I am sure that in peacetime these same scientists would have viewed such a plan as barbaric; they would not have contemplated it even for a moment. Yet during the war it was considered quite seriously and, I presume, abandoned only because it was technically infeasible.

Disturbing News

After I told Chadwick that I wished to leave the project, he came back to me with very disturbing news. When he conveyed my wish to the intelligence chief at Los Alamos, he was shown a thick dossier on me with highly incriminating evidence. It boiled down to my being a spy: I had arranged with a contact in Santa Fe to return to England, and then to be flown to and parachuted onto the part of Poland held by the Soviets, in order to give them the secrets of the atom bomb. The trouble was that within this load of rubbish was a grain of truth. I did indeed meet and converse with a person during my trips to Santa Fe. It was for a purely altruistic purpose, nothing to do with the project, and I had Chadwick's permission for the visits. Nevertheless, it contravened a security regulation, and it made me vulnerable.

Fortunately for me, in their zeal the vigilant agents had included in their report details of conversations with dates, which were quite easy to refute and to expose as complete fabrications. The chief of intelligence was rather embarrassed by all this and conceded that the dossier was worthless. Nevertheless, he insisted that I not talk to anybody about my reason for leaving the project. We agreed with

Chadwick that the ostensible reason would be a purely personal one: that I was worried about my wife whom I had left in Poland.

And so, on Christmas Eve 1944, I sailed for the United Kingdom, but not without another incident. Before leaving Los Alamos I packed all my documents—research notes as well as correspondence and other records—in a box made for me by my assistant. En route I stayed for a few days with the Chadwicks in Washington. Chadwick personally helped me to put the box on the train to New York. But when I arrived there a few hours later, the box was missing. Nor, despite valiant efforts, was it ever recovered.

The work on the Manhattan Project, as I said at the outset, has had an enduring effect on my life. Indeed, it radically changed my scientific career and the carrying out of my obligations to society.

Work on the atom bomb convinced me that even pure research soon finds applications of one kind or another. If so, I wanted to decide myself how my work should be applied. I chose an aspect of nuclear physics which would definitely be beneficial to humanity: the applications to medicine. Thus I completely changed the direction of my research and spent the rest of my academic career working in a medical college and hospital.

Spreading the Word

While this gave me personal satisfaction, I was increasingly concerned about the political aspects of the development of nuclear weapons, particularly the hydrogen bomb, about which I knew from Los Alamos. Therefore, I devoted myself both to arousing the scientific community to the danger, and to educating the general public on these issues. I was instrumental in setting up the Atomic Scientists Association in the United Kingdom, and within its framework organized the Atom Train, a travelling exhibition which explained to the public the good and evil aspects of nuclear energy. Through these activities I came to collaborate with Bertrand Russell. This association led to the foundation of the Pugwash Conferences, where I met again with colleagues from the Manhattan Project, who were also concerned about the threat to mankind that has arisen partly from their work.

After 40 years one question keeps nagging me: have we learned enough not to repeat the mistakes we made then? I am not sure even about myself. Not being an absolute pacifist, I cannot guarantee that I would not behave in the same way, should a similar situation arise. Our concepts of morality seem to get thrown overboard once military action starts. It is, therefore, most important not to allow such a situation to develop. Our prime effort must concentrate on the prevention of nuclear war, because in such a war not only morality but the whole fabric of civilization would disappear. Eventually, however, we must aim at eliminating all kinds of war.

Scientists Look Back on the Manhattan Project

William L. Laurence

On the twentieth anniversary of the dropping of the atom bombs on Hiroshima and Nagasaki, William L. Laurence asked some of the scientists and political and military leaders involved with the Manhattan Project if they believed they made the right decision to make and use the atom bomb. All those interviewed by Laurence maintain that developing the bomb was essential to the war effort and national security, and have no regrets about their role in the project. However, Laurence notes that there continues to be differences in opinion about whether Japan should have been warned about the bomb before it was used. Some believe Japan would have surrendered after seeing a demonstration of the bomb's power, while others maintain that using the bomb was the best way to end a long and bloody war.

William L. Laurence was the science editor for the *New York Times*. In the spring of 1945 he was asked by the War Department to come to Los Alamos to observe and write about the development of the atom bomb. Laurence flew on the mission that dropped the atom bomb on Nagasaki on August 9, 1945. He won the Pulitzer Prize for his series of articles on the atomic bomb, which appeared in the *New York Times* in September and October 1945.

There is a story about one of our great atomic physicists—a story for whose authenticity I cannot vouch, and therefore I will not mention his name. . . . This man, one of the chief

Excerpted from "The Scientists: Their Views Twenty Years Later," by William L. Laurence, in *Hiroshima Plus 20*, prepared by *The New York Times*, introduction by John W. Finney. Copyright © 1945, 1951, 1963, 1964, 1965, by The New York Times Company.

architects of the atomic bomb, so the story runs, was out wandering in the woods one day with a friend when he came upon a small tortoise. Overcome with pleasurable excitement, he took up the tortoise and started home, thinking to surprise his children with it. After a few steps he paused and surveyed the tortoise doubtfully.

"What's the matter?" asked his friend.

Without responding, the great scientist slowly retraced his steps as precisely as possible, and gently set the turtle down upon the exact spot from which he had taken him up.

Then he turned solemnly to his friend. "It just struck me," he said, "that perhaps, for one man, I have tampered enough with the universe." He turned, and left the turtle to wander on its way.

—Loren Eiseley, from *The Firmament of Time*, 1960

"Why Did You Help Make the Bomb?"

"Knowing what you do now, would you do the same again?"

Repeatedly, the scientists and the military and civilian leaders who participated in the decision to build and use the atomic bomb are asked such questions. A number of the leading protagonists have died since 1945. The dead, all of whom agreed that the bomb be used without prior warning or demonstration, include Enrico Fermi, Ernest O. Laurence and Arthur H. Compton, among the scientists; Sir Winston Churchill, Henry L. Stimson, General George C. Marshall, Admiral Ernest King and General Henry H. Arnold, among the civilian and military leaders. Very few who played equal roles in arriving at the great decision are left. Hence the twentieth anniversary of the fateful date on which the decision was carried out over Hiroshima suggested itself as a propitious time for asking leading representatives among these survivors whether, in contemplating the past in the light of more recent knowledge, they would do it again. The men and their replies:

Dr. J. Robert Oppenheimer

[Director, Institute for Advanced Study, Princeton, N.J. Headed the Los Alamos team—the greatest scientific team ever assembled—which designed, developed and fabricated the atomic bomb. Later opposed the development of the hydrogen bomb.]

Q.: *After what has happened during these past twenty years, would you, under conditions as they were in 1942, accept once again the invitation to work on the development of the atomic bomb?*

A.: Yes.

Q.: *Even after Hiroshima?*

A.: Yes.

Q.: *Do you think it was necessary to drop the two atomic bombs over Japan when Japan was already on her knees?*

A.: From what I know today, I do not believe that we could have known with any degree of certainty that the atomic bomb was necessary to end the war. But that was not the view of those who had studied the situation at the time and who were thinking of an invasion of Japan. Probably they were wrong. Japan had already approached Moscow to sound out the United States about terms of peace. Probably a settlement could have been reached by political means. But the men who made the decision—and I am thinking particularly of Secretary [of War Henry L.] Stimson and President Truman—were sure that the choice was either invasion or the bomb. Maybe they were wrong, but I am not sure that Japan was ready to surrender.

Dr. Oppenheimer added:

I never regretted, and do not regret now, having done my part of the job. I have a deep, continuing, haunting sense of the damage done to European culture by the two world wars. The existence of the bomb has reduced the chance of World War III and has given us valid hope.

I believe it was an error that Truman did not ask Stalin to carry on further talks with Japan, and also that the warning to Japan was completely inadequate.

But I also think that it was a damn good thing that the bomb was developed, that it was recognized as something important and new, and that it would have an effect on the course of history. In that world, in that war, it was the only thing to do. I only regret that it was not done two years earlier. It would have saved a million or more lives.

Dr. Edward Teller

[Lawrence Radiation Laboratories of the University of California at Berkeley. A member of the Los Alamos team. Known as "the father of the hydrogen bomb."]

To develop the bomb was right. To drop it was wrong. We could have used the bomb to end the war without bloodshed by exploding it high over Tokyo at night without prior warning. If it had been exploded at an altitude of 20,000 feet, instead of the low altitude of 2,000 feet (as was the case at Hiroshima and Nagasaki), there would have been a minimum loss of life, if any, and hardly any damage to property, but there would have been tremendous sound and light effects. We could then have said to the Japanese leaders: "This was an atomic bomb. One of them can destroy a city. Surrender or be destroyed!"

I believe they would have surrendered just as they did following the destruction of the two cities. If that had happened it would have been a tremendous moral as well as military victory. We could have said to the world: "See what science can do? It has ended the war without shedding a drop of blood!" On the other hand, if they had failed to surrender they would have given us good reason for using the bomb as we did, though we might have waited a longer interval before we dropped the second bomb.

Like most of the other scientists, Dr. Teller worked on the bomb because he believed we were in a race against the Nazi scientists. But, he said:

Even when it was found out that there was no race, I still wanted to continue working on the bomb as an instrument to end the war, but without unnecessary bloodshed.

Dr. Teller added:

I was positive then, and I am positive now, that we made a mistake dropping the bomb without a previous bloodless demonstration. But I am quite willing to work on such a project again because I believe that in a democratic government such mistakes are the exception rather than the rule.

To abstain from progress is a medieval idea. I am in favor

The Scientific Panel's Recommendations on the Use of Atomic Weapons

In the spring of 1945, Harry S. Truman appointed an Interim Committee to study the feasibility of using an atomic bomb in the war. The committee appointed a panel of scientists who were involved in designing and making the bomb to help the committee understand scientific issues. On June 16, 1945, the Scientific Panel gave its recommendations on the new weapon to the Interim Committee. The following is an excerpt from their report:

You have asked us to comment on the initial use of the new weapon. This use, in our opinion, should be such as to promote a satisfactory adjustment of our international relations. At the same time, we recognize our obligation to our nation to use the weapons to help save American lives in the Japanese war. . . .

The opinions of our scientific colleagues on the initial use of these weapons are not unanimous: they range from the proposal of a purely technical demonstration to that of the military application best designed to induce surrender. Those who advocate a purely technical demonstration would wish to outlaw the use of atomic weapons, and have feared that if we use the weapons now our position in future negotiations will be prejudiced. Others emphasize the opportunity of saving American lives by immediate military use, and believe that such use will improve the international prospects, in that they are more concerned with the prevention of war than with the elimination of this specific weapon. We find ourselves closer to these latter views; we can propose no technical demonstration likely to bring an end to the war; we see no acceptable alternative to direct military use.

Michael B. Stoff, Jonathan F. Fanton, R. Hal Williams, eds., *The Manhattan Project: A Documentary Introduction to the Atomic Age*, 1991.

of any advance in knowledge or any development of the greater power of man. I believe in such advances because I feel that on the whole they will be used in the right way by democratic nations.

Does a scientist have a choice? In an emergency, it is obvious that everyone's choice is more restricted. The pressures are greatly increased. Everyone's responsibility is greater. However, an emergency does not eliminate any individual's responsibility, choice or conscience.

Dr. Eugene P. Wigner

[Princeton University. One of the group, led by Enrico Fermi, who lighted the first atomic pile under a squash court at the University of Chicago on December 2, 1942. The only winner of the world's three major honors in physics—the Fermi Award of the U.S. Atomic Energy Commission, the Atoms for Peace Award and the Nobel Prize.]

On the basis of admittedly scant information at the time the use of the nuclear weapon against Japan was contemplated, I came to the conclusion that Japan would surrender without its use, and that such use was unnecessary. For this reason I signed the so-called Franck petition [the report of a group of scientists headed by James Franck, Nobel Prize–winner in physics, opposing the use of the bomb].

Subsequently, particularly as a result of my reading Herbert Feis's book *Japan Subdued*, serious doubts concerning this question have raised in my mind. I am now inclined to believe that the use of the nuclear bomb to terminate the war was a more humane way and led to less suffering and loss of life than any other way that was contemplated.

There was no difference in my attitude concerning the possible use of a nuclear weapon against Germany, on the one hand, and against Japan, on the other. In both cases my attitude would have been governed at that time by the view of whether peace could be obtained without the use of a nuclear weapon.

I signed the Franck petition because I believed at the time that it would be possible to terminate the war without the use of the nuclear weapon. Today I would try to avoid responsibility for using it or not using it. I would leave it to other people to decide, on the grounds that it was not my job.

As for my participation in making the bomb, there was no choice. The original discovery that made it possible was made in Germany, and we had believed that the German scientists were ahead of us in the development of a nuclear weapon. I shudder to think what would have happened if Germany had been first to acquire the weapon.

I had volunteered for the Army as a soldier, but was refused. I knew I had to leave the ivory tower and go out into the world, because what was at stake in the war was just too much.

Believing as I did that the use of the weapon was unnecessary, I was very unhappy about it, and I would have been equally unhappy had I believed that it was necessary to use it. But I had no sense of guilt, since I did not make the decision.

The scientist in a democracy has the right to refuse to do anything distasteful to him. But as long as scientists in totalitarian countries have no such choice, it would not be right to exercise such legal rights for, if one did, there soon would not be any democracy. The scientist, like any other civilian, should not act in such a way as to make democracy impossible.

Dr. Emilio Segre

[University of California at Berkeley. One of Fermi's original associates at the University of Rome. Winner of the Nobel Prize in Physics.]

Q.: *If you knew then what you know now, would you have worked on the bomb?*

A.: Under the circumstances prevailing at the time, yes. We had Hitler around. We knew the Nazis would make the bomb and were working on it. We would have been crazy not to make the bomb under the circumstances. We could not be sure atomic bombs would not start dropping on us. If that had happened, Hitler would have won the war.

Q.: *Did you approve the use of the bomb?*

A.: The President had hardly any alternative. On the basis

of the information available—the probability that the war would go on for a long time—I thought, and still think, the decision was the only one possible. But I am glad I was not the President.

Dr. Luis W. Alvarez

[University of California at Berkeley. Played a major role on the Los Alamos team and served as a key member of the group that assembled the two nuclear weapons on Tinian. Flew aboard the B-29 *Enola Gay* on its atomic-bomb run over Hiroshima.]

Q.: *Did you approve the use of the bomb in 1945?*

A.: Of course. We had been in the war a long time. It seemed certain to continue for a long time, with enormous loss of life on both sides. We had the means to end the war quickly, with a great saving of human life. I believed it was the only sensible thing to do, and I still do.

Q.: *Would you do it over again? Would you still work on the bomb?*

A.: Of course. The weapon was possible. So far as we knew, we were in a race with the Germans. We had to beat them to it, or risk losing the war.

Q.: *Would you have done it, knowing subsequent history?*

A.: Yes. I am proud to have had a part in a program that by most modern estimates saved a million lives, both Japanese and American, that would otherwise have been lost in the projected invasion. This pride is reinforced by the knowledge that the world has not had a major war in the past 20 years, and that most responsible people feel the risk of a World War III has diminished steadily with time in these same years. I am confident that both of these admirable situations are directly traceable to the existence of nuclear weapons.

Lieutenant General Leslie R. Groves, U.S. Army Retired

[As head of the Manhattan Project, in less than two and a half years built the $2 billion industrial empire which produced the atomic bomb on schedule.]

There was never any question as to the use of the bomb, if it was successfully developed, on the part of anyone who was in a top position on the project and who knew what was going on. One group that objected to the use of the bomb did not object until after V-E Day. That group was mostly centered around people who were bitterly anti-Germany and who did not appear to feel the same way toward Japan.

John J. McCloy

[Attorney and civic leader. Former U.S. Military Governor and High Commissioner for Germany. As Assistant Secretary of War under Stimson, participated in the wartime inner councils.]

Q.: *We made the A-bomb because we believed we were in a race with the Nazis. Would we have made it if we had known, as we know now, that the Nazis were actually very far from making the A-bomb?*

A.: Yes, we would have done it because of the mere fact that atomic energy was in the air. I don't believe you could have checked it. We couldn't afford to take a chance that somebody wouldn't come along and do it.

We were in a race with ideas. At that stage, under the pressure of war, we would have gone ahead anyway. Here there was something to end the war, to bring about peace, to prevent war in the future.

Q.: *Knowing what you know today, would you approve dropping the bomb as we did?*

A.: I tried to tell Stimson to advise the Japanese that we had the bomb. I am absolutely convinced that had we said they could keep the Emperor, together with the threat of the atomic bomb, they would have accepted and we would never have had to drop the bomb.

However, if they had refused our offer, then there is no question that we should have used the bomb.

The final decision was that there was no alternative; that neither air bombardment nor blockade would end the war. It was either invasion or the bomb. It was decided not to mention the bomb because it was still not known whether it would work (it was before Alamogordo) and because there was at that time an inhibition against talking about it.

Under the circumstances we had to go ahead with it, because an invasion would have cost terrible casualties. However, I wish we had given them better notice about the Emperor and the bomb. Then our position before the world would have been better.

As to my own position, it was to bring the war to an end sooner than it would otherwise be ended, and thus to save American lives. We were losing about 250 men a day in the Pacific. The estimated American casualties for landing on Japanese shores were anywhere between 250,000 and 1,000,000, while the Japanese casualties were conservatively estimated to run as high as 10 million. We were therefore faced with a very serious question: Should we go on with the war and face the American soldiers who were subjected to unnecessary danger and the families of all those who were killed after we could have stopped the war?

The Demonstration Debate

The reason that we did not have a demonstration of the bomb was, first, that it would have completely wiped out the element of surprise, which in my opinion was extremely important. As it turned out, that was one of the reasons why Japan surrendered so quickly. They weren't prepared for it. It was a bolt out of heaven. There has never been a surprise to equal it since the Trojan horse.

Also, if we had had a demonstration or warning, and if neither had any effect—and I don't believe they would have—then the Japanese would have made every effort to see that the plane that carried the bomb was brought down, and it would have increased the hazards of the men who were carrying the bomb manyfold.

Above all else was the very strong feeling on the part of President Truman, which was the same feeling that the rest of us who knew about it had, that it was criminal and morally wrong for us to have means to bring this war to a proper conclusion and then not use the means.

It is true we didn't need the bomb to win, but we needed it to save American lives.

Remember this, that when the bomb was used, before it was used and at the time it was used, we had no basic concept of the damage that it would do. We thought it would do a great deal, but we didn't know at that time whether the explosion might not be a little too high or a little too low. We didn't know whether the fusing would work. The bomb used over Hiroshima had never been tested. A lot of features had been tested, but only of the gun-part—it was a gun-type bomb in which a projectile of uranium-285 was fired into a uranium-235 target. We had no real knowledge that the thing would work. The fact that the bomb had exploded at Alamogordo—the implosion type, the kind used over Nagasaki—was no indication that the Hiroshima type would go off.

Also, the one tested in New Mexico was put up on a tower. It had none of the mechanisms that were necessary to set it off at the proper height. The actual proximity fusing for control of the height at which it would be exploded was tested in the United States about 48 hours before it was actually used over Nagasaki. It was tested over the Tinian area 24 hours ahead of time. And nobody could tell just what was going to happen, and particularly we couldn't tell how severe the explosion would be and how many people would be injured.

The decisions recommending the use of the bomb, made by the interim committee formed by President Truman, were reached after thorough exploration of every possible angle: Could you have a demonstration? What would that mean? How and where would you have a demonstration? What would be its effects? We had not at that time seen the explosion at Alamogordo, but I can just say that if I had been a Japanese observer and had seen the bomb go off at Alamogordo, I would not have advised surrender. It's one thing to see something go off, causing no damage at all but creating a great ball of fire and obviously tremendous power, but it's another thing to say: "Well, now, they set this off on a tower; maybe it weighs 50 tons. How do we know they can deliver it? That they can get all the mechanisms perfected to deliver it?" And I am sure that anyone who was a sound thinker would have said: "No, that doesn't convince us. In the first place, would they have another?" For example, the German scientists believed that it would be impossible for us to make an atomic bomb, and that if we did we could make only one. The Germans thought of an atomic bomb as something that would have to contain as much as 20 tons of uranium-235, a practically impossible quantity.

Scientists Must Be Morally Responsible for Their Work

John A. Simpson

The development of the atom bomb gave the world a new and powerful weapon. John A. Simpson recounts how, during the bomb's construction and even after the war, many scientists believed that they must use their knowledge of the bomb to influence how the bomb should be used. He contends that those who work on weapons of mass destruction have a responsibility to ensure that the bombs are not used to destroy the world. Education, he maintains, is the best way to get this information across to the public, and many Americans are embracing the message.

John A. Simpson, a scientist who worked on the Manhattan Project, is an astrophysicist at the University of Chicago. He was also the chairman of the Atomic Scientists of Chicago and a founder of the *Bulletin of the Atomic Scientists*, a bimonthly publication of the Educational Foundation for Nuclear Science.

In December 1945 I was 29 years old and testifying before the U.S. Senate on how nuclear energy, under civilian control, could benefit the world, not destroy it. As I began, Sen. Warren Austin leaned over and asked me, "How old are you?" This was a natural question. Many of us involved in the Manhattan Engineer District—the World War II atom bomb project—were very young.

Immediately after the war we had a brief and unique window of opportunity as "atomic scientists" to get our message across to the public and policy-makers. For example, during

Excerpted from "A Challenge for the Twenty-First Century," by John A. Simpson, *The Bulletin of the Atomic Scientists*, November/December 1995. Copyright © 1998 by the Educational Foundation for Nuclear Science, 6042 S. Kimbark, Chicago, IL 60637, USA. A one-year subscription is $28. Reprinted with permission from *The Bulletin of the Atomic Scientists*.

the war I was a group leader in the secret Metallurgical Laboratory (plutonium project) at the University of Chicago and joined the faculty as the war ended. One day in September, Chancellor Robert Hutchins invited me and Eugene Rabinowitch, another Manhattan Project scientist (and future editor of the *Bulletin of the Atomic Scientists*) to meet a friend of his: Henry Luce, publisher of *Time*, *Life*, and *Fortune*. After hearing our story, Luce offered us two full pages in *Life* to tell it. In those pre-TV days, two pages in *Life* gave access to virtually every thoughtful person in the nation.

The Scientists Movement

Our story was actually a distillation of ideas that many Manhattan Project scientists had been working on for some time—in the case of the Chicago group, since the summer of 1944.

Joined by David Hill, also a project scientist, we wrote in the October 29, 1945, issue of *Life* that "having convinced the [reluctant] authorities, scientists developed a weapon that was of a different order of magnitude from the discoveries of gunpowder, dynamite, poison gas or radar." We were entering a new world in which, we hoped, world wars would be obsolete. Scientists for the first time had recognized a moral responsibility "to carry the warning of this danger to all the people of our country and to all the other nations on earth."

Even before the bomb was tested many Manhattan Project scientists had concluded that they were morally compelled to try to influence, within the constraints of secrecy, how the bomb would be used in the war, or even *whether* it should be used at all. In the spring and summer of 1945, before the Trinity test, many of us at the Chicago Met Lab tried to do just that. We did not want to see the bomb used against Japan unless that nation was fully warned. We suggested through various secret channels that a demonstration could be carried out which would be witnessed by Japanese representatives.

Nuclear Weapons Must Not Be Used

Our efforts failed. Years after the war, as layers of secrecy were lifted and the full military and political aspects came into focus, we realized that the use of the bomb was not likely to have been influenced by a few dozen scientists in Chicago. But that did not stop us after the war from pursuing our basic idea: scientists and engineers no longer could remain aloof from the consequences of their own work. Those who had participated in bringing forth the nuclear age had an inescapable responsibility now—and in the future—to do everything possible to make certain that humankind did not self-destruct. Nuclear weapons must be brought under international control and must never be used again.

Not All Felt Responsible

Leo Szilard, a physicist with the Manhattan Project in Chicago, questioned the need to continue with the atom bomb after Germany's surrender. He also promoted the idea of demonstrating the bomb's destructive power before dropping it on Japan. He urged many of his colleagues to oppose the use of the atom bomb and to let the president know of their opposition. Not all his coworkers shared his sense of moral responsibility, however. Physicist Edward Teller, who worked on the Manhattan Project and who was a strong advocate for developing the hydrogen bomb, wrote a letter to Szilard explaining why he felt no responsibility for the bomb.

Since our discussion I have spent some time thinking about your objections to an immediate military use of the weapon we may produce. I decided to do nothing. I should like to tell you my reasons.

First of all let me say that I have no hope of clearing my conscience. The things we are working on are so terrible that no amount of protesting or fiddling with politics will save our souls.

This much is true: I have not worked on the project for a very selfish reason and I have gotten much more trouble than pleasure out of it. I worked because the problems interested me and I should have felt it a great restraint not to go ahead. I can not claim that I simply worked to do my duty. A sense of duty

Our best tool for achieving that goal was education—to get across to policy-makers as well as ordinary citizens the realization that nuclear weapons were not just another weapon of war.

That is an old story now. The *Bulletin*, which evolved from the Atomic Scientists of Chicago, has been telling it for 50 years. So has the Federation of American Scientists, which was also founded 50 years ago, initially as the Federation of Atomic Scientists. The international Pugwash Conferences have been telling the story for nearly 40 years; the Council for a Livable World for more than 30 years.

---

could keep me out of such work. It could not get me into the present kind of activity against my inclinations. If you should succeed in convincing me that your moral objections are valid, I should quit working. I hardly think that I should start protesting.

But I am not really convinced of your objections. I do not feel that the there is any chance to outlaw any one weapon. If we have a slim chance of survival, it lies in the possibility to get rid of wars. The more decisive a weapon is the more surely it will be used in any real conflict and no agreements will help.

Our only hope is in getting the facts of our results before the people. This might help to convince everybody that the next war would be fatal. For this purpose actual combat-use might even be the best thing.

And this brings me to the main point. The accident that we worked out this dreadful thing should not give us the responsibility of having a voice in how it is to be used. This responsibility must in the end be shifted to the people as a whole and that can be done only by making the facts known. This is the only cause for which I feel entitled in doing something: the necessity of lifting the secrecy at least as far as the broad issues of our work are concerned. My understanding is that this will be done as soon as the military situation permits it.

Spencer R. Weart and Gertrud Weiss Szilard, eds., *Leo Szilard: His Version of the Facts*, vol. II, 1978.

The story has lost some of its freshness over the decades, but only because many of the principles and policies proposed by the early atomic scientists movement have been widely accepted. Treaties are remarkably successful. Most important is the fact that nuclear and biological weapons are no longer regarded by policy-makers in most nations as usable weapons of war; scientists and engineers contributed to winning that battle.

A Worthy Mission

But we still have tens of thousands of nuclear weapons, a few of which might become available to rogue states. The great challenge for the twenty-first century is to reduce this overall threat while simultaneously enhancing the many beneficial uses of nuclear energy for all nations. The youth of today still have a mission worthy of their talent.

The United States Was Right to Build the Hydrogen Bomb

Edward Teller

Although the United States should have demonstrated the awesome power of the atom bomb to the Japanese before using it, Edward Teller argues that the nation was right to develop the bomb. The chance to increase knowledge should never be denied, Teller asserts. For that reason, he maintains that the United States was absolutely correct to develop the hydrogen bomb, a bomb even more powerful than the atom bomb. Teller asserts that by delaying the development of the hydrogen bomb, the United States fell behind the Soviet Union in its nuclear arsenal and has never caught up. Therefore, he concludes, it is important that the United States continue its quest for knowledge and develop a defense to destroy enemy missiles.

Edward Teller is a physicist who worked on the atom bomb in Chicago and Los Alamos, New Mexico. Teller was appointed director of a second nuclear weapons laboratory in Livermore as a branch of the University of California Radiation Laboratory. He was a strong advocate for the development of the hydrogen bomb and of thermonuclear weapons testing.

Should we have built the atomic bomb? Should the bomb used at Hiroshima have been followed by the development of another one, a thousand times more powerful? Should we establish a defense against missiles carrying such bombs?

Of those three controversies, the first arose not before the weapon was developed but many years after the bomb had been used. The second controversy was ended by a

Excerpted from *Better a Shield Than A Sword: Perspectives on Defense and Technology,* by Edward Teller. Copyright © 1987 by The Free Press. Reprinted with the permission of The Free Press, a division of Simon & Schuster, Inc.

Presidential decision, but its repercussions have not subsided. The controversy over strategic defense is raging today. In all three debates, many of the same people are participants. That is to be expected. The variety of the arguments is more surprising.

The Atomic Bomb

Intensive work on the atomic bomb began during the darkest hours of World War II. Not only did Vice President Harry S. Truman know nothing of the project, but the nature of the work was kept secret even from many of the people working on the Los Alamos mesa.

One evening during a trip down from the laboratory, the Fifty-Minute WAC (a woman soldier who could drive any distance in fifty minutes) glumly commented: "My girl friend will come home from Africa and tell our acquaintances, 'I drove a munitions truck to the crucial battle of El Alamein.' I will say, "I stayed in the States and drove Mr. Teller [even the fact that I had a doctorate in physics was classified] to Santa Fe." Not until after Hiroshima was announced did I see the Fifty-Minute WAC smile.

Forty years later, in 1985, not many people smile. Many of the scientists who planned the first atomic bombs made up their minds never to work on weapons again. Before Hiroshima, one of those scientists recommended that the United States wait until a dozen atomic bombs were available and then drop them all on the same day; that would surely win the war. Today he opposes Strategic Defense.

In retrospect, it is clear that no atomic bomb should have been dropped before its incredible power had been demonstrated to the Japanese. Hiroshima did not change a single vote in the Japanese War Cabinet, which was responsible for decisions about the war. It did affect Emperor Hirohito, who broke with tradition and the Japanese constitution and appealed directly to the people for peace. A demonstration of the bomb and the power of science, 30,000 feet above Tokyo Bay, would not have hurt anyone. It would have been seen by Hirohito, would have ended the war, and would have left behind a world more reasonable and secure.

We developed the bomb in fear that the Nazis might have it first. Actually, the Germans under the leadership of Werner Heisenberg barely tried. Soviet work on the project was curtailed by wartime shortages. But had not a democracy been the first to succeed, it is a foregone conclusion that a totalitarian state would have succeeded not many years later. Critics of the atomic bomb development fail to mention that our inaction would have set the stage for world dictatorship.

The United States as sole possessor of the first atomic weapons did not use their immense new power to create a world empire. Restraint was exercised because the first development took place in a democracy. I do not claim that the United States makes no mistakes, but only that in our country discussion and reason have a chance.

Increasing knowledge and progress, including progress in the military field, are unavoidable. Los Alamos did not change the world by developing the atomic bomb. It did change world history by placing the first bomb in the hands of those who value peace more than power.

The Hydrogen Bomb

Why develop the hydrogen bomb? Wasn't the atomic bomb destructive enough?

Obviously, weapons have been too destructive since a man first used a rock to kill another man. A more pertinent question concerns ignorance. Can lack of knowledge ever contribute to stability or safety? The hydrogen bomb controversy marked the first time that a large group of scientists argued for remaining ignorant of technical possibilities.

But if the United States ceased to develop destructive weapons, would others follow suit? In late October 1949, that hope was formally raised by the General Advisory Committee (GAC) of the Atomic Energy Committee. According to Andrei Sakharov, the physicist instrumental in the development of the Soviet hydrogen bomb, the Soviet effort had been under way for at least a year and a half when the American hope of delaying development was voiced.

The public debate on the hydrogen bomb ended after a

few weeks with President Truman's decision to proceed with development. At the beginning of the debate, two great scientists, Enrico Fermi and I.I. Rabi, made a statement that had a lasting effect on public opinion. They said: "The fact that no limit exists to the destructiveness of this weapon makes its very existence and the knowledge of its construction a danger to humanity as a whole."

The much greater explosive yield of a thermonuclear weapon proved to be an alarming reality—the thousandfold increase in explosive power provided by the atomic bomb was followed by a further thousandfold increase. However, contrary to expectation, destructiveness does have limits. The limits are both technical and deliberate.

A very big explosive blows the atmosphere within a diameter of 10 miles into space. With a further increase in the size of the explosive, practically the same mass of air will be blown into space at a higher velocity. The lateral effects along the ground expand to an exceedingly small extent. Thus, further escalation in the power of the explosive is ineffectual and useless.

Actually, the megatonnage in the U.S. stockpile peaked in the mid-1960s and has decreased steadily from that time to one-quarter of its maximum value as the accompanying graph shows. Current U.S. weapons do not include any of multimegaton size. The Soviet nuclear stockpile has increased in megatonnage and exceeds the U.S. explosive power severalfold at this time.

Other Arguments

An additional argument against developing the hydrogen bomb was the critics' claim that fusion, unlike fission, had no potential peacetime applications. Other arguments were that clusters of fission bombs were militarily more effective; that the hydrogen bomb was unnecessary because plans were already under way to build an atomic bomb with a 500,000-ton equivalent TNT yield; that the fusion weapon might be impossible to develop; and that even if possible, it would be unwieldy and expensive.

The thermonuclear explosive produces less radioactivity.

It can therefore be used in construction and mining work, as the Soviets have demonstrated. Contrary to predictions, the thermonuclear weapon turned out to be less expensive and much smaller in weight and size. That meant rockets could easily be used for their delivery, a fact that caused the United States to make a large-scale effort to catch up with Soviet rocket technology.

One final argument against development was that if the Soviets did produce a thermonuclear weapon, the United States could close the gap quickly. How we would gauge Russian progress or gather support for matching a secret Soviet effort was not specified.

No one can be happy about the balance of terror that fol-

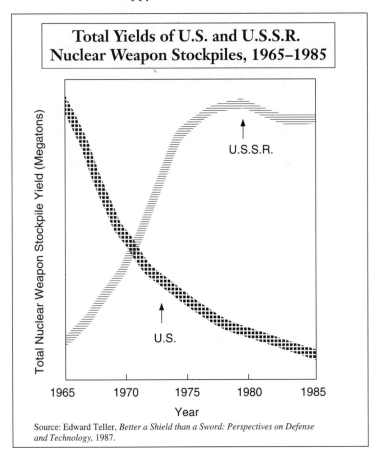

Total Yields of U.S. and U.S.S.R. Nuclear Weapon Stockpiles, 1965–1985

Source: Edward Teller, *Better a Shield than a Sword: Perspectives on Defense and Technology,* 1987.

lowed the development of thermonuclear weapons, but a Soviet monopoly on intercontinental missiles carrying thermonuclear weapons would have been worse. . . .

Then and Now

In 1949, the United States had the strongest military arsenal in the world. Had we made a mistake then and recognized the peril in the early 1950s, we might possibly have caught up again. In 1985, the Soviet Union is stronger in every quantitative sense. If we make a mistake today, we have no margin to absorb the consequences.

In 1949, I advocated work on the hydrogen bomb, a weapon of attack. I am now arguing for the development of the means to defend against those weapons. The change is due to new understandings, which have arisen from increased technical knowledge. Now as then, my argument is for knowledge and against ignorance. Now as then, I offer no detailed proposals as to how the knowledge, once acquired, should be used. Scientists have the responsibility to make knowledge available and to explain its possible applications. The decision as to which uses should be adopted, now as then, should belong to the entire community. That is indeed the main principle on which a democratic society rests.

Epilogue

The *Enola Gay* Controversy

Michael J. Hogan

On August 6, 1945, at 8:15 A.M., a B-29 bomber named the *Enola Gay* dropped an atomic bomb on Hiroshima, Japan. Following the war, the *Enola Gay* languished unattended in airfields around the United States until the Smithsonian Institution purchased it to restore it and make it a part of an exhibition commemorating the fiftieth anniversary of the dropping of the bomb and the end of World War II.

The Smithsonian's exhibit was to have included a historical analysis of Harry S. Truman's decision to drop the atom bomb on Japan, an examination of how the bomb affected Japan, and a follow-up of how the bomb contributed to hostile postwar relations with the Soviet Union. According to Michael J. Hogan, many war veterans' groups were outraged over the presentation, contending that the planned exhibit was unbalanced and inaccurate in its portrayal of American and Japanese troops fighting in the Pacific theater. Hogan writes that attempts at compromise between the museum and veterans were unsuccessful, and in the end, the exhibit was cancelled. Even fifty years after the fact, Americans still cannot agree on the relevance and necessity of the atom bomb.

Michael J. Hogan is a history professor at Ohio State University. He has written and edited several books on war and diplomacy, including *Hiroshima in History and Memory*.

It was an "eerie sight," reported the *Washington Post* on Thanksgiving Day 1994. Two nights before, observers in the nation's capital had been dumbstruck to see the fuselage of a

Excerpted from "The Enola Gay Controversy: History, Memory, and the Politics of Presentation," by Michael J. Hogan, in *Hiroshima in History and Memory*, edited by Michael J. Hogan. Copyright © 1996 by Michael J. Hogan. Reprinted with permission from the Cambridge University Press.

B-29 bomber being hauled down Independence Avenue to the Smithsonian's Air and Space Museum. It was the *Enola Gay*, the giant four-engine Superfortress that had dropped the atomic bomb on Hiroshima, Japan, in the early morning of 6 August 1945. Named after the mother of its pilot, Colonel Paul W. Tibbets, the *Enola Gay* had disappeared from sight after its deadly mission. Stored outdoors in three states, it had been home to field mice and other critters before taking up residence in Building 20 at the Smithsonian's storage yard in Suitland, Maryland. There, technicians had worked for years to restore the bomber before shrink-wrapping its fuselage for protection and moving it to the Air and Space Museum for an exhibit that was to open in May 1995.

Competing Symbols

Shrouded in white plastic as it traveled down Independence Avenue, the fuselage looked vaguely like a blowup of the "Little Boy" atomic bomb it had dropped on Hiroshima. A group of demonstrators assembled near the museum to protest the public display of a warplane whose payload had taken the lives of so many Japanese soldiers and civilians. For them, the *Enola Gay* was a symbol of the atomic carnage that had ended World War II and launched the Cold War. For others, however, the giant B-29 bomber was a lifesaver, a peacemaker, "a totem of American technological triumph," as Arthur Hirsch reported in the *Baltimore Sun*, that deserved center stage in an exhibit marking the fiftieth anniversary of the atomic bombing of Japan.

These competing symbols were at the heart of a bitter controversy over the proposed exhibit, finally entitled "The Last Act: The Atomic Bomb and the End of World War II." At stake in this controversy was whether the exhibit would commemorate the atomic bombing of Japan or investigate the circumstances surrounding that event. Would Hiroshima loom as the last act in a bloody struggle or the first in a long and dangerous arms race? The answers to these and similar questions would determine whose story the exhibit recounted. Although American veterans wanted an exhibit that spoke for them, it was not at all clear if their memories could be reconciled with a careful analysis of the motives that drove President Harry S. Truman's resort to atomic warfare. Nor would it be easy to balance their narrative of the war against the silent voices of those who had perished at Hiroshima and Nagasaki, the Japanese city that was destroyed by a second atomic bomb three days after Hiroshima.

To a large extent, everything depended on who controlled the process by which the exhibit was framed. Curators at the Air and Space Museum based their right to interpret the past on their scholarly credentials, on their mastery of the historical record, and on the advice they received from professional historians. American veterans appealed to the authenticity of personal experience. They equated their collective memory with historical reality and asserted their authority over that of the curators. These differences might have been reconciled, and some balance between history and memory achieved, had it not been for the intervention of organized interests, including the American Legion, the Air Force Association, and conservative politicians in Congress. These groups appropriated the memory of American veterans to defend a conventional, patriotic picture of the past. Determined to deny history if it subverted their sense of American identity, they censored alternative voices and forced the Smithsonian to cancel its original plans. To be sure, the fuselage of the *Enola Gay* would still be displayed at the Smithsonian's Air and Space Museum, but the exhibit would no longer tell the bomber's story or recount the memories, and commemorate the sacrifices, of American veterans.

Walking a Tightrope

The curators at the National Air and Space Museum understood better than most that historical commemorations are socially constructed and often contested events. At stake in such commemorations is nothing less than the control of history itself, or at least the process by which historical representation gives voice to the past. The question is: Whose voice will be heard? In addressing this question the curators knew they were walking a "tightrope," to borrow a word from Tom D. Crouch, chair of the museum's aeronautics department and a leading figure in the *Enola Gay* controversy. "On both sides of the Pacific, the sensitivities on this subject run very deep," he said. "There's very little middle ground." Crouch's colleagues agreed. "When we began discussions of the exhibit," Martin O. Harwit, the museum's director, told a reporter for the *Baltimore Sun*, "there were two points everyone agreed on. One, this is a historically significant aircraft. Two, no matter what the museum did, we'd screw it up."

Harwit worried from the beginning about Japan's reaction to the proposed exhibit and was anxious to include a Japanese voice in the Smithsonian's plans. Early in 1994, Crouch and other curators met with a delegation of Japanese officials from Hiroshima and Nagasaki. The Smithsonian hoped for their cooperation in the commemoration, particularly the contribution of a number of artifacts that could illustrate the awesome power of the atomic bomb and the death and destruction it had brought to Japan. For their part, the Japanese did not want the exhibit to glorify the atomic assault on their homeland or arouse anti-Japanese sentiments in the United States. One Japanese resident in Washington wrote the mayor of Hiroshima that the *Enola Gay* belonged in "the Holocaust Museum," not in the Air and Space Museum. Japanese-Americans had similar concerns, which officials at the Smithsonian tried to assuage. The proposed exhibit, they explained on every occasion, would "reflect all the many arguments" about the atomic bombing of Hiroshima and Nagasaki. To be sure, it would be "an American exhibition," said Michael J. Neufeld, the exhibit's principal curator, but it would nonetheless "present all the differing views."

Unpopular with the Veterans

It was this aspect of the Smithsonian's plan that got it into so much trouble with American veterans of the Second World War. Neufeld had said at the start that he and his collaborators "must be careful not to offend our own veterans." But this was going to be difficult if the curators also acknowledged Japanese concerns and perceptions or addressed some of the controversial issues that have bothered historians for years, which is exactly what they decided to do. For example, early drafts of the exhibit's script dealt with the diplomatic as well as the strategic aspects of Truman's decision to use the atomic bomb, especially with whether that decision had been driven in part by a desire to intimidate the Soviet Union with American military power. They also presented evidence on the degree to which Truman's decision might have been motivated by racist perceptions of the Japanese and by a desire to avenge the Japanese attack on Pearl Harbor. They summarized recent historical studies that question whether an invasion of Japan would have cost hundreds of thousands of American and Japanese lives, and they asked if the atomic bombing of Hiroshima and Nagasaki was the only alternative to such an invasion. Might the Japanese have been induced to surrender by a test demonstration of the bomb, by Soviet entry into the war, or by revising the American demand for unconditional surrender in order to safeguard the position of the Japanese emperor? Historians have been dealing with these difficult issues since 1945, and the curators wanted those who viewed the exhibit to tackle them as well. Visitors would be encouraged to take sides in the historiographical debates, as the curators themselves appeared to do in certain cases. They seemed convinced, for example, that diplomatic considerations had played a part in Truman's decision, and they had their doubts about whether the atomic bomb was the best way to end the war. "In the end," said Neufeld, "there's still a case to be made that the bomb was a better alternative than invading, but it's not as clear-cut as some would say. . . . There are a lot more questions and unknowns."

An Exercise in Thinking

For the curators, in other words, the exhibit would be much more than a display of historical artifacts; it would be an exercise in historical thinking. Besides the motives behind Truman's decision, they wanted visitors to view that decision less in the context of the Pacific war, more as a prelude to the postwar era, and to grapple with its consequences. As a result, the exhibit would begin with the last year of the war, by which time the Japanese were clearly on the defensive. From this beginning, visitors would move through a second section of the exhibit on the American decision to drop the bomb and a third section on the wartime bombing of Japan and the training of the 509th Composite Group, an elite corps of Army Air Force crewmen that included the crew of the *Enola Gay*. This section would feature the fuselage of the *Enola Gay* and a replica of the "Little Boy" atomic bomb it dropped on Hiroshima. The fourth section would constitute the "emotional center" of the exhibit. It would illustrate the destruction at Ground Zero with life-size pictures of Japanese dead and wounded, personal narratives of those who survived, and a variety of artifacts, including a watch with its hands frozen on the moment when the bomb exploded over Hiroshima. A final section would focus on the nuclear arms race that followed the war. This section would speak to the children and grandchildren of those who had lived through World War II, for whom Hiroshima and Nagasaki marked the start of a fabulously expensive arms race with "megaton warheads, the DEW line, 45-minute warnings, first strike, Mutually Assured Destruction," radioactive fallout, and the danger of nuclear winter. "Part of the purpose of the exhibition," Crouch told National Public Radio, was "to get people to think about the origins" of the "nuclear age and everything that's come with it over the past half-century."

The Vets' Vision

Veterans envisioned a different history altogether. While the curators wanted visitors to analyze the Hiroshima bombing and wrestle with the horrors of war and the dangers of a nuclear arms race, veterans wanted an exhibit that commemorated the sacrifices they had made in a just cause. From their perspective, these sacrifices would be obscured by the exhibit's emphasis on the last year of the struggle, on the death and destruction at Ground Zero, and on the role that diplomatic considerations, racism, and the spirit of vengeance had played in Truman's decision. Instead of commemorating their sacrifices, the exhibit, in their opinion, would portray the Japanese as victims of American aggression and the atomic bombings as unnecessary, wrongful acts. The Smithsonian's plans were an "insult to every soldier, sailor, marine and airman who fought the war against Japan," complained W. Burr Bennett, Jr., a veteran from Illinois. "They're trying to evaluate everything in the context of today's beliefs," explained Brigadier General Paul Tibbetts, who flew the *Enola Gay* on that fateful day, and it's "a damn big insult." Instead of taking up the questions that historians have debated, Bennett, Tibbets, and other veterans urged the Smithsonian to display the bomber "proudly and patriotically," much as it displayed the Wright Brothers' first airplane or Lindbergh's *Spirit of St. Louis*.

As the veterans saw it, the curators were recounting the end of the war from a perspective that privileged a Japanese narrative over their own experience. They were particularly offended by the curators' decision to emphasize the destruction at Hiroshima and Nagasaki. Neufeld and Crouch could not imagine an exhibit that stopped "the story when the bomb leaves the bomb bay." Veterans, Crouch complained, were reluctant to "tell the whole story." Not so, said Bennett. What troubled the veterans was the exhibit's "accent on the effects of the bombing rather than the fact that the bombing ended the war in nine days." By stressing the death and destruction at Ground Zero, the exhibit, according to the veterans, made the Japanese look like victims. "It will leave you with the impression that you have to feel sorry for those poor Japanese," said Tibbets, "because they were only defending their way of life." Still worse, the curators' perspective made American soldiers look like ruthless aggressors rather than selfless heroes. "History has been denigrated," Tibbets complained. "The *Enola Gay* has been miscast and a group of valiant Americans . . . have been denied a historically correct representation to the public." Other veterans made the same point. Manny Horowitz, a B-29 navigator, did not want "school children and their parents born after World War II" to leave the exhibit "with a distorted and incorrect understanding of this important part of our country's history." Ben Nicks, another B-29 pilot who flew his last mission on the day of the Hiroshima bombing, was more specific. The *Enola Gay* was a symbol to generations for whom World War II was only a memory, said Nicks, and he and other veterans wanted a symbol "that reflects credit on us."

To veterans and other critics it was especially galling to see the Air and Space Museum discounting the experiences of those who had lived through the war and whose collective memories supposedly added up to the nation's history. "Let the Smithsonian listen to the voices of those who fought," said the son of a war veteran, not to historians who would "place the legacy" of the veterans in "a specific ideological camp." Historians had no business challenging "the views of history of those who actually lived it." They could "read the words of their research," but they could not interpret that research "in the atmosphere of the past." By ignoring the authentic voices of the past, according to the critics, the curators had failed to properly contextualize the bombing of Hiroshima and Nagasaki. They had ignored the record of Japan's aggression, the brutality of its war policy, and the fanaticism of its soldiers. Most importantly, they had failed to appreciate how Truman's decision to drop the bomb had saved countless lives that would have been spent in an American invasion of the Japanese home islands. . . .

Caught Between Memory and History

In the end, however, the historians were no match for the American Legion and its friends on Capitol Hill. On 24 January, Republican Representative Peter Blute of Massachusetts and his two allies were joined by seventy-eight other members of Congress in a letter to Smithsonian Secretary Ira Michael Heyman that demanded cancellation of the exhibit and the dismissal of Martin Harwitt. The representatives also promised a congressional investigation of the entire controversy, as did Senator Bob Dole of Kansas, the new Republican majority leader in the Senate. Running for cover, Heyman suspended work on the exhibit and asked the Smithsonian's Board of Regents to take up the issue. Meeting on 30 January 1995, the board decided to cancel the original exhibit and accede to the Legion's demand that the *Enola Gay* be displayed without historical commentary. The planned exhibit of ten thousand square feet would be scrapped and the B-29 Superfortress would be displayed with little more than a plaque identifying the giant bomber and its crew. Dr. Robert K. Musil, a historian and director of Physicians for Social Responsibility, called the decision a "tragic capitulation to political pressure . . . reminiscent of the McCarthy era." Heyman viewed the results differently. Veterans and their families, he said in a statement announcing the board's decision, were expecting an exhibit that would "commemorate their valor and sacrifice." They "were not looking for analysis," and the Smithsonian, frankly, had not given "enough thought to the intense feelings such analysis would evoke."

The *Enola Gay* exhibit had been "caught between memory and history," wrote historian Edward Linenthal shortly after the exhibit was cancelled, between "the commemorative voice and the historical voice." On one side of this divide were the curators, who were "looking for analysis," to borrow Heyman's phrase. Citing their professional credentials, and backed by the authority of professional historians, they claimed a right to interpret the past in an exhibit that would challenge the historical consciousness of its viewers. They wanted viewers to wrestle with the doubts and debates that had occupied historians for half a century, to grapple with the complexities of an important historical event, and to appreciate its consequences for later generations. On the other side of the struggle were the veterans of World War II, who spoke not with the authority of the historian but with "the authority of the witness," as Linenthal put it. The veterans wanted an exhibit that squared with their collective memory, and with their sense of personal heroism and American exceptionalism. They wanted an exhibit that privileged their story over that of the Japanese, that commemorated their sacrifices in a noble cause, not the destruction at Ground Zero, and that remembered "the atomic bomb as the redemptive ending of a horrible war," not as the beginning of the nuclear arms race. This was the history re-

counted not only by the American Legion and other organized veterans groups, but by individual veterans in letters
written to the editors of newspapers all across the country.

In the end, the commemorative voice prevailed over the
historical voice, in part because veterans groups could
muster more political power than the historians, in part because of a conservative political climate called the very practice of history into question. One of the most fascinating aspects of the *Enola Gay* controversy was the degree to which
critics in Congress and the press, particularly conservative
critics, discounted the authority of professional historians
with whom they disagreed. Professional historians, including the curators, were dismissed as the agents of political
correctness, multiculturalism, postmodernism, or historical
revisionism—all phrases used more-or-less interchangeably
in a conservative critique that ranged from the *Enola Gay* exhibit to the National Standards for American History. If the
critics needed experts on their side of the story they pointed
invariably to the authors of popular histories, such as David
McCullough, or to military historians, who were seen as
somehow uncorrupted by the "revisionist" disease. But
mostly the critics were their own experts or found them
among American veterans, whose collective memory constituted a more authentic past than the archival accounts of
professional scholars. . . .

Contested Terrain

The *Enola Gay* controversy proved again that history is contested terrain, particularly when public presentations of the
past collide with living memory. In hindsight, it is easy to
wish that Neufeld, Crouch, and the other curators had tried
harder, and earlier, to contextualize the atomic bombings in
the long and bloody history of the Second World War. And
maybe they could have struck a better balance between the
narrative of Japanese suffering and the record of Japanese
aggression, between the commemorative voice and the historical voice. As Heyman concluded, the curators had not
thought enough about the feelings of individual veterans,
who were less concerned about the politics of the *Enola Gay*

controversy than they were about how their wartime sacrifices would be remembered by generations to come.

Still, the curators had been willing to share their work with the Air Force Association and other interested parties, had sought their advice, and had made adjustments accordingly. What is more, it is difficult to see how any degree of balance between history and memory would have satisfied critics like *Air Force Magazine* editor-in-chief John T. Correll, who was determined to censor all voices but his own. Second-guessing the curators also sidesteps the central issue in the *Enola Gay* controversy, on which Professor Alfred F. Young of Northern Illinois University had the last word. The issue is whether or not the nation's history can be openly and critically discussed or whether organized political pressure will encourage censorship and promote a false consciousness about the past. Historians will always disagree over the past, Young wrote, but they should respect their disagreements and defend the right of public historians to represent the past without political interference. Defending that right is particularly important in an age when so many critics are determined to reduce history to "bunk," to borrow a famous phrase from Henry Ford, who, like Correll, sought to build a romanticized version of the past as an alternative to the one offered by historians.

Appendix

Excerpts from Original Documents Pertaining to the Atom Bomb

Document 1: Albert Einstein Urges Franklin D. Roosevelt to Consider Developing Atom Bombs

During the summer of 1939, physicist Leo Szilard became convinced that a nuclear chain reaction was possible. The next step, he reasoned, would be to construct a bomb using atomic energy. Fearful that the Germans were already working on developing an atomic bomb, Szilard contacted Alexander Sachs, Franklin D. Roosevelt's science adviser, and the two of them met with Albert Einstein to explain their fears. Einstein agreed that there was cause to worry, and signed a letter drafted by Sachs and Szilard to Roosevelt explaining the implications of atomic energy. When Roosevelt read the letter, he immediately established the Advisory Committee on Uranium which granted $6,000 to Columbia University a few months later, and government research into atomic energy began.

Some recent work by E. Fermi and L. Szilard, which has been communicated to me in manuscript, leads me to expect that the element uranium may be turned into a new and important source of energy in the immediate future. Certain aspects of the situation which has arisen seem to call for watchfulness and, if necessary, quick action on the part of the Administration. I believe therefore that it is my duty to bring to your attention the following facts and recommendations:

In the course of the last four months it has been made probable—through the work of Joliot in France as well as Fermi and Szilard in America—that it may become possible to set up a nuclear chain reaction in a large mass of uranium by which vast amounts of power and large quantities of new radium-like elements would be generated. Now it appears almost certain that this could be achieved in the immediate future.

This new phenomenon would also lead to the construction of bombs, and it is conceivable—though much less certain—that extremely powerful bombs of a new type may thus be constructed. A single bomb of this type, carried by boat and exploded in a port, might very well destroy the whole port together with some of the surrounding territory. However, such bombs might very well prove to be too heavy for transportation by air.

The United States has only very poor ores of uranium in moderate quantities. There is some good ore in Canada and the former Czechoslovakia, while the most important source of uranium is the Belgian Congo.

In view of this situation you may think it desirable to have some permanent contact maintained between the Administration and the group of physicists working on chain reactions in America. One possible way of achieving this might be for you to entrust with this task a person who has your confidence and who could perhaps serve in an inofficial capacity. His task might comprise the following:

a) to approach Government Departments, keep them informed of the further development, and put forward recommendations for Government action, giving particular attention to the problem of securing a supply of uranium ore for the United States,

b) to speed up the experimental work, which is at present being carried on within the limits of the budgets of University laboratories, by providing funds, if such funds be required, through his contacts with private persons who are willing to make contributions for this cause, and perhaps also by obtaining the co-operation of industrial laboratories which have the necessary equipment.

I understand that Germany has actually stopped the sale of uranium from the Czechoslovakian mines which she has taken over. That she should have taken such early action might perhaps be understood on the ground that the son of the German Under-Secretary of State, von Weizsäcker, is attached to the Kaiser-Wilhelm-Institut in Berlin where some of the American work on uranium is now being repeated.

Spencer R. Weart and Gertrud Weiss Szilard, eds., *Leo Szilard: His Version of the Facts*. Cambridge, MA: MIT Press, 1978, pp. 94–96.

Document 2: The "Official" Explanation of the Los Alamos Project

The Manhattan Project was one of America's most closely guarded secrets. Most of the workers at Los Alamos had no idea of the project's true purpose. The scientific director of the Manhattan Project, J. Robert Oppenheimer, wrote a memo to Leslie R. Groves, the military director of the atom bomb project, on how speculation about the project by the outside community could be eased.

In accordance with our discussion of last week, I have given some thought to the question of a story about the Los Alamos Project which, if disseminated in the proper way, might serve somewhat to reduce the curiosity of the local population, and at least to delay the dissemination of the truth.

We propose that it be let known that the Los Alamos Project is working on a new type of rocket and that the detail be added that this is a largely electrical device. We feel that the story will have a certain credibility; that the loud noises which we will soon be making here will fit in with the subject; and that the fact, unfortunately not kept completely secret, that we are installing a good deal of electrical equipment, and the further fact that we have a large group of civilian specialists would fit in quite well. We further believe that the remoteness of the site for such a development and the secrecy which has surrounded the project would both be appropriate, and that the circumstance that a good deal of work is in fact being done on rockets, together with the appeal of the word, makes this story one which is both exciting and credible.

Alice Kimball Smith and Charles Weiner, *Robert Oppenheimer: Letters and Recollections.* Cambridge, MA: Harvard University Press, 1980, p. 256.

Document 3: The British and Americans Join Forces

The Americans were not alone in attempting to develop an atomic bomb. The British had begun their own project, code-named Tube Alloys. In Quebec, Canada, in August 1943, Franklin D. Roosevelt met with England's prime minister, Winston Churchill, to discuss combining American and English efforts on the atom bomb. The Quebec Agreement outlines the collaboration expected between the United States and the United Kingdom.

Whereas it is vital to our common safety in the present War to bring the Tube Alloys project to fruition at the earliest moment; and whereas this may be more speedily achieved if all available British and American brains and resources are pooled; and whereas owing to war conditions it would be an improvident use of war resources to duplicate plants on a large scale on both sides of the Atlantic and therefore a far greater expense has fallen upon the United States;

It is agreed between us

First, that we will never use this agency against each other.

Secondly, that we will not use it against third parties without each other's consent.

Thirdly, that we will not either of us communicate any information about Tube Alloys to third parties except by mutual consent.

Fourthly, that in view of the heavy burden of production falling upon the United States as the result of a wise division of war effort, the British Government recognize that any post-war advantages of an industrial or commercial character shall be dealt with as between the United States and Great Britain on terms to be specified by the President of the United States to the Prime Minister of Great Britain. The Prime Minister expressly disclaims any interest in these industrial and commercial aspects beyond what may be considered by the President of the United States to be fair and just and in harmony with the economic welfare of the world.

Foreign Relations of the United States: The Conferences at Washington and Quebec 1943. Washington, DC: U.S. Government Printing Office, 1970, pp. 1117–19.

Document 4: Roosevelt and Churchill Discuss the Bomb

Franklin Roosevelt and Winston Churchill met frequently during the war years. In September 1944 they discussed their countries' joint atom bomb project. Tube Alloys is the code name for the British atom bomb project.

The suggestion that the world should be informed regarding Tube Alloys, with a view to an international agreement regarding its control and use, is not accepted. The matter should continue to be regarded as of the utmost secrecy; but when a 'bomb' is finally available, it might perhaps, after mature consideration, be used against the Japanese, who should be warned that this bombardment will be repeated until they surrender.

2. Full collaboration between the United States and the British Government in developing Tube Alloys for military and commercial purposes should continue after the defeat of Japan unless and until terminated by joint agreement.

3. Enquiries should be made regarding the activities of Professor Bohr and steps taken to ensure that he is responsible for no leakage of information particularly to the Russians.

Margaret Gowing, *Britain and Atomic Energy 1939–1945.* New York: St. Martin's Press, 1964, p. 447.

Document 5: Harry S. Truman Learns About the Manhattan Project

The Manhattan Project was so secret that not even Vice President Harry S. Truman knew what it was about, despite his several requests to Secretary of War Henry L. Stimson to be filled in on the secret project. Although Truman was sworn in as president after Franklin Roosevelt's death on April 12, 1945, Stimson did not inform Truman about the atom bomb for two more weeks. On April 25 Stimson wrote a memorandum outlining what he had told Truman about the bomb.

1. Within four months we shall in all probability have completed the most terrible weapon ever known in human history, one bomb of which could destroy a whole city.

2. Although we have shared its development with the UK, physically the US is at present in the position of controlling the resources with which to construct and use it and no other nation could reach this position for some years.

3. Nevertheless it is practically certain that we could not remain in this position indefinitely. . . .

4. As a result, it is indicated that the future may see a time when such a weapon may be constructed in secret and used suddenly and effectively with devastating power by a wilful nation or group against an unsuspecting nation or group of much greater size and material power. With its aid even a very powerful unsuspecting nation might be conquered within a very few days by a very much smaller one, although probably the only nation which could enter into production within the next few years is Russia.

5. The world in its present state of moral advancement compared with its technical development would be eventually at the mercy of such a weapon. In other words, modern civilization might be completely destroyed.

6. To approach any world peace organization of any pattern now likely to be considered, without an appreciation by the leaders of our country of the power of this new weapon, would seem to be unrealistic. No system of control heretofore considered would be adequate to control this menace. Both inside any particular country and between the nations of the world, the control of this weapon will undoubtedly be a matter of the greatest difficulty and would involve such thorough-going rights of inspection and internal controls as we have never heretofore contemplated.

7. Furthermore, in the light of our present position with reference to this weapon, the question of sharing it with other nations and, if so shared, upon what terms, becomes a primary question of our foreign relations. Also our leadership in the war and in the development of this weapon has placed a certain moral responsibility upon us which we cannot shirk without very serious responsibility for any disaster to civilization which it would further.

8. On the other hand, if the problem of the proper use of this weapon can be solved, we would have the opportunity to bring the

world into a pattern in which the peace of the world and our civilization can be saved.

Michael B. Stoff, Jonathan F. Fanton, R. Hal Williams, eds., *The Manhattan Project: A Documentary Introduction to the Atomic Age.* New York: McGraw-Hill, 1991, pp. 95–96.

Document 6: The Interim Committee Considers Targets for the Atom Bomb

In May 1945 an all-civilian committee known as the Interim Committee was appointed by Secretary of War Henry L. Stimson to discuss how and when the atom bomb should be used. In a memorandum to Leslie R. Groves, the military director of the project, the committee proposed and discussed five potential targets for the first atomic bomb.

A. Dr. [Joyce C.] Stearns described the work he had done on target selection. He has surveyed possible targets possessing the following qualifications: (1) they be important targets in a large urban area of more than three miles diameter, (2) they be capable of being damaged effectively by a blast, and (3) they are likely to be unattacked by next August. Dr. Stearns had a list of five targets which the Air Forces would be willing to reserve for our use unless unforeseen circumstances arise. These targets are:

(1) *Kyoto*—This target is an urban industrial area with a population of 1,000,000. It is the former capital of Japan and many people and industries are now being moved there as other areas are being destroyed. From the psychological point of view there is the advantage that Kyoto is an intellectual center for Japan and the people there are more apt to appreciate the significance of such a weapon as the gadget. (Classified as an AA Target)

(2) *Hiroshima*—This is an important army depot and port of embarkation in the middle of an urban industrial area. It is a good radar target and it is such a size that a large part of the city could be extensively damaged. There are adjacent hills which are likely to produce a focusing effect which would considerably increase the blast damage. Due to rivers it is not a good incendiary target. (Classified as an AA Target)

(3) *Yokohama*—This is an important urban industrial area which has so far been untouched. Industrial activities include aircraft manufacture, machine tools, docks, electrical equipment and oil refineries. As the damage to Tokyo has increased additional industries have moved to Yokohama. It has the disadvantage of the most important target areas being separated by a large body of water and of being in the heaviest anti-aircraft concentration in Japan. For us it has the advantage as an alternative target for use in

case of bad weather of being rather far removed from the other targets considered. (Classified as an A Target)

(4) *Kokura Arsenal*—This is one of the largest arsenals in Japan and is surrounded by urban industrial structures. The arsenal is important for light ordnance, anti-aircraft and beach head defense materials. The dimensions of the arsenal are 4100' x 2000'. The dimensions are such that if the bomb were properly placed full advantage could be taken of the higher pressures immediately underneath the bomb for destroying the more solid structures and at the same time considerable blast damage could be done to more feeble structures further away. (Classified as an A Target)

(5) *Niigata*—This is a port of embarkation on the N.W. coast of Honshu. Its importance is increasing as other ports are damaged. Machine tool industries are located there and it is a potential center for industrial dispersion. It has oil refineries and storage. (Classified as a B Target)

(6) The possibility of bombing the Emperor's palace was discussed. It was agreed that we should not recommend it but that any action for this bombing should come from authorities on military policy. It was agreed that we should obtain information from which we could determine the effectiveness of our weapon against this target.

B. It was the recommendation of those present at the meeting that the first four choices of targets for our weapon should be the following:

a. Kyoto
b. Hiroshima
c. Yokohama
d. Kokura Arsenal

Michael B. Stoff, Jonathan F. Fanton, R. Hal Williams, eds., *The Manhattan Project: A Documentary Introduction to the Atomic Age.* New York: McGraw-Hill, 1991, pp. 100–101.

Document 7: Scientists Question the Use of the Bomb

When it became clear in 1945 that Germany would surrender before the atom bomb would be ready for use, some of the scientists involved in the project began to question whether the bomb should be used at all. James Franck, a German Jew refugee who joined the Manhattan Project in 1942, chaired a committee of six other scientists—Donald Hughes, James J. Nickson, Eugene Rabinowitch, Glenn T. Seaborg, Joyce C. Stearns, and Leo Szilard—who were to discuss and report on the social and political implications of dropping the atom bomb on Japan. The

Franck Report, excerpted here, argued against dropping the bomb without warning Japan first.

The way in which the nuclear weapons now being secretly developed in this country are first revealed to the world appears to be of great, perhaps fateful importance.

One possible way—which may particularly appeal to those who consider nuclear bombs primarily as a secret weapon developed to help win the present war—is to use them without warning on an appropriately selected object in Japan. It is doubtful whether the first available bombs, of comparatively low efficiency and small size, will be sufficient to break the will or ability of Japan to resist, especially given the fact that the major cities like Tokyo, Nagoya, Osaka and Kobe already will largely have been reduced to ashes by the slower process of ordinary aerial bombing. Although important tactical results undoubtedly can be achieved by a sudden introduction of nuclear weapons, we nevertheless think that the question of the use of the very first available atomic bombs in the Japanese war should be weighed very carefully, not only by military authorities, but by the highest political leadership of this country. If we consider international agreement on total prevention of nuclear warfare as the paramount objective, and believe that it can be achieved, this kind of introduction of atomic weapons to the world may easily destroy all our chances of success. Russia, and even allied countries which bear less mistrust of our ways and intentions, as well as neutral countries may be deeply shocked. It may be very difficult to persuade the world that a nation which was capable of secretly preparing and suddenly releasing a weapon as indiscriminate as the rocket bomb and a million times more destructive, is to be trusted in its proclaimed desire of having such weapons abolished by international agreement. We have large accumulations of poison gas, but do not use them, and recent polls have shown that public opinion in this country would disapprove of such a use even if it would accelerate the winning of the Far Eastern war. It is true that some irrational element in mass psychology makes gas poisoning more revolting than blasting by explosives, even though gas warfare is in no way more "inhuman" than the war of bombs and bullets. Nevertheless, it is not at all certain that American public opinion, if it could be enlightened as to the effect of atomic explosives, would approve of our own country being the first to introduce such an indiscriminate method of wholesale destruction of civilian life.

Thus, from the "optimistic" point of view—looking forward to an international agreement on the prevention of nuclear warfare—the military advantages and the saving of American lives achieved by the sudden use of atomic bombs against Japan may be outweighed by the ensuing loss of confidence and by a wave of horror and repulsion sweeping over the rest of the world and perhaps even dividing public opinion at home.

From this point of view, a demonstration of the new weapon might best be made, before the eyes of representatives of all the United Nations, on the desert or a barren island. The best possible atmosphere for the achievement of an international agreement could be achieved if America could say to the world, "You see what sort of a weapon we had but did not use. We are ready to renounce its use in the future if other nations join us in this renunciation and agree to the establishment of an efficient international control."

After such a demonstration the weapon might perhaps be used against Japan if the sanction of the United Nations (and of public opinion at home) were obtained, perhaps after a preliminary ultimatum to Japan to surrender or at least to evacuate certain regions as an alternative to their total destruction. This may sound fantastic, but in nuclear weapons we have something entirely new in order of magnitude of destructive power, and if we want to capitalize fully on the advantage their possession gives us, we must use new and imaginative methods.

Michael B. Stoff, Jonathan F. Fanton, R. Hal Williams, eds., *The Manhattan Project: A Documentary Introduction to the Atomic Age.* New York: McGraw-Hill, 1991, pp. 143–45.

Document 8: The State of Japan

The atom bomb was a weapon that had never been used before and no one was quite sure if it would work or how effective it would be. The War Department had drawn up a contingency plan to invade the Japanese islands in November 1945 and in the spring of 1946 if Japan had not surrendered by then. However, the Japanese were known to be extremely tenacious fighters and astronomical casualties were expected. In the following memo written by Secretary of War Henry L. Stimson to Harry S. Truman, Stimson describes the situation in Japan and suggests that the country might be persuaded to surrender if it is given a warning about a powerful new weapon that would be used against it.

1. The plans of operation up to and including the first landing have been authorized and the preparations for the operation are now actually going on. This situation was accepted by all members of your conference on Monday, June 18th.

2. There is reason to believe that the operation for the occupa-

tion of Japan following the landing may be a very long, costly and arduous struggle on our part. The terrain, much of which I have visited several times, has left the impression on my memory of being one which would be susceptible to a last ditch defense such as has been made on Iwo Jima and Okinawa and which of course is very much larger than either of those two areas. According to my recollection it will be much more unfavorable with regard to tank maneuvering than either the Philippines or Germany.

3. If we once land on one of the main islands and begin a forceful occupation of Japan, we shall probably have cast the die of last-ditch resistance. The Japanese are highly patriotic and certainly susceptible to calls for fanatical resistance to repel an invasion. Once started in actual invasion, we shall in my opinion have to go through with an even more bitter finish fight than in Germany. We shall incur the losses incident to such a war and we shall have to leave the Japanese islands even more thoroughly destroyed than was the case with Germany. This would be due both to the difference in the Japanese and German personal character and the differences in the size and character of the terrain through which the operations will take place.

4. A question then comes: Is there any alternative to such a forceful occupation of Japan which will secure for us the equivalent of an unconditional surrender of her forces and a permanent destruction of her power again to strike an aggressive blow at the "peace of the Pacific"? I am inclined to think that there is enough such chance to make it well worthwhile our giving them a warning of what is to come and a definite opportunity to capitulate. As above suggested, it should be tried before the actual forceful occupation of the homeland islands is begun and furthermore the warning should be given in ample time to permit a national reaction to set in.

We have the following enormously favorable factors on our side—factors much weightier than those we had against Germany:

Japan has no allies.

Her navy is nearly destroyed and she is vulnerable to a surface and underwater blockade which can deprive her of sufficient food and supplies for her population.

She is terribly vulnerable to our concentrated air attack upon her crowded cities, industrial and food resources.

She has against her not only the Anglo-American forces but the rising forces of China and the ominous threat of Russia.

We have inexhaustible and untouched industrial resources to

bring to bear against her diminishing potential.

We have great moral superiority through being the victim of her first sneak attack. . . .

5. It is therefore my conclusion that a carefully timed warning be given to Japan by the chief representatives of the United States, Great Britain, China and, if then a belligerent, Russia, calling upon Japan to surrender and permit the occupation of her country in order to insure its complete demilitarization for the sake of the future peace.

This warning should contain the following elements:

The varied and overwhelming character of the force we are about to bring to bear on the islands.

The inevitability and completeness of the destruction which the full application of this force will entail.

The determination of the allies to destroy permanently all authority and influence of those who have deceived and misled the country into embarking on world conquest.

The determination of the allies to limit Japanese sovereignty to her main islands and to render them powerless to mount and support another war.

The disavowal of any attempt to extirpate the Japanese as a race or to destroy them as a nation. . . .

6. Success of course will depend on the potency of the warning which we give her. She has an extremely sensitive national pride and, as we are now seeing every day, when actually locked with the enemy will fight to the very death. For that reason the warning must be tendered before the actual invasion has occurred and while the impending destruction, though clear beyond peradventure, has not yet reduced her to fanatical despair. If Russia is a part of the threat, the Russian attack, if actual, must not have progressed too far. Our own bombing should be confined to military objectives as far as possible.

Michael B. Stoff, Jonathan F. Fanton, R. Hal Williams, eds., *The Manhattan Project: A Documentary Introduction to the Atomic Age.* New York: McGraw-Hill, 1991, pp. 168–70.

Document 9: The Military Explains the Sights and Sounds of the Trinity Test

The first atomic bomb test at the Alamogordo Army Air Base in New Mexico was seen and heard up to hundreds of miles away. The following news story, released by the Manhattan Project to area newspapers to allay any fears or questions about the test, appeared in the Albuquerque Tribune *July 16, 1945.*

Alamogordo, N.M., July 16—William O. Eareckson, commanding officer of the Alamogordo Army Air Base, made the following statement today:

"Several inquiries have been received concerning a heavy explosion which occurred on the Alamogordo Air Base reservation this morning.

"A remotely located ammunition magazine containing a considerable amount of high explosive and pyrotechnics exploded.

"There was no loss of life or injury to anyone, and the property damage outside of the explosives magazine itself was negligible.

"Weather conditions affecting the content of gas shells exploded by the blast may make it desirable for the Army to evacuate temporarily a few civilians from their homes."

Michael B. Stoff, Jonathan F. Fanton, R. Hal Williams, eds., *The Manhattan Project: A Documentary Introduction to the Atomic Age*. New York: McGraw-Hill, 1991, p. 193.

Document 10: A Petition to the President

After Germany surrendered in May 1945, some scientists questioned the morality of using an atom bomb against Japan. Leo Szilard, who was a member of the Franck Committee which issued a report arguing against the use of the bomb, circulated a petition among the scientists of the Manhattan Project and collected sixty-eight signatures. He then forwarded the petition on to Harry S. Truman, but it is believed that Truman did not see it before Hiroshima and Nagasaki were bombed.

Discoveries of which the people of the United States are not aware may affect the welfare of this nation in the near future. The liberation of atomic power which has been achieved places atomic bombs in the hands of the Army. It places in your hands, as Commander-in-Chief, the fateful decision whether or not to sanction the use of such bombs in the present phase of the war against Japan.

We, the undersigned scientists, have been working in the field of atomic power. Until recently we have had to fear that the United States might be attacked by atomic bombs during this war and that her only defense might lie in a counterattack by the same means. Today, with the defeat of Germany, this danger is averted and we feel impelled to say what follows:

The war has to be brought speedily to a successful conclusion and attacks by atomic bombs may very well be an effective method of warfare. We feel, however, that such attacks on Japan could not be justified, at least not until the terms which will be imposed after the war on Japan were made public in detail and Japan were given an opportunity to surrender.

If such public announcement gave assurance to the Japanese that they could look forward to a life devoted to peaceful pursuits in their homeland and if Japan still refused to surrender our nation might then, in certain circumstances, find itself forced to resort to the use of atomic bombs. Such a step, however, ought not to be made at any time without seriously considering the moral responsibilities which are involved.

The development of atomic power will provide the nations with new means of destruction. The atomic bombs at our disposal represent only the first step in this direction, and there is almost no limit to the destructive power which will become available in the course of their future development. Thus a nation which sets the precedent of using these newly liberated forces of nature for purposes of destruction may have to bear the responsibility of opening the door to an era of devastation on an unimaginable scale.

If after the war a situation is allowed to develop in the world which permits rival powers to be in uncontrolled possession of these new means of destruction, the cities of the United States as well as the cities of other nations will be in continuous danger of sudden annihilation. All the resources of the United States, moral and material, may have to be mobilized to prevent the advent of such a world situation. Its prevention is at present the solemn responsibility of the United States—singled out by virtue of her lead in the field of atomic power.

The added material strength which this lead gives to the United States brings with it the obligation of restraint and if we were to violate this obligation our moral position would be weakened in the eyes of the world and in our own eyes. It would then be more difficult for us to live up to our responsibility of bringing the unloosened forces of destruction under control.

In view of the foregoing, we, the undersigned, respectfully petition: first, that you exercise your power as Commander-in-Chief to rule that the United States shall not resort to the use of atomic bombs in this war unless the terms which will be imposed upon Japan have been made public in detail and Japan knowing these terms has refused to surrender; second, that in such an event the question whether or not to use atomic bombs be decided by you in the light of the consideration presented in this petition as well as all the other moral responsibilities which are involved.

Spencer R. Weart and Gertrud Weiss Szilard, *Leo Szilard: His Version of the Facts.* Cambridge, MA: MIT Press, 1978, pp. 211–12.

Document 11: The Allies' Terms for a Japanese Surrender

In late July 1945, Harry S. Truman, Winston Churchill, and Joseph Stalin met in the Berlin suburb of Potsdam to finalize their decisions over the administration and government of Germany. At the end of the conference, on July 26, 1945, the United States, England, and China issued an ultimatum to Japan. The Potsdam Declaration gave Japan the opportunity to surrender or face total annihilation.

(1) We, the President of the United States, the Prime Minister of Great Britain, and the President of the Republic of China, representing the hundreds of millions of our countrymen, have conferred and agree that Japan shall be given an opportunity to surrender on the terms we state herein.

(2) The prodigious land, sea and air forces of the United States, the British Empire and of China, many times reinforced by their armies and air fleets from the west are poised to strike the final blows upon Japan. This military power is sustained and inspired by the determination of all the Allied nations to prosecute the war against Japan until her unconditional capitulation.

(3) The result of the futile and senseless German resistance to the might of the aroused free peoples of the world stands forth in awful clarity as an example before Japan. The might that now converges on Japan is immeasurably greater than that which, when applied to the resisting Nazis, necessarily laid waste to the lands, the industry and the method of life of the whole German people. The full application of our military power backed by our resolve means the inevitable and complete destruction of the Japanese armed forces and just as inevitably the utter devastation of the Japanese homeland.

(4) Is Japan so lacking in reason that it will continue blindly to follow the leadership of those ridiculous militaristic advisers whose unintelligent calculations have brought the Empire of Japan to the threshold of annihilation? The time has come to decide whether to continue on to destruction or to follow the path of reason.

(5) Following are our terms. We will not deviate from them. They may be accepted or not. There are no alternatives. We shall not tarry on our way.

(6) There must be eliminated for all time the authority and influence of those who have deceived and misled the country into embarking on world conquest, for we insist that a new order of peace, security and justice will be impossible until irresponsible militarism is driven from the world.

(7) Until such a new order is established Japanese lands must be

occupied and the exercise of our authority shall continue until there is convincing proof that Japan's war-making power is destroyed.

(8) The terms of the Cairo Declaration shall be carried out and Japanese sovereignty shall be limited to the islands of Honshu, Hokkaido, Kyushu, Shikoku and such adjacent minor islands as we determine.

(9) The Japanese military forces shall be completely disarmed and returned to their homes and peaceful and productive lives.

(10) The Japanese shall not be enslaved as a race or destroyed as a nation, but stern justice will be meted out to all war criminals including those who have visited cruelties upon our prisoners. Democratic tendencies found among the Japanese peoples [sic] shall be supported and strengthened. Freedom of speech, of religion and of thought, as well as respect for the fundamental human rights shall be established.

(11) Japan shall be permitted to maintain only such industries as will not enable her to rearm herself for war but which can produce a sustaining economy. To this end, access to, as distinguished from control of, raw materials shall be permitted. Eventual Japanese participation in world trade relations shall be permitted.

(12) The occupying forces of the Allies shall be withdrawn from Japan as soon as our objectives are accomplished and there has been established beyond doubt a peacefully inclined, responsible government of a character representative of the Japanese people. This may include a constitutional monarchy under the present dynasty if it be shown to the complete satisfaction of the world that such a government will never again aspire to aggression.

(13) We call upon those in authority in Japan to proclaim now the unconditional surrender of all the Japanese armed forces under the authority of the Japanese Government and High Command, and to provide proper and adequate assurances of their good faith in such action.

Foreign Relations of the United States Diplomatic Papers: The Conference of Berlin (The Potsdam Conference). 1945, Vol. I. Washington, DC: U.S. Government Printing Office, 1960, pp. 893–94.

Document 12: Conclusions Drawn from the Trinity Test

The results of the world's first atom bomb test at the Trinity site in Alamogordo, New Mexico, continued to be studied long after the actual explosion. On July 30, 1945, General Leslie R. Groves, the military director of the Manhattan Project, wrote a memo to George C. Marshall, the U.S. Army chief of staff, informing him of the bomb's effect and how such information could be used in a combat situation.

1. The following additional conclusions have been drawn from the test in New Mexico with respect to the probable effects of the combat bomb which will be exploded about 1800 feet in the air:

a. Measured from the point on the ground directly below the explosion the blast should be lethal to at least 1000 feet. Between 2500 and 3500 feet, blast effects should be extremely serious to personnel. Heat and flame should be fatal to about 1500 to 2000 feet.

b. At 10 miles for a few thousandths of a second the light will be as bright as a thousand suns; at the end of a second, as bright as one or possibly two suns. The effect on anyone about a half mile away who looks directly at the explosion would probably be permanent sight impairment; at one mile, temporary blindness; and up to and even beyond ten miles, temporary sight impairment. To persons who are completely unshielded, gamma rays may be lethal to 3500 feet and neutrons to about 2000 feet.

c. No damaging effects are anticipated on the ground from radioactive materials. These effects at New Mexico resulted from the low altitude from which the bomb was set off.

d. Practically all structures in an area of one or two square miles should be completely demolished and a total area of six to seven square miles should be so devastated that the bulk of the buildings would have to have major repairs to make them habitable.

e. At New Mexico tanks could have gone through the immediate explosion area at normal speeds within thirty minutes after the blast. With the explosion at the expected 1800 feet, we think we could move troops through the area immediately, preferably by motor but on foot if desired. The units should be preceded by scouts with simple instruments. The nearest exposed personnel should not be nearer to the blast than six miles plus the necessary allowance for bombing inaccuracy and they would require a high order of discipline and special but simple instructions. As an extra precaution, extra special dark glasses might be issued to all commanders of units as large as a platoon. If dropped on the enemy lines, the expected effect on the enemy would be to wipe out his resistance over an area 2000 feet in diameter; to paralyse it over an area a mile in diameter; and to impede it seriously over an area five miles in diameter. Troops which were in deep cave shelters at distances of over a mile should not be seriously affected. Men in slit trenches within 800 feet should be killed by the blast.

Philip L. Cantelon, Richard G. Hewlett, and Robert C. Williams, eds., *The American Atom: A Documentary History of Nuclear Policies from the Discovery of Fission to the Present.* Philadelphia: University of Pennsylvania Press, 1984, 1991, pp. 59–61.

Document 13: The White House Announces the Attack on Hiroshima

Shortly after the United States dropped the atom bomb on Hiroshima on August 6, 1945, Harry S. Truman announced the fact to the world.

Sixteen hours ago an American airplane dropped one bomb on Hiroshima, an important Japanese Army base. That bomb had more power than 20,000 tons of T.N.T. It had more than two thousand times the blast power of the British "Grand Slam" which is the largest bomb ever yet used in the history of warfare.

The Japanese began the war from the air at Pearl Harbor. They have been repaid many fold. And the end is not yet. With this bomb we have now added a new and revolutionary increase in destruction to supplement the growing power of our armed forces. In their present form these bombs are now in production and even more powerful forms are in development.

It is an atomic bomb. It is a harnessing of the basic power of the universe. The force from which the sun draws its power has been loosed against those who brought war to the Far East.

Before 1939, it was the accepted belief of scientists that it was theoretically possible to release atomic energy. But no one knew any practical method of doing it. By 1942, however, we knew that the Germans were working feverishly to find a way to add atomic energy to the other engines of war with which they hoped to enslave the world. But they failed. We may be grateful to Providence that the Germans got the V-1's and V-2's late and in limited quantities and even more grateful that they did not get the atomic bomb at all.

The battle of the laboratories held fateful risks for us as well as the battles of the air, land and sea, and we have now won the battle of the laboratories as we have won the other battles. . . .

We are now prepared to obliterate more rapidly and completely every productive enterprise the Japanese have above ground in any city. We shall destroy their docks, their factories, and their communications. Let there be no mistake; we shall completely destroy Japan's power to make war.

It was to spare the Japanese people from utter destruction that the ultimatum of July 26 was issued at Potsdam. Their leaders promptly rejected that ultimatum. If they do not now accept our terms they may expect a rain of ruin from the air, the like of which has never been seen on this earth. Behind this air attack will follow sea and land forces in such numbers and power as they have not yet seen and with the fighting skill of which they are already well aware.

Public Papers of the Presidents of the United States: Harry S. Truman. Containing the Public Messages, Speeches, and Statements of the President April 12 to December 31, 1945. Washington, DC: U.S. Government Printing Office, 1961, pp. 197–200.

Document 14: The Japanese Account of the Bombing of Hiroshima

Although the atom bomb dropped on Hiroshima almost completely destroyed the city, the Japanese government kept this news from its people outside of the city. On August 7, the Pacific branch of the Office of War Information picked up a Japanese broadcast about the bombing of Hiroshima, a transcript of which is provided here.

A small number of B-29s penetrated into Hiroshima city a little after eight A.M. yesterday morning and dropped a small number of bombs. As a result, a considerable number of homes were reduced to ashes and fires broke out in various parts of the city.

To this new type of bomb are attached parachutes, and it appears as if these new bombs exploded in the air. Investigations are now being made with regard to the effectiveness of this bomb, which should not be regarded as slight.

The enemy has exposed his cold-bloodedness and atrocious nature more and more in killing innocent people by the use of this new type bomb. It is believed that the enemy, being faced with difficult conditions, is feeling rushed to turn the war into one of short duration. Hence he has begun to use this type of bomb.

The use of this new type of bomb by the enemy in the future can be expected. As for measures to cope with this bomb, it is anticipated that they will be disclosed as soon as possible. Until these measures are disclosed by the government authorities, it is necessary for the general public to strengthen the present air defense system.

As frequently pointed out in the past, the people must watch themselves against underrating the enemy simply because he has carried out raids with a small number of planes. The enemy has been carrying out large-scale propaganda on the effectiveness of this new type bomb since using these bombs, but as long as we formulate strong steel-like measures to cope with this type of bomb, it will be possible to keep the damage at a minimum.

We must be careful at all times so that we will not fall victim to the enemy's machinations.

Fletcher Knebel and Charles W. Bailey II, *No High Ground*, New York: Harper & Row, 1960.

Document 15: The United States Warns the Japanese About the Atom Bomb

Although the United States did not give the Japanese people any warning about the atom bomb prior to the bombing of Hiroshima, it did give some of them a warning before it bombed Nagasaki. Allied radio stations in Saipan began broadcasting warnings about the atom bomb on August 8. In addition, leaflets were dropped on forty-seven Japanese cities with populations of more than 100,000. However, due to the huge number of leaflets that had to be printed, Nagasaki did not receive its leaflets before it was bombed.

TO THE JAPANESE PEOPLE:

America asks that you take immediate heed of what we say on this leaflet.

We are in possession of the most destructive explosive ever devised by man. A single one of our newly developed atomic bombs is actually the equivalent in explosive power to what 2000 of our giant B-29's can carry on a single mission. This awful fact is one for you to ponder and we solemnly assure you it is grimly accurate.

We have just begun to use this weapon against your homeland. If you still have any doubt, make inquiry as to what happened to Hiroshima when just one atomic bomb fell on that city.

Before using this bomb to destroy every resource of the military by which they are prolonging this useless war, we ask that you now petition the Emperor to end the war. Our President has outlined for you the thirteen consequences of an honorable surrender: We urge that you accept these consequences and begin the work of building a new, better, and peace-loving Japan.

You should take steps now to cease military resistance. Otherwise, we shall resolutely employ this bomb and all our other superior weapons to promptly and forcefully end the war.

EVACUATE YOUR CITIES

Dennis Merrill, ed., *Documentary History of the Truman Presidency: Vol. 1: The Decision to Drop the Atomic Bomb on Japan.* Bethesda, MD: University Publications of America, 1995, p. 194.

Document 16: Japan Protests the Use of the Atom Bomb

Using the Swiss government as an intermediary, the Japanese government sent an official protest to the United States over the dropping of the atom bomb on Hiroshima. Weapons such as gas had been outlawed by the Geneva Conventions as inhumane, and according to the Japanese, the atomic bomb was just as cruel and uncivilized a weapon as gas.

The Legation of Switzerland in charge of Japanese interests has received an urgent cable from the authorities abroad, requesting that the Department of State be immediately apprised of the following communication from the Japanese Government, reading, in translation, as follows:

> On August 6, 1945, American airplanes released on the residential district of the town of Hiroshima bombs of a new type, killing and injuring in one second a large number of civilians and destroying a great part of the town. Not only is the city of Hiroshima a provincial town without any protection or special military installations of any kind, but also none of the neighboring region of this town constitutes a military objective.
>
> In a declaration President Truman has asserted that he would use these bombs for the destruction of docks, factories, and installations of transportation. However, this bomb, provided with a parachute, in falling has a destructive force of a great scope as a result of its explosion in the air. It is evident, therefore, that it is technically impossible to limit the effect of its use to special objectives such as designated by President Truman, and the American authorities are perfectly aware of this. In fact, it has been established on the scene that the damage extends over a great area and that combatant and non-combatant men and women, old and young, are massacred without discrimination by the atmospheric pressure of the explosion, as well as by the radiating heat which results therefrom. Consequently there is involved a bomb having the most cruel effects humanity has ever known, not only as far as the extensive and immense damage is concerned, but also for reasons of suffering endured by each victim.
>
> It is an elementary principle of international public law that in time of war the belligerents do not have unlimited right in the choice of the means of attack and that they cannot resort to projectile arms or any other means capable of causing the enemy needless suffering. These principles are stipulated in the Convention respecting the laws and customs of war on land and in Article 22, as well as under letter

(E) of Article 23 of the rules concerning the laws and customs of war on land. Since the beginning of the present war, the American Government has declared on various occasions that the use of gas or other inhuman means of combat were considered illegal in the public opinion of civilized human society and that it would not avail itself of these means before enemy countries resorted to them. The bombs in question, used by the Americans, by their cruelty and by their terrorizing effects, surpass by far gas or any other arm the use of which is prohibited by the treaties for reasons of their characteristics.

The Americans have effected bombardments of towns in the greatest part of Japanese territory, without discrimination massacring a great number of old people, women, children; destroying and burning down Shinto and Buddhist temples, schools, hospitals, living quarters, etc. This fact alone means that they have shown complete defiance of the essential principles of humanitarian laws, as well as international law. They now use this new bomb, having an uncontrollable and cruel effect much greater than any other arms or projectiles ever used to date. This constitutes a new crime against humanity and civilization. The Government of Japan, in its own name and at the same time in the name of all of humanity and civilization, accuses the American Government with the present note of the use of an inhuman weapon of this nature and demands energetically abstinence from its use.

Michael B. Stoff, Jonathan F. Fanton, R. Hal Williams, eds., *The Manhattan Project: A Documentary Introduction to the Atomic Age.* New York: McGraw-Hill, 1991, p. 244.

Document 17: The Russians Test an Atom Bomb

Sometime in August 1949, the Russians tested their first atomic bomb and the arms race between the United States and the Soviet Union officially began. Early supporters of atomic energy had argued for international control of nuclear weapons, in which an international agency would control and inspect nuclear weapons. The Soviet Union objected, however, to allowing other nations to determine its nuclear weapons policy. In the following document, Harry S. Truman informs the American public on September 23, 1949, that the Soviet Union has tested its first atom bomb.

I believe the American people, to the fullest extent consistent with national security, are entitled to be informed of all developments in the field of atomic energy. That is my reason for making public the following information.

We have evidence that within recent weeks an atomic explosion occurred in the U.S.S.R.

Ever since atomic energy was first released by man, the eventual development of this new force by other nations was to be expected. This probability has always been taken into account by us.

Nearly four years ago I pointed out that "scientific opinion appears to be practically unanimous that the essential theoretical knowledge upon which the discovery is based is already widely known. There is also substantial agreement that foreign research can come abreast of our present theoretical knowledge in time." And, in the Three-Nation Declaration of the President of the United States and the Prime Ministers of the United Kingdom and of Canada, dated November 15, 1945, it was emphasized that no single nation could in fact have a monopoly of atomic weapons.

This recent development emphasizes once again, if indeed such emphasis were needed, the necessity for that truly effective enforceable international control of atomic energy which this Government and the large majority of the members of the United Nations support.

Public Papers of the Presidents of the United States: Harry S. Truman. Containing the Public Messages, Speeches, and Statements of the President January 1 to December 31, 1949. Washington, DC: U.S. Government Printing Office, 1964, p. 485.

Document 18: Nagasaki Commemorates Its Bombing with a Peace Declaration

The residents of Hiroshima and Nagasaki have become adamant about the necessity of abolishing nuclear weapons. Every year there are ceremonies to mark the anniversary of the bombing. In 1980, on the thirty-fifth anniversary of the bombing of Nagasaki, Mayor Hitoshi Motoshima released a declaration in which he urged the international community to give up its nuclear arsenal and learn to live in peace with its neighbors.

On August 9, 1945, the city of Nagasaki turned into an inferno beyond human imagination, and more than 70,000 precious lives were obliterated.

Even now, 35 years from that event, a great number of surviving victims are still suffering under the persistent shadow of death.

While the losses and cruelties of the war experienced by the Japanese people, both physical and spiritual, have gradually disappeared, the painful struggle of the atomic bomb victims becomes deeper and more intense with the passing of the months and years.

Now here this common gathering of surviving victims and relatives, youngsters, citizens of Nagasaki, and people from all over our country and from other countries, has paid respect to the souls of the ones who lost their lives on account of the atomic bomb, and, from the bottom of our hearts, we have prayed for their eternal rest and happiness. Out of the sorrow and hate of our relatives and friends who fell victim to the atomic bomb, we have to engrave deeply on our hearts a prayer for peace. Historians of the generations to come will undoubtedly record the cruel atomic bombing as one of the darkest moments of the twentieth century.

The citizens of Nagasaki, now recovered from the suffering and anger of the bombing, have the obligation, the responsibility, and the mission of continuing to urge a stop in the race of nuclear arms proliferation and to advocate total disarmament.

Let us remind ourselves of the existing tense relations between neighboring countries in the world and of how even the light of the dawn of peace has almost been extinguished, how the race of nuclear arms has so fiercely intensified, how the nuclear tests have this year exceeded by far the number of tests held last year. The city of Nagasaki for the last eleven years has protested against the 188 different nuclear tests, but her protests have been totally ignored. Under the pretension of doing it to avoid war, the nations which possess nuclear weapons have expanded them more and more each year. We are sure that unless this dangerous course is reversed, no true peace nor progress will ever be attained on earth.

The world's arsenal of immensely powerful nuclear weapons is capable of erasing several times the whole of mankind. The danger of a technical or supervisory miss leading to an accidental ignition of a nuclear war is a strong reality. Is mankind entering the road of self-destruction? Time is pressing. People of goodwill from all over the world should now give ears to the voice of Nagasaki, open their eyes to wisdom, and stand up with actions and efficient means to stop the proliferation of nuclear arms and to make a reality the total ban of wars. Not only the descendants of the ones who experienced the atomic bomb—the citizens of Nagasaki and Hiroshima—but all our countrymen, and moreover, all mankind should advance in all strength on the way to complete this task. For the realization of true peace we must go beyond countries' borders, beyond beliefs and faiths, in an all-out cooperation.

We now strongly appeal to the government of Japan for a new resolution to stop totally the production of nuclear weapons and for total disarmament, and for the certainty of a policy to help the atomic bomb victims, following the spirit of state compensation.

Here we pray for the eternal repose of the atomic bomb victims and in the name of the citizens of Nagasaki we appeal for a firm advancement in the realization of everlasting world peace and of a total ban on nuclear arms.

Committee for the Compilation of Materials on Damage Caused by the Atomic Bombs in Hiroshima and Nagasaki, *Hiroshima and Nagasaki: The Physical, Medical, and Social Effects of the Atomic Bombings.* New York: Basic Books, 1981, pp. 613–14.

Glossary

alpha particle (or ray) A positively charged sub-atomic particle consisting of two protons and two neutrons that is identical to the nucleus of a helium atom. Alpha particles are the result of spontaneous radioactive decay of radioactive elements. Alpha particles are not very penetrating; they can be stopped by a sheet of paper.

atom The smallest unit of matter that cannot be split by chemical means. Each atom consists of a nucleus of positively charged protons and neutral neutrons surrounded by an equal number of negatively charged electrons.

atom bomb (atomic bomb) A bomb that uses the energy released from fission of uranium or plutonium to produce its explosive power.

atomic number The number of protons in an atom's nucleus. Each element has its own atomic number.

atomic weight The mass of an atom. Atomic weight is approximately equal to the total of an atom's protons and neutrons.

beta particle (or ray) An electron, especially one that is emitted during radioactive decay. Beta particles are one hundred times more penetrating than alpha particles but less penetrating than gamma rays.

chain reaction A series of nuclear fissions, in which the neutrons produced by the splitting of an atom cause other atoms to fission, which release more neutrons, and so on. A nuclear explosion is an uncontrolled chain reaction. A nuclear reactor is fueled by controlled chain reactions.

control rod A rod made of an element or material that absorbs neutrons. A control rod is inserted into a nuclear reactor to control the rate of fission.

critical mass The smallest amount of a material such as plutonium or uranium that will sustain a nuclear reaction.

cyclotron A subatomic particle accelerator. An electrical charge in a vacuum chamber accelerates subatomic particles along a circular path until the particles have enough energy to split an atom's nucleus.

electron A negatively charged subatomic particle that orbits an atom's nucleus.

element A material that cannot be broken down further by chemical means. There are ninety-two naturally occurring elements.

fallout Radioactive material that is produced by and released into the air after a nuclear explosion.

fission The splitting of an atom into two new elements of roughly equal atomic weights with an accompanying release of energy. A nuclear reaction caused by fission can be controlled.

fusion A nuclear reaction in which two nuclei of light atomic weights, such as hydrogen, join together to form a heavier nucleus and energy is released. A fusion-type bomb releases more energy than a fission-type bomb.

gamma rays An extremely penetrating electromagnetic radiation, similar to x rays. Gamma rays can destroy human tissue and cause death, although they are also used in nuclear medicine to diagnose and treat disease.

ground zero The point on the earth's surface directly below a nuclear explosion.

hydrogen bomb A bomb that uses nuclear fusion of hydrogen isotopes to produce its energy.

hypocenter   The point on the earth's surface directly below a nuclear explosion.

isotope   An atom of an element which has the same atomic number but a different atomic weight. U-235 and U-238 are isotopes of uranium with a difference of three neutrons.

kiloton   A measure of explosive power. One kiloton is equivalent to one thousand tons of TNT. Fission bombs are generally measured in kilotons.

megaton   One megaton equals one million tons of TNT.

moderator   A material, such as water or graphite, that is used in a nuclear reaction to reduce the speed of neutrons emitted during fission. Slow-moving neutrons are much more likely to cause fission than fast-moving neutrons.

neutron   A subatomic particle found in an atom's nucleus (except hydrogen's) that has no electrical charge. A neutron's mass is slightly heavier than a proton.

nuclear energy   The energy released through fission, fusion, or radioactive decay.

nuclear reactor   An apparatus in which nuclear fission can be maintained and controlled for the production of nuclear energy in the form of heat.

pile   The original term for a nuclear reactor.

plutonium   A radioactive, manmade element used as a fuel in nuclear reactors and weapons.

proton   A subatomic particle in an atom's nucleus with a positive electrical charge.

RAD   Radiation Absorbed Dose. A measurement formerly used to measure the cumulative dose of radiation absorbed by the flesh. One RAD is equivalent to the radiation dose of five mammograms. Nuclear power plant workers are limited to an exposure of five RADs per year.

radiation   The release of energy in the form of heat, light, or alpha, beta, or gamma rays.

radioactive decay   A process, also known as disintegration or transmutation, in which a nucleus emits radiation and changes from one element to another.

radioactivity   The spontaneous decay of an atomic nucleus accompanied by the emission of alpha and beta particles or gamma rays.

rem   Roentgen Equivalent, Man. A measure of the amount of radiation absorbed that reflects the extent of tissue damage. Some forms of radiation are more damaging than others, and some organs and tissues are more susceptible to radiation damage. Rems are calculated by multiplying the RAD dose by a modifying factor that reflects the tissue sensitivity to radiation. Low-level radiation is measured in millirems (mrems), which is one-thousandth of a rem. The average environmental background dose of radiation is 200 mrems. A mammogram x-ray produces 700 mrems and a dental x ray, 1,000 mrems.

roentgen   A unit of measurement of radiation dosage named after the German physicist Wilhelm Konrad Roentgen. Normal environmental background radiation varies from three to eight microroentgens (one-thousandth of a roentgen) per hour.

subatomic particles   Particles that are smaller than an atom, such as protons, neutrons, or electrons.

transuranic elements   Manmade elements with an atomic number higher than that of uranium, 92.

uranium   The heaviest, naturally occurring, radioactive element in nature with an atomic number of 92. Its isotope U-235 is fissionable, but makes up only 0.7 percent of all uranium.

Discussion Questions

Chapter 1: The Development of the Bomb

1. C.P. Snow identifies the components of an atom and their characteristics. What is the difference between atomic weight and atomic number? What were scientists expecting to find when they bombarded uranium atoms with neutrons, according to Snow? What did they find instead? Why is fission so important to the theory of an atom bomb?

2. Laura Fermi talks about the work her husband, Enrico Fermi, did in designing and constructing the world's first nuclear reactor, which he called a pile. Why were water and other hydrogen-based materials unacceptable for a moderator in the pile? What did Fermi end up using instead, and what was his biggest problem with that moderator?

3. Robert C. Batchelder describes the situation in the United States and Europe leading up to the establishment of the Manhattan Project. According to Batchelder, what was the primary driving force behind the U.S. decision to build an atom bomb?

4. According to Richard Rhodes, an atom bomb using plutonium as its energy source must be built differently than a bomb that uses uranium as its energy source. Why must a plutonium bomb be different from the gun-type uranium bomb, and how did the Manhattan Project scientists solve the problem?

5. Once the Manhattan Project was established, research and development on the atom bomb proceeded very quickly, about two and a half years from the time scientists moved to their secret laboratory in Los Alamos, New Mexico, to the first test of an atom bomb on July 16, 1945. In your opinion, why did it take nearly three years to set up the Manhattan Project from the time Roosevelt received Einstein's letter?

Chapter 2: The Decision to Drop the Bomb

1. Alan Cranston argues that there was never any specific decision to drop the bomb because it had always been assumed by everyone involved in the project that the bomb would be used against the enemy when it was ready. What in this book contra-

dicts his argument? Why might Cranston be excused for his assertion?

2. Henry L. Stimson was secretary of war during World War II. As such, he was extremely involved in all the decisions made about the atom bomb, including the decision to use it. He asserts that the time, money, and effort expended on the bomb could only be justified if the bomb was used. Do you agree with his statement? Why or why not? According to Stimson, why was it impractical to demonstrate the bomb's destructive power before using it on Japan?

3. Hanson W. Baldwin asserts that by using the atom bomb on Japan, the United States was just as guilty as Japan and Germany in committing war atrocities. This action, he claims, has forced the United States to give up its position as the world's moral leader. Do you accept Baldwin's contention? Why or why not? In your opinion, has the atom bomb affected the world's opinion of the United States? Explain your answer.

4. Gar Alperovitz is a revisionist who contends that the United States dropped the atom bomb on Japan not to speed up the end of the war, but to intimidate the Soviet Union in the post-war negotiations. What evidence does Alperovitz present to support his view? Do you agree with his conclusions? Why or why not?

5. Many historians assert that for many years there was little dissent about the appropriateness or morality of dropping the atom bombs to end World War II. What have you read that challenges this assertion? Consider the effects and consequences of dropping the atom bomb and the alternatives to its use. Do you agree or disagree with the decision to use the bomb? Explain your answer.

Chapter 3: Aftermath

1. Atsuko Tsujioka describes what it was like in Hiroshima minutes after the atom bomb fell on the city. How does her experience and journey to her home reinforce the conclusion, reached by the Committee for the Compilation of Materials on Damage Caused by the Atomic Bombs in Hiroshima and Nagasaki, that the atom bomb destroys society?

2. Charles W. Sweeney is the pilot of the B-29 bomber that dropped the atomic bomb on Nagasaki. He visited the city within a few weeks of dropping the bomb, and, despite the devastation he

saw, had no regrets over the decision to use the bomb or his role in dropping it. According to Sweeney, what were his feelings as he stood in the rubble below where the bomb exploded?

3. The Committee for the Compilation of Materials and Damage Caused by the Atomic Bombs in Hiroshima and Nagasaki asserts that an atomic bomb attack differs from conventional bombing in several key ways. What are the three features of an atomic bombing, according to the committee? How do the authors characterize the magnitude of the killing?

Chapter 4: America in the Cold War

1. Henry L. Stimson argued in chapter two that the military considered the atom bomb as just another weapon available to fight wars. Eight years after the atom bombs were dropped on Japan, the U.S. military was using American troops as test subjects in atom bomb tests in the Nevada desert and on islands in the South Pacific. According to Michael Uhl and Tod Ensign, what was the purpose of the tests? Were the tests successful in meeting their objectives, according to the military?

2. Paul Boyer argues that the public's fear of the atom bomb and nuclear destruction tends to be cyclical. When did Americans first begin to fear the bomb and nuclear destruction? What was the cause behind their fear, in Boyer's opinion? What does Boyer credit for causing American attitudes of apathy and neglect toward the bomb from 1963 into the 1970s?

Chapter 5: In Retrospect: The Scientists' Views on the Bomb

1. How did Joseph Rotblat convince himself that it was morally acceptable to work on the atom bomb project? What changed his mind? Do you agree with his reasons for going ahead on the project and/or leaving the project? Why or why not?

2. Twenty years after the bomb was dropped, William L. Laurence interviewed many of the scientists involved in the Manhattan Project. Some of their views had changed in the preceding years, and some had not. What is J. Robert Oppenheimer's only regret about the atom bomb? Why does Edward Teller believe that scientists must always work on developing new ideas? Why did Eugene P. Wigner change his mind about dropping the bomb on Japan?

3. In chapter three, Atsuko Tsujioka argues that science should not be used to develop inventions which do not benefit humanity. John A. Simpson believes that scientists should be morally responsible for what they produce. Do you agree with these authors? Why or why not? Now consider some manmade inventions that have both harmful and useful applications. Should these products never have been invented? Explain your answer.

Chapter 6: Epilogue

1. Fifty years after the atom bombs were dropped on Japan, the Smithsonian Institution was embroiled in controversy over its planned exhibit of the *Enola Gay* and the atomic bomb. Should the museum have interpreted the bombing of Japan according to what historians know and believe years later; according to what was known and believed at the time; or should the exhibit be presented in a straightforward, factual manner with no editorial commentary? Does the fact that the Smithsonian receives funding from Congress through tax dollars influence your answer? Explain your answers.

Chronology

1933

January 30—Hitler is appointed chancellor of Germany.

Spring–Summer—Physicists James Franck, Edward Teller, Leo Szilard, Eugene Wigner, and Albert Einstein are persecuted for their Jewish ancestry and leave Germany.

1938

November—Fleeing Benito Mussolini's fascist regime, Italian physicist Enrico Fermi travels to Sweden to accept his Nobel Prize and immediately emigrates to the United States with his family.

December—Otto Hahn and Fritz Strassmann, two German physicists, successfully split uranium into two separate, lighter elements by bombarding the uranium atoms with neutrons. The fission of uranium created energy and additional neutrons, the basis behind the atom bomb.

1939

Summer—Germany cuts off all exports of uranium ore from mines in Czechoslovakia.

August 2—Albert Einstein signs a letter drafted by physicist Leo Szilard that is delivered to Franklin D. Roosevelt telling him an atomic bomb is possible.

September 1—Germany invades Poland, starting World War II.

October 21—First meeting of Roosevelt's advisory committee on uranium.

1940

Spring—Rudolf Peierls and Otto Frisch, two German physicists working in Birmingham, England, write a paper in which they conclude that an atomic bomb could be fueled by a nuclear chain reaction from fission of uranium. Szilard and Fermi receive a grant of $6,000 from the U.S. government to begin work on developing an atomic pile at Columbia University.

1941

February—Glenn T. Seaborg and Emilio Segré discover a new element, plutonium, that shows promise of replacing uranium as a fissile fuel in nuclear chain reactions.

July 15—British committee known as the MAUD Committee releases its report concluding that an atomic bomb using fission is indeed possible.

December 6—Franklin D. Roosevelt commits the U.S. government to building an atomic bomb.

December 7—Japanese surprise attack on Pearl Harbor, Hawaii.

December 8—United States declares war on Japan.

December 11—Germany and Italy declare war on United States.

1942
January 25—The Metallurgical Laboratory (Met. Lab) is established at the University of Chicago. The scientists there work on producing a nuclear chain reaction and plutonium.

June—Fermi moves from Columbia University to the University of Chicago to continue his work on developing an atomic pile and the first controlled nuclear chain reaction.

September 17—General Leslie R. Groves is appointed director of the Manhattan Engineer District, which later becomes known as the Manhattan Project.

October—J. Robert Oppenheimer is named scientific director of the Manhattan Project.

December 2—Fermi supervises the first controlled nuclear chain reaction at the Met. Lab.

December 7—Los Alamos Ranch School in New Mexico becomes the home of the future Los Alamos Laboratory and the Manhattan Project.

1943
April—A secret laboratory, part of the Manhattan Project, is established in Los Alamos, New Mexico, for the design and manufacture of atomic weapons.

June 17—Secretary of War Henry L. Stimson refuses to tell Senator Harry S. Truman the purpose of the plutonium-producing plant in Hanford, Washington.

August 19—Quebec Agreement is signed by the United States and

Great Britain, in which the two countries agree to work together on developing the atom bomb.

December—*Alsos* mission, a secret U.S. military project to gather information on the German atom bomb effort, arrives in Italy.

1944

March 13—Stimson again refuses to tell Truman about the Manhattan Project.

August 9—*Alsos* mission lands in France to investigate the German uranium project.

November 7—Franklin D. Roosevelt is re-elected to a fourth term as president with Truman as his vice president.

December—Klaus Fuchs, a German-born, naturalized British physicist, arrives at Los Alamos.

1945

Spring—American B-29 bombers drop incendiary bombs on Tokyo, Yokohama, and other Japanese cities.

February—Fuchs passes atomic secrets to a Soviet agent.

March—German scientists nearly succeed in their effort to produce a nuclear chain reaction.

April 12—Roosevelt dies and Truman is sworn in as president.

April 24—*Alsos* mission discovers the German atomic pile in a cave near Haigerloch and dismantles it.

April 25—Truman learns about the Manhattan Project and the attempt to develop the atomic bomb.

May 7—Germany surrenders.

May 8—Allies designate this V-E (Victory in Europe) Day.

May 16—Pilots arrive at Tinian Island to prepare for bomb drop on Hiroshima.

June—Fuchs gives more atomic secrets to a Soviet agent.

June 12—The Franck Report, written by a committee of seven scientists chaired by physicist James Franck, is delivered to Stimson. The report warns that using the atom bomb against Japan is "inadvisable" and suggests a warning demonstration instead.

July 2—Stimson writes Truman urging him to use the atom bomb only as a warning for the Japanese.

mid-July—Japan's emperor Hirohito sends out peace feelers to Russia.

July 14—Little Boy (uranium) atomic bomb leaves Los Alamos for Tinian Island.

July 16—First atomic bomb is tested at Trinity Test Site in Alamogordo, New Mexico.

July 17—Szilard sends a petition to the president, signed by sixty-eight Manhattan Project scientists, urging Truman not to use the bomb against Japan.

July 17–August 2—Truman, Joseph Stalin, and Winston Churchill meet at Potsdam, Germany, to discuss the occupation of Germany and the war against Japan.

July 25—General Carl Spaatz, the commanding officer of the 509th Composite Group, 20th Air Force, receives official orders directing him to drop the atom bomb any time after August 3.

July 26—The United States, Britain, and China issue the Potsdam Declaration, an ultimatum to Japan to surrender.

July 28—Fat Man (plutonium) atomic bomb arrives on Tinian Island.

August 6—The United States drops the first atom bomb (Little Boy) on Hiroshima.

August 8—Soviet Union declares war on Japan.

August 9—The United States drops the second atom bomb (Fat Man) on Nagasaki.

August 10—Japan offers to surrender.

August 14—Japan accepts Allied conditions for surrender.

August 15—V-J (Victory over Japan) Day is declared.

August 28—U.S. occupation forces land in Japan.

September 2—Japanese sign peace treaty aboard the U.S.S. *Missouri.*

November 1—First phase of land invasion against Japan, Operation Olympic, was to have been launched.

December—The McMahon Bill, establishing the Atomic Energy Commission, is presented to Congress.

1946
March 1—Second phase of land invasion against Japan, Operation Coronet, was to have begun.

July 1—First atomic test on Bikini Atoll.

1947
January 1—The Atomic Energy Commission is formed and takes over responsibility for atomic energy and nuclear weapons.

1949
August—Soviet Union successfully tests an atom bomb.

1950
February—Klaus Fuchs is arrested by Great Britain for passing atomic secrets to Soviet Union.

For Further Research

Books

Documentary History

Robert H. Ferrell, ed., *Harry S. Truman and the Bomb: A Documentary History*. Worland, WY: High Plains Publishing, 1996.

Dennis Merrill, ed., *Documentary History of the Truman Presidency, vol. I: The Decision to Drop the Atomic Bomb on Japan*. Bethesda, MD: University Publications of America, 1995.

Michael B. Stoff, Jonathan F. Fanton, and R. Hal Williams, eds., *The Manhattan Project: A Documentary Introduction to the Atomic Age*. New York: McGraw-Hill, 1991.

Robert C. Williams and Philip L. Cantelon, eds., *The American Atom: A Documentary History of Nuclear Policies from the Discovery of Fission to the Present 1939–1984*. Philadelphia: University of Pennsylvania Press, 1984.

General History

Michael Blow, *The History of the Atomic Bomb*. New York: American Heritage Publishing, 1968.

Frank W. Chinnock, *Nagasaki: The Forgotten Bomb*. New York: World, 1969.

Leslie R. Groves, *Now It Can Be Told: The Story of the Manhattan Project*. New York: Harper, 1962.

Burt Hirschfeld, *A Cloud over Hiroshima: The Story of the Atomic Bomb*. New York: Messner, 1967.

James W. Kunetka, *City of Fire: Los Alamos and the Atomic Age 1943–1945*. Albuquerque: University of New Mexico Press, 1979.

Dan Kurzman, *Day of the Bomb: Countdown to Hiroshima*. New York: McGraw-Hill, 1986.

K.D. Nichols, *The Road to Trinity*. New York: William Morrow, 1987.

John Francis Purcell, *The Best-Kept Secret: The Story of the Atomic Bomb*. New York: Vanguard Press, 1963.

Richard Rhodes, *The Making of the Atomic Bomb*. New York: Simon and Schuster, 1986.

Charles W. Sweeney, James A. Antonucci, and Marion K. Antonucci, *War's End: An Eyewitness Account of America's Last Atomic Mission*. New York: Avon, 1997.

Ferenc Morton Szasz, *The Day the Sun Rose Twice: The Story of the Trinity Site Nuclear Explosion July 16, 1945*. Albuquerque: University of New Mexico Press, 1984.

Gordon Thomas and Max Morgan Witts, *Enola Gay*. New York: Stein and Day, 1977.

Peter Wyden, *Day One: Before Hiroshima and After*. New York: Simon and Schuster, 1984.

Marion Yass, *Hiroshima*. New York: Putnam, 1972.

The German Effort to Build the Bomb

Jeremy Bernstein, *Hitler's Uranium Club: The Secret Recordings at Farm Hall*. Woodbury, NY: American Institute of Physics, 1996.

David John Cawdell, *The German Atomic Bomb: The History of Nuclear Research in Nazi Germany*. New York: Simon and Schuster, 1967.

Dan Kurzman, *Blood and Water: Sabotaging Hitler's Bomb*. New York: Henry Holt, 1997.

Malcolm MacPherson, *Time Bomb: Fermi, Heisenberg, and the Race for the Atomic Bomb*. New York: Berkley Books, 1987.

Thomas Powers, *Heisenberg's War: The Secret History of the German Bomb*. New York: Knopf, 1993.

Paul Lawrence Rose, *Heisenberg and the Nazi Atomic Bomb Project: A Study in German Culture*. Berkeley: University of California Press, 1998.

Mark Walker, *Nazi Science: Myth, Truth, and the German Atomic Bomb*. New York: Plenum Press, 1995.

The Scientists

Lawrence Badash, Joseph O. Hirschfelder, and Herbert P. Broida, eds., *Reminiscences of Los Alamos 1943–1945*. Boston: Reidel Publishing, 1980.

Robert Jungk, *Brighter than a Thousand Suns: A Personal History of the Atomic Scientists*. New York: Harcourt, Brace, 1958.

Alice Kimball Smith, *A Peril and a Hope: The Scientists' Movement in America 1945–1947*. Cambridge, MA: MIT Press, 1971.

C.P. Snow, *The Physicists*. Boston: Little, Brown, 1981.

Jane Wilson, ed., *All in Our Time: The Reminiscences of Twelve Nuclear Pioneers.* Chicago: Bulletin of the Atomic Scientists, 1975.

The Decision to Drop the Bomb

Thomas B. Allen and Norman Polmar, *Code-Name Downfall: The Secret Plan to Invade Japan and Why Truman Dropped the Bomb.* New York: Simon and Schuster, 1995.

Gar Alperovitz, *The Decision to Use the Atomic Bomb and the Architecture of an American Myth.* New York: Knopf, 1995.

Paul R. Baker, ed., *The Atomic Bomb: The Great Decision.* Hinsdale, IL: Dryden Press, 1976.

Barton J. Bernstein, ed., *The Atomic Bomb: The Critical Issues.* Boston: Little, Brown, 1976.

Len Giovannitti and Fred Freed, *The Decision to Drop the Bomb.* New York: Coward-McCann, 1965.

Robert James Maddox, *Weapons for Victory: The Hiroshima Decision Fifty Years Later.* Columbia: University of Missouri Press, 1995.

Ronald Takaki, *Hiroshima: Why America Dropped the Atomic Bomb.* Boston: Little, Brown, 1995.

Dennis D. Wainstock, *The Decision to Drop the Atomic Bomb.* Westport, CT: Praeger, 1996.

The Survivors

Michihiko Hachiya, *Hiroshima Diary: The Journal of a Japanese Physician, August 6–September 30, 1945.* Chapel Hill: University of North Carolina Press, 1995.

John Hersey, *Hiroshima.* New York: Knopf, 1985.

Michael J. Hogan, ed., *Hiroshima in History and Memory.* New York: Cambridge University Press, 1996.

Averill A. Liebow, *Encounter with Disaster: A Medical Diary of Hiroshima 1945.* New York: W.W. Norton, 1970.

Robert Jay Lifton, *Death in Life: Survivors of Hiroshima.* New York: Random House, 1967.

Rachelle Linner, *City of Silence: Listening to Hiroshima.* Maryknoll, NY: Orbis, 1995.

Richard H. Minear, ed., *Hiroshima: Three Witnesses.* Princeton, NJ: Princeton University Press, 1990.

Toyofumi Ogura, *Letters from the End of the World: A Firsthand Ac-*

count of the Bombing of Hiroshima. New York: Kodansha America, 1997.

Sue Rabbitt Roff, *Hotspots: The Legacy of Hiroshima and Nagasaki.* New York: Cassell, 1995.

Lequita Vance-Watkins and Aratani Mariko, eds., *White Flash, Black Rain: Women of Japan Relive the Bomb.* Minneapolis: Milkweed Editions, 1995.

The Bomb's Legacy and the Cold War

Hans Albrecht Bethe, *The Road from Los Alamos.* New York: Simon and Schuster, 1991.

Kai Bird and Lawrence Lifschultz, *Hiroshima's Shadow.* Stony Creek, CT: Pamphleteer's Press, 1998.

Paul S. Boyer, *By the Bomb's Early Light: American Thought and Culture at the Dawn of the Atomic Age.* Chapel Hill: University of North Carolina Press, 1994.

Ruth Faden, *The Human Radiation Experiments: Final Report of the Advisory Committee on Human Radiation Experiments.* New York: Oxford University Press, 1996.

Martin Harwit, *An Exhibit Denied: Lobbying the History of Enola Gay.* New York: Copernicus, 1996.

Margot A. Henriksen, *Dr. Strangelove's America: Society and Culture in the Atomic Age.* Berkeley: University of California Press, 1997.

Richard G. Hewlett, *Atoms for Peace and War 1953–1961: Eisenhower and the Atomic Energy Commission.* Berkeley: University of California Press, 1989.

Phyllis La Farge, *The Strangelove Legacy: Children, Parents, and Teachers in the Nuclear Age.* New York: Harper and Row, 1987.

Robert Jay Lifton, *Hiroshima in America: Fifty Years of Denial.* New York: Putnam's Sons, 1995.

Edward T. Linenthal and Tom Engelhardt, eds., *History Wars: The Enola Gay and Other Battles for the American Past.* New York: Metropolitan Books, 1996.

Howard L. Rosenberg, *Atomic Soldiers: American Victims of Nuclear Experiments.* Boston: Beacon Press, 1980.

Michael Uhl and Tod Ensign, *GI Guinea Pigs: How the Pentagon Exposed Our Troops to Dangers More Deadly than War: Agent Orange and Atomic Radiation.* New York: Playboy Press, 1980.

Allan M. Winkler, *Life Under a Cloud, American Anxiety About the Atom*. New York: Oxford University Press, 1993.

Periodicals

Hans Bethe and Leila Conners, "Present at the Detonation," *New Perspectives Quarterly*, Fall 1995.

Ian Buruma, "The War over the Bomb," *New York Review of Books*, September 21, 1995.

E.L. Doctorow, "Mythologizing the Bomb," *Nation*, August 14–21, 1995.

Tom Engelhardt, "Fifty Years under a Cloud," *Harper's*, January 1996.

Donald Kagan, "Why America Dropped the Bomb," *Commentary*, September 1995.

Michael B. King, "Bombs Away," *National Review*, November 6, 1995.

Arjun Makhijani, "'Always' the Target?" *Bulletin of Atomic Scientists*, May/June 1995.

Greg Mitchell, "A Hole in History," *Progressive*, August 1995.

Gerald Parshall, "Shock Wave," *U.S. News & World Report*, July 31, 1995.

Richard Rhodes, "Atomic Physicist Enrico Fermi," *Time*, March 29, 1999.

———, "The Experiment of the Century," *American Heritage*, April 1999.

Technology Review, "The Atomic Age at Fifty," August/September 1995.

Evan Thomas, "Why We Did It," *Newsweek*, July 24, 1995.

Index